HTML5
Games

D1072908

HTML5 Games

CREATING FUN WITH HTML5, CSS3, AND WEBGL

Jacob Seidelin

Publisher's Acknowledgements

Some of the people who helped bring this book to market include the following:

Editorial and Production

VP Consumer and Technology Publishing Director:
Michelle Leete

Associate Director–Book Content Management:
Martin Tribe

Associate Publisher:
Chris Webb

Associate Commissioning Editor:
Ellie Scott

Project Editor:
Sydney Argenta

Copy Editor:
Melba Hopper

Technical Editor:
Andrew Wooldridge

Editorial Manager:
Jodi Jensen

Senior Project Editor:
Sara Shlaer

Editorial Assistant:
Annie Sullivan

Marketing

Marketing Manager:
Lorna Mein

Marketing Assistant:
Polly Thomas

About the Author

JACOB SEIDELIN is a freelance web developer with 15 years of experience working with back-end programming, graphics design, and front-end technology. When not working with clients he enjoys JavaScript and HTML5, web game development, and generally pushing the limit of what is possible in the browser. Thee results of his adventures in web development can be witnessed at his website at http://www.nihilogic.dk/.

Acknowledgments

I'd like to acknowledge a few people who helped in the making of this book. I want to thank my editors Sydney Argenta and Melba Hopper and the rest of the Wiley team. A big thanks to Andrew Wooldridge, my technical editor, whose keen eye for technical details kept me on my toes. It has been a pleasure working with all of you. Thanks also to the people who helped in the making of the first edition, Linda Morris, Brian Herrmann, and Charles Hutchinson.

I'd also like to extend my gratitude to the web development community in general for the never-ending inspiration and motivation. The same goes for the hard-working people at W3C, Khronos, and other organizations trying to make the Web a better place through open standards. Keep fighting the good fight.

Finally, thanks to my beautiful Ulla for the endless support and patience. Thank you for believing.

Contents

Introduction

"ALL THIS IS done in HTML5, by the way!" exclaimed Steve Jobs, the mind and face of the Apple success story, as he walked the audience through the new HTML5-powered ad system at the iPhone OS 4.0 Keynote, receiving cheers, laughs, and applause in return. The recent developments in open, standards-based web technologies are moving the web forward at an increasing pace, and Apple's embrace of HTML5, including the blocking of Flash on all iOS devices, is just another symbol of the power of this movement. Although Apple's love for HTML5 might in part be fueled by business motives, it is clear that the open web is on the move and exciting things are happening on an almost daily basis, making it an exciting time for web and game developers alike.

The world of web and game development wasn't always this exciting, however. Building games for the browser could be a frustrating experience and has traditionally meant having to choose between using feature-rich plugin-based technologies or settling for a more low-tech approach, trying to fit the square peg of HTML and JavaScript into the round hole of game development. Disagreeing or downright broken implementations of various standards have only made the consistent and predictable environment of, for instance, Flash more appealing.

By opting for plugins like Flash, developers and game designers gain access to frameworks that are suitable for advanced game development, featuring dynamic graphics, sounds, and even 3D, but doing so also disconnects the game from the technologies surrounding it. Although technologies such as Flash, Java, and Silverlight all have means to communicate with the rest of the page, they remain isolated objects with limited capabilities for mixing with the surrounding content.

In contrast, using HTML, JavaScript, and CSS — the native building blocks of the web — means your game will fit naturally within the context of a web page, but with them comes other compromises, not the least of which is a lack of suitable elements and APIs. When the first editions of the HTML standard were published in the mid-1990s, it is doubtful that anyone had rich Internet applications in mind, and HTML's document-centric nature meant that it was much more suitable for marking up pages of text and images than for application and game development. Even as these pages slowly became more and more interactive as JavaScript and the Document Object Model (DOM) evolved, graphics were still limited to static images and styled HTML elements, and audio was pretty much nonexistent. Only recently have the specifications for HTML5, CSS3, and other related standards evolved in the direction of actual applications, allowing developers to build experiences more akin to desktop applications than the traditional page-based web site. Naturally, these developments also apply to web games, and many of the recent advancements are a perfect fit for games and other interactive entertainment applications.

Who this book is for

HTML, JavaScript, and CSS are no longer limited to building web sites; web apps can be deployed on the web, as desktop widgets, and on mobile devices and many other places. If you are in any way interested in developing games for these targets and want to leverage your existing web development skills to do so, this is the book for you.

You probably already know a good deal about web development and have worked with HTML, CSS, and JavaScript previously. *HTML5 Games* is not a general guide to HTML5, and it does not teach you how to build web sites, so it is generally assumed throughout the book that you have some basic experience with traditional HTML and have at least heard of the new elements and APIs. Not all aspects of HTML5 are covered either, simply because they are not very relevant to games. You do not need to be an expert programmer, but you should have some experience with JavaScript. The new JavaScript APIs introduced with HTML5 are, of course, covered and explained, but it is otherwise expected that you have a good grasp of the language itself.

HTML5 Games is also not a book about game design. Many excellent books are available that deal with all conceivable aspects of game development more in depth than what this book can offer you. Trying to cover topics as diverse as artificial intelligence, physics simulation, and advanced graphics programming with enough detail to do them justice would leave little room to talk about HTML5 and web development. That being said, you don't need any prior experience with game development, nor do you need to be a mathematician or a great artist to use this book. *HTML5 Games* stays in the shallow end in terms of game development theory, and any nontrivial math and programming concepts that are used are explained as they are introduced. An interest in games and web development, a bit of high school math, and the ability to create very basic graphics should get you through the book just fine.

What this book is about

HTML5 Games is about taking your skills in web development and applying them to game development. It doesn't matter if you are a web developer looking to move into the game development field, a Flash game developer interested in the new open web technologies, or if you possess an entirely different goal, *HTML5 Games* shows you how to use the tools you already know to bridge the divide between traditional web sites and fun game experiences.

During the course of the book, you go through the development of a complete web game from the initial white page to the final product, ready to play in both the browser as well as on your iPhone or Android device. You see how to utilize new elements such as `canvas` and `audio` to make games that fit naturally in the context of the web without relying on plugins or ugly hacks. You learn how to add multiplayer functionality using Web Sockets and Node. js, how to store game data on the client with Web Storage, and how to manipulate graphics down to the pixel level using `canvas`. You also see how the game can easily be moved to mobile devices, taking advantage of touch input. In addition, you see how your applications can be made available offline with the new application cache. Finally, *HTML5 Games* examines the options available for deploying and distributing the finished game. When you finish the book, you will be able to take these lessons and apply them to your own projects, creating smashing web games that fully exploit today's open web technologies.

Most of the code you will encounter throughout the book is available from the book's companion web site, which you will find at `www.wiley.com/go/html5games.com`. From there, you can download an archive containing all the code for the example game as well as many smaller, independent examples. Inside the archive, you will find a folder for each chapter of the book. These folders contain the example web game as it exists at the end of each chapter. If the given chapter has any examples not related to the game, you will find those in a sub-folder called *examples*.

As you work your way through the book, I encourage you to try building the game from the ground up but if you prefer to just examine the sample code, that's perfectly fine as well. In any case, I hope you will have fun.

Now, let's get started. Game on.

Part I

Getting Started with HTML5 Games

Chapter 1
Gaming on the Web

In This Chapter

- Finding out what HTML5 is and where it came from
- Seeing HTML5 within the context of games
- Looking at important new features
- Enabling feature detection and dealing with legacy browsers

BEFORE I DIVE into code, I want to establish the context of the technology we use. In this first chapter, I discuss what HTML5 is as well as some of the history that led to the HTML5 specification.

One of the most interesting aspects of HTML5 is how game developers can profit from many of its new features. In this chapter, I introduce you to some of those features and give you a few quick examples of how to use them. I talk about the canvas element and WebGL and the huge improvement they make in creating dynamic graphics. I also cover the audio element and the added multiplayer possibilities created by the WebSocket specification.

Everybody likes new toys, but remember that in the real world, old and outdated browsers keep many users from taking advantage of these cutting-edge features. In this chapter, I discuss a few tools that can help you detect which features you can safely use as well as how you can use these feature tests to load appropriate fallback solutions when necessary.

Finally, I briefly introduce the puzzle game that I use throughout the rest of the book to take you through the creation of a complete HTML5 game.

Tracing the History of HTML5

HTML, the language of the web, has gone through numerous revisions since its invention in the early 1990s. When Extensible Markup Language (XML) was all the rage around the turn of the millennium, a lot of effort went into transforming HTML into an XML-compliant language. However, lack of adoption, browser support, and backward compatibility left the web in a mess with no clear direction and a standards body that some felt was out of touch with the realities of the web.

When the W3C finally abandoned the XHTML project, an independent group had already formed with the goal of making the web more suitable for the type of web applications you see today. Instead of just building upon the last specification, the Web Hypertext Application Technology Working Group (WHATWG) began documenting existing development patterns and non-standard browser features used in the wild. Eventually, the W3C joined forces with the WHATWG. The two groups now work together to bring new and exciting features to the HTML5 specification. Because this new specification more closely reflects how web developers already use the web, making the switch to HTML5 is easy, too. Unlike previous revisions, HTML5 doesn't enforce a strict set of syntax rules. Updating a page can often be as easy as changing the document type declaration.

But what is HTML5? Originally, it referred to the latest revision of the HTML standard. Nowadays, it's harder to define; the term has gone to buzzword hell and is now used to describe many technologies that aren't part of the HTML5 specification. Even the W3C got caught up in the all-inclusiveness of HTML5. For a brief period, they defined it as including, for example, Cascading Style Sheets (CSS) and Scalable Vector Graphics (SVG). This only added to the confusion. Fortunately, the W3C backed away from that stance and went back to the original, stricter definition that refers only to the actual HTML5 specification. In a somewhat bolder move, the WHATWG simply dropped the numeral 5, renaming it simply *HTML*. This actually brings it much closer to reality, in the sense that specifications such as HTML are always evolving and never completely supported by any browser. In this book, I just use the term *HTML* for the most part. You can assume that any mention of HTML5 refers to the actual W3C specification called HTML5.

Using HTML5 for Games

Many features from the HTML5 specification have applications in game development, but one of the first features to gain widespread popularity was the canvas element. The visual nature of this element without a doubt helped it spread quickly when the first interactive animations and graphics effects started appearing. More advanced projects soon followed, giving the new standard a dose of good publicity and promising a future with a more dynamic and visually interesting web.

Canvas

Hobbyist game developers were also among the first to embrace HTML5, and for good reason. The `canvas` element provides web game developers with the ability to create dynamic graphics, giving them a welcome alternative to static images and animated GIFs.

Sure, people have created more or less ingenious (and/or crazy) solutions in lieu of better tools for creating dynamic graphics. Entire drawing libraries rely on nothing more than colored `div` elements—that may be clever, but that approach isn't sufficient for doing anything more than drawing a few simple shapes.

Uniform Resource Identifier (URI) schemes let you assign source files to `img` elements, for example, using a base64-encoded data string, either directly in the HTML or by setting the `src` or `href` property with JavaScript. One of the clever uses of this `data` URI scheme is to generate images on the fly and thus provide a dynamically animated image, which isn't a great solution for anything but small and simple images.

Wolf 5K, the winner of the 2002 The 5K contest, which challenged developers to create a website in just five kilobytes, used a somewhat similar technique. The game, a small 3D maze game, generated black and white images at runtime and fed them continuously to the image `src` property, relying on the fact that `img` elements can also take a JavaScript expression in place of an actual URL.

Graphics drawn on a `canvas` surface can't be declared with HTML markup; instead, they must be drawn with JavaScript using a simple Application Programming Interface (API). Listing 1-1 shows a basic example of how to draw a few simple shapes. Note that the full API provides much more functionality than the small portion shown in this example.

Listing 1-1 Drawing shapes with the canvas API

```
<canvas id="mycanvas"></canvas>
<script>
    var canvas = document.getElementById("mycanvas"),
        ctx = canvas.getContext("2d");

    canvas.width = canvas.height = 200;

    // draw two blue circles
```

continued

Listing 1-1   continued

```
    ctx.fillStyle = "blue";
    ctx.beginPath();
    ctx.arc(50, 50, 25, 0, Math.PI * 2, true);
    ctx.arc(150, 50, 25, 0, Math.PI * 2, true);
    ctx.fill();

    // draw a red triangle
    ctx.fillStyle = "red";
    ctx.beginPath();
    ctx.moveTo(100, 75);
    ctx.lineTo(75, 125);
    ctx.lineTo(125, 125);
    ctx.fill();

    // draw a green semi-circle
    ctx.strokeStyle = "green";
    ctx.beginPath();
    ctx.scale(1, 0.5);
    ctx.arc(100, 300, 75, Math.PI, 0, true);
    ctx.closePath();
    ctx.stroke();
</script>
```

The code produces the drawing shown in Figure 1-1.

FIGURE 1-1: This simple canvas drawing was created with JavaScript.

I revisit the `canvas` element in Chapter 6 and explore it in detail when I use it to create game graphics and special effects.

Audio

The new `audio` element is just as welcome to a web game developers' toolbox as the `canvas` element. Finally, you have native audio capabilities in the browser without resorting to plug-ins. Not too long ago, if a website had audio, some form of Flash was involved. Libraries like the SoundManager 2 project (`www.schillmania.com/projects/soundmanager2`) provide full JavaScript access to most of the audio features of Flash. But even if such a bridge allows your own code to stay on the JavaScript side, your users still need to install the plug-in. The HTML5 `audio` element solves this problem, making access to audio available in browsers out of the box using only plain old HTML and JavaScript.

The `audio` element still has a few unresolved issues, however. The major browser vendors all seem to agree on the importance of the element and have all adopted the specification, but so far they've failed to agree on which audio codecs should be supported. So, while the theory of the `audio` element is good, reality has left developers with no other option than to provide audio files in multiple formats to appease all the browser vendors.

The `audio` element can be defined in the mark-up or created dynamically with JavaScript. (The latter option is of more interest to you as an application and game developer.) Listing 1-2 shows a basic music player with multiple source files, native user interface (UI) controls, and a few keyboard hotkeys that use the JavaScript API.

Listing 1-2   A simple music player with HTML5 audio

```
<audio controls id="myaudio">
    <source src="Prelude In E Minor, Op. 28.ogg"/>
    <source src="Prelude In E Minor, Op. 28.mp3"/>
</audio>
<script>
    var audio = document.getElementById("myaudio");
    document.onkeydown = function(e) {
        if (e.keyCode == 83) {
            audio.pause(); // Key pressed was S
        } else if (e.keyCode == 80) {
            audio.play(); // Key pressed was P
        }
    };
</script>
```

TIP The W3C is currently working on expanding HTML5 with the Web Audio API, which enables advanced audio synthesizing and processing. Because this API is still experimental, I won't be using it for the game in this book, although I briefly examine the possibilities it presents in Chapter 10 when I dive into HTML5 audio.

WebSockets

Ajax and the `XMLHttpRequest` object at its heart brought new life to the web with the Web 2.0 explosion in the early 2000s. Despite the many great things it has enabled, however, it is still painfully limited. Being restricted to the HTTP protocol, the action is rather one-sided, as the client must actively ask the server for information. The web server has no way of telling the browser that something has changed unless the browser performs a new request. The typical solution has been to poll the server repeatedly, asking for updates, or alternatively to keep the request open until there is something to report. The umbrella term *Comet* (http://en.wikipedia.org/wiki/Comet_(programming)) is sometimes used to refer to these techniques. In many cases, that is good enough, but these solutions are rather simple and often lack the flexibility and performance necessary for multiplayer games.

Enter WebSockets. With WebSockets, you're a big step closer to the level of control necessary for efficient game development. Although it isn't a completely raw socket connection, a WebSocket connection does allow you to create and maintain a connection with two-way communication, making implementation of real-time multiplayer games much easier. As Listing 1-3 demonstrates, the interface for connecting to the server and exchanging messages is quite simple.

Listing 1-3   Interacting with the server with WebSockets
```
// Create a new WebSocket object
var socket = new WebSocket("ws://mygameserver.com:4200/");

// Send an initial message to the server
socket.onopen = function () {
    socket.send("Hello server!");
};

// Listen for any data sent to us by the server
socket.onmessage = function(msg) {
    alert("Server says: " + msg);
};
```

Of course, using WebSockets requires that you also implement a server application that's compatible with the WebSockets protocol and capable of responding to the messages you send to it. This doesn't have to be a complex task, however, as I show you in Chapter 13 when you build a simple chat application using WebSockets and Node.js.

Web Storage

Cookies are the usual choice when web applications need to store data on the client. Their bad reputation as spyware-tracking devices aside, cookies have also given developers a much-needed place to store user settings and web servers a means of recognizing returning clients, which is a necessary feature for many web applications because of the stateless nature of the HTTP protocol.

Originally a part of HTML5 but later promoted to its own specification, Web Storage can be seen as an improvement on cookies and can, in many cases, directly replace cookies as a larger storage device for key-value type data. There is more to Web Storage than that, however. Whereas cookies are tied only to the domain, Web Storage has a local storage that's similar to cookies and a session storage that's tied to the active window and page, allowing multiple instances of the same application in different tabs or windows. Unlike cookies, Web Storage lives on only the client and isn't transmitted with each HTTP request, allowing for storage space measured in megabytes instead of kilobytes.

Having access to persistent storage capable of holding at least a few megabytes of data comes in handy when you want to store any sort of complex data. Web Storage can store only strings, but if you couple it with a JavaScript Object Notation (JSON) encoder/decoder, which is natively available in most browsers today, you can easily work around this limitation to hold structures that are more complex. In the game that you develop during the course of this book, you use local Web Storage to implement a Save Game feature as well as to store local high score data.

Listing 1-4 shows the simple and intuitive interface to the storage.

Listing 1-4   Saving local data with Web Storage

```
// save highscore data
localStorage.setItem("highscore", "152400");

// data can later be retrieved, even on other pages
var highscore = localStorage.getItem("highscore");

alert(highscore); // alerts 154200
```

WebGL

WebGL is OpenGL for the web. It's based on OpenGL ES 2.0. The most widely used graphics API is now available for web developers to create online 3D graphics content. Of course, this has major implications for the kind of web games that are now possible. As a testament to this significance, Google developers released a WebGL port of the legendary first-person shooter, "Quake II," on April 1, 2010, to general disbelief because of both the carefully chosen release date and the achievement itself.

REMEMBER Using WebGL requires you to be very aware of the platforms you plan to target. Neither Android nor iOS currently supports WebGL, limiting you to desktop browsers. Furthermore, Internet Explorer prior to IE 11 supports only the 2D canvas context. In this book, I show you how to create the game graphics using both WebGL and 2D canvas.

HTML5 and Flash

Ever since the arrival of the `canvas` element and the improved JavaScript engines, the Internet has seen discussions and good old flame wars over whether the new standards would replace Flash as the dominant delivery method for multimedia applications on the web. Flash has long been the favorite choice when it comes to online video, music, and game development. Although competing technologies such as Microsoft's Silverlight have tried to beat it, they've made only a small dent in the Flash market share. HTML5 and its related open technologies now finally look like a serious contender for that top spot.

Adobe, the company behind Flash, has also shifted its priorities toward HTML5 and recently released Adobe Edge (`http://html.adobe.com/edge`), a development environment very similar to Flash but based fully on HTML5, CSS3, and JavaScript. Add to this the fact that Adobe Flash Professional CS6 introduced the option to publish directly to HTML5, and it seems all but certain that the proprietary Flash format will be phased out in favor of HTML5 and the open web.

REMEMBER HTML5 isn't a drop-in replacement for Flash. You must know where the new standards fall short and when alternative solutions like Flash might be more appropriate. Flash is still very handy for ensuring backward compatibility with older browsers, which I talk about next.

Creating Backward Compatibility

As with most other new technologies, issues with backward compatibility inevitably show up when working with HTML5. HTML5 isn't one big, monolithic thing: Browsers support *features*, not entire specifications. No browsers today can claim 100 percent support for all of the HTML5 feature sets, and Internet Explorer, still the most widely used browser, has only recently caught up with the rest of the browsers with features such as WebGL.

However, even if the current crop of browsers fully supports HTML5 and the related standards, you still have to think about legacy browsers. With browsers like Internet Explorer 8 still seeing significant use today you can't safely assume that the users of your applications and games can take advantage of all the features of HTML5 for many years to come. I recommend using the CanIUse website (`http://caniuse.com/`), which keeps tabs on most features and their past, current, and future browser support. A similar site, Mobile HTML5 (`http://mobilehtml5.org/`) focuses on feature support in mobile browsers.

Using feature detection

No one says that the applications and games you build today must support all browsers ever released—doing so would only lead to misery and hair-pulling. You shouldn't just forget about those users, though. The least you can do is try to tell whether the user is able to play the game or use a certain feature and then handle whatever problems you detect. Browser sniffing—that is, detecting what browser the user is using by examining its user agent string—has almost gone out of style. Today, the concept of feature detection has taken its place. Testing for available properties, objects, and functions is a much saner strategy than relying on a string that users can change and assuming a set of supported features.

With so many discrepancies in the various implementations and features that can be tricky to detect, adequate feature detection is no simple task. Fortunately, you don't usually need to reinvent the wheel because many clever tricks for detecting feature support have already been developed and aggregated in various libraries. One collection of these detectors is available in the Modernizr library (`www.modernizr.com`). Modernizr provides an easy-to-use method of testing whether a certain feature is available. You can detect everything from the `canvas` element and WebGL to web fonts and a whole slew of CSS features, allowing you to provide fallback solutions where features aren't supported and to degrade your application gracefully.

Filling the gaps with polyfills

Beginning in the early 2000s, a popular trend has been to favor so-called *progressive enhancement* when adding new features to websites. This strategy calls for websites to target the lowest common denominator in terms of supported features. Any technology that isn't supported across the board should be used only to add enhancements to the site, never critical functionality. This ensures that everyone can access and use the website. If the user has a modern browser, he simply has a better experience.

Progressive enhancement is a sound strategy in many cases, but sometimes you simply need to use a certain feature. If some browsers don't have native support for that feature, that hole must be plugged, even if it means using less than ideal or even hackish fallback solutions. These fallbacks are sometimes called *polyfills*, named after the spackling paste Polyfilla because their function is somewhat similar. They fill the cracks in the supported feature sets when you're running your code in actual browsers, bridging the gap between specifications and the reality of dealing with imperfect browsers. As an example, Internet Explorer had no support for `canvas` until IE9, but several polyfills exist that provide various amounts of `canvas` functionality for legacy browsers.

The ExplorerCanvas project from Google (`http://code.google.com/p/explorer canvas/`) was one of the earliest of these polyfills. It uses Vector Markup Language (VML), an old Microsoft developed XML-based language, to simulate a `canvas` element. Because it provides enough 2D drawing functionality, it's been used successfully in many projects. Some features are missing, however, because VML doesn't perfectly overlap the `canvas` specification and lacks support for patterns and clipping paths, for example.

Other polyfills use Flash or Silverlight to get even closer to the full `canvas` API, letting you use advanced features like image data access and compositing effects. With all these different options, picking the right fallback solutions is no easy task. Depending on the target platforms, sometimes even the polyfills need fallbacks.

Building a Game

Starting with Chapter 2 and throughout the rest of the book, I take you through the process of developing an HTML5 web game from scratch. I show you how to create a match-three gem-swapping game in the style of Bejeweled or Puzzle Quest, casual games that have been very popular on many platforms over the past decade. This type of game has tried-and-tested game mechanics, allowing you to focus your attention on the use of web technologies in the context of game development. Additionally, these games play well on desktop browsers and on mobile devices such as smart phones and tablets, all of which give you the opportunity to explore multiplatform web game development.

The game you'll develop takes advantage of several features from the HTML5 specification and also uses related technologies such as web fonts and CSS3 for building the UI. Although the game may not be revolutionary, it allows me to cover many of the newest advances in open web technology. Among other things, I use the `canvas` element to generate some of the game graphics, and I show you how to add sound effects using HTML5 audio. The finished game will be playable on a desktop browser, and I show you how to ensure that it plays just as well on mobile devices and even offline. I show you how to use Web Storage to save high-score data and to allow players to pick up where they left off.

The `canvas` element lets you create interesting dynamic graphics, but it isn't always suitable for creating user interfaces. You don't really need any new tools for that part, however, because traditional HTML and CSS give you all you need to build a great UI. With the latest additions to the CSS specification, you can add animations, transforms, and other features that bring life to the UI experience. In Chapters 6 and 7, I show you how to build the display module with the canvas element. Later on, in Chapter 11, I take you a bit further as I show you how to use WebGL to add 3D graphics to the game.

In Chapter 13, I show you how to create a simple chat application using WebSockets. For this purpose, I also show you how to develop a small server application using the Node.js framework (`http://nodejs.org`). WebSockets are supported in most modern browsers, one notable exception being the Android browser, which as of Android 4.3, still doesn't support this feature.

Summary

It's been a bumpy road but it finally looks like HTML and the web in general are on the right track again. The WHATWG brought in some fresh perspective on the standards process, and web developers are now beginning to enjoy the fruits of this undertaking in the plethora of new tools and an HTML standard that's more in line with how the web is used today. As always, using new features requires dealing with older browsers but many polyfills that you can use to ensure cross-browser compatibility are already available.

Many of the new additions are of special interest to game developers because real alternatives to Flash-based web games are now available. Canvas and WebGL bring dynamic- and hardware-accelerated graphics to the table; the `audio` element has finally enabled native sound; and with WebSockets, it's now possible to create multiplayer experiences that more closely match desktop games than was possible just a few years ago. Advances in other, related areas like CSS and the increasing support for web fonts let you create richer UI experiences using open, standardized tools.

Chapter 2
Taking the First Steps

In This Chapter

- Setting out the rules and mechanics of the game
- Identifying various stages of the game
- Setting up the basic HTML
- Creating the first JavaScript modules
- Making a splash screen using web fonts

WITH THE BACKGROUND and technological context covered in the previous chapter, it's now time to get your hands dirty. However, before you start writing code and markup, it's important to understand the project. In the first part of this chapter, I describe the rules, goals, and mechanics of the game. I also define the key stages of the game and identify the individual screens that make up the application.

With the game clearly defined, you can finally start putting down some code. Starting with the basics, I show you how to set up an HTML page with some simple structure to support the game. From there, I add some preliminary CSS and show how you can use JavaScript to control dynamic loading of extra scripts. I also introduce the first two JavaScript modules, the main application module, and a helper module to make Document Object Model (DOM) manipulation easier.

Finally, I turn to the first of the game stages and use web fonts to create a splash screen with a fancy game logo.

Understanding the Game

The game I walk you through in this book is a match-three puzzle game, a game type made popular mainly by the Bejeweled game series by casual game developer PopCap Games. I have named the game Jewel Warrior; feel free to pick a better and more creative name as you go through the process.

Before you begin actually building the game, you explore the components and processes of the game—the core mechanics and rules of the game and the different stages of the game. From the initial launch of the application to the point where the player exits the game, the users see different stages of the application that all behave differently. Take a look at the mechanics of the actual game and leave other key stages such as menus and loading screens for later.

Swapping jewels

The core of the game revolves around an 8x8 grid filled with jewels of various shapes and colors. When the game begins, each of the 64 cells holds a random jewel type. The goal of the game is to score points by matching jewels of the same kind in sets of three or more. The player can swap two adjacent jewels by selecting first one and then the other.

Matching three

A swap is legal only if it produces a match of three or more jewels of the same color; any illegal swaps are reversed automatically. When the player performs a valid swap, all jewels included in the matching set are removed. If any jewels are above the resulting gaps, these jewels fall down, and new, randomly picked jewels enter the game area from the top. The simplest match is a match with three identical jewels, but it's also possible to create chains of four or five matching jewels. The more jewels the player matches in a single row or column, the more points he or she receives.

Triggering chain reactions reward the player with additional points. After a valid swap, the falling jewels can produce even more groups of matching jewels, which are then subject to a bonus multiplier. By carefully examining the board, the player can even trigger these chain reactions intentionally to score extra points.

During the course of a game, the player can also face a situation where no valid moves are left. If no swaps can produce a set of at least three identical jewels, the game board must be reshuffled. The board is cleared of jewels, and new ones are brought in using the same randomized fill routing that was used when the board was initially set up.

Level progression

To create a sense of urgency, I introduce a timer that slowly counts down. If the timer reaches zero, the game ends. The player can progress to the next level by reaching a specified number of points before the timer runs out. This triggers a refill of the jewel board, resets the timer, and raises the number of points needed to advance to the next level. This might keep players on their toes, but without modification, a skilled player can keep playing indefinitely. To make the game harder and harder as time goes by, the point gap between levels increases each time the player advances. Eventually, even the best jewel swapper fails to gather enough points in the allotted time.

Identifying Game Stages

The game-playing stage of the application is by far the most complicated stage and is where the player will be spending most of his or her time. You do need a few additional stages, however, because you shouldn't dump the player straight into the game.

Splash screen

The very first thing the player sees is a splash screen. This screen serves two purposes: First, it introduces the player to the game by displaying the game logo front and center. Second, by adding a progress bar, it provides a nice waiting area while the game's assets are preloaded behind the curtain. Not all assets need to be preloaded right away, but it creates a better impression if all the graphics for the next stage are immediately available when the stage is activated. Figure 2-1 shows a sketch of what the splash screen will look like.

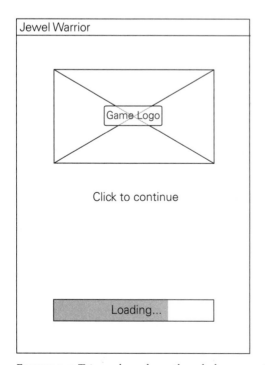

FIGURE 2-1: This mock up shows the splash screen with preloader.

Main menu

After the player clicks through the splash screen, she is taken to the main menu. This is a simple menu with just a few items. Most importantly, the menu gives access to the actual game but also features buttons for displaying the high score, more info about the game, and an option to exit the game. If the player selects a new or previous game, the game begins right away. Figure 2-2 shows a sketch of the main menu.

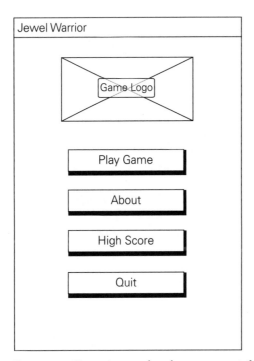

FIGURE 2-2: The main menu lets the user access information about the game.

Playing the game

When the actual game begins, the game elements—the jewel board, player name, and current score—occupy most of the screen, but the player needs to be able to exit back to the main menu. I enable this by using a small slice of the screen to make a status or toolbar. See Figure 2-3 for a sketch of the game area.

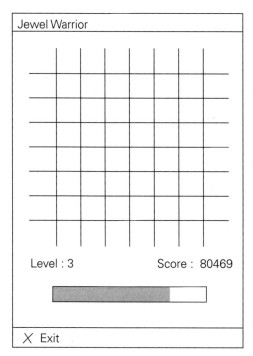

FIGURE 2-3: The sketch of the game screen includes a grid and space for a toolbar.

High score

When the game ends, the application switches to a high score list showing the top scores along with the player names. If the player achieved a score that's high enough, he's asked to enter his name, after which the score is entered into the list. This screen has an option to return to the main menu. The game uses a locally stored high score list based on WebStorage. The sketch in Figure 2-4 shows the basic layout of the high score list.

Jewel Warrior		
High Scores		
1	AAA	256000
2	BBB	128000
3	CCC	64000
4	DDD	32000
5	EEE	16000
6	FFF	8000
7	GGG	4000
8	HHH	2000
9	III	1000
10	JJJ	500
	↰ Main menu	

FIGURE 2-4: This sketch shows a typical high score list.

Creating the Application Skeleton

You don't need special tools or applications to follow the development of the game. When you get to the WebSocket discussion in Chapter 13, you do need to install Node.js and set it up on your web server. For everything else, however, your favorite text editor and a simple image editor will do.

Many web developers use libraries such as jQuery and Prototype so they don't have to deal with the trivial parts of web development, such as selecting and manipulating DOM elements. Often, you'll find that these libraries include a lot of functionality that you aren't using. It's sometimes a good idea to ask yourself if you really need a 50–100K library or if something simpler and smaller will do, especially when developing for mobile platforms where a fast Internet isn't guaranteed.

I generally don't use third-party libraries in this book in order to better show the core fundamentals. Feel free to use other libraries to make things easier in your own projects, but pay attention to what functionality you actually need so you don't add unnecessary bloat to your project. The MicroJS website (`http://microjs.com`) features a collection of micro libraries that focuses on particular areas rather than elaborate frameworks.

Okay, time to get started. Create an empty folder for the game project and create two sub-folders: `scripts` and `styles`. Later in the process, a few extra folders are added, but these two are enough for now.

Setting up the HTML

The foundation of the game is just a regular HTML document. Create a new file, name it `index.html`, and put it in the project folder. Listing 2-1 shows the initial content of `index.html`.

Listing 2-1   The empty HTML document

```
<!DOCTYPE HTML>
<html lang="en-US">
<head>
    <meta charset="UTF-8">
    <title>Jewel Warrior</title>
</head>
<body>
    <div id="game">
        <!-- game goes here -->
    </div>
</body>
</html>
```

Notice the dead simple document type declaration. Compare this to, for example, the HTML 4.01 Strict `DOCTYPE`:

```
<!DOCTYPE HTML PUBLIC "-//W3C//DTD HTML 4.01//EN"
  "http://www.w3.org/TR/html4/strict.dtd">
```

Gone are the monstrosities of yesteryear. The `DOCTYPE` is now simple enough that you can actually memorize it. The `meta` tag used for declaring the character encoding got a similar treatment. Hooray for keeping things simple!

Back to the HTML document. The `div` tag in the body is the overall game container. The rest of the game markup goes inside this tag. The next level of markup contains the various game screens listed earlier in this chapter. A `div` container with the CSS class `screen` signifies a game screen, and each screen has a unique `id` that is used to refer to that particular game screen. Listing 2-2 shows the first few screens added to the game container.

Listing 2-2   Adding screen elements to the game container

. . .

```
<div id="game">
    <div class="screen" id="splash-screen"></div>
    <div class="screen" id="main-menu"></div>
    <div class="screen" id="game-screen"></div>
    <div class="screen" id="high-scores"></div>
</div>
```

. . .

I return to the splash screen later in this chapter, but for now, you have enough structure in place that you can start adding some CSS.

Adding a bit of style

You'll find a few different style sheets throughout the book. The first style sheet, `main.css`, contains rules for styling the overall structure of the game application. Listing 2-3 shows the style sheet added to the `head` element.

Listing 2-3   Adding the main style sheet

. . .

```
<head>
    <meta charset="UTF-8">
    <title>Jewel Warrior</title>

    <link rel="stylesheet" href="styles/main.css" />
</head>
```

. . .

REMEMBER   HTML5 defines a default value of `text/css` for the `type` attribute when the `rel` attribute is set to `stylesheet`. That means you no longer need to set the `type` attribute explicitly.

For now, the style sheet targets desktop browsers. In Chapter 3, I discuss how to deal with mobile browsers and show how you can use CSS media queries to load different style sheets for different devices and resolutions. Initially, you only need a few simple rules in the main style sheet. Listing 2-4 shows the CSS rules in `main.css`.

Listing 2-4 **The initial content of the main style sheet**

```
body {
    margin : 0;
    overflow : hidden;
}

#game {
    position : absolute;
    left : 0;
    top : 0;
    width : 320px;
    height : 480px;
    background-color : rgb(30,30,30);
}

#game .screen {
    position : absolute;
    width : 100%;
    height : 100%;
    display : none;
    z-index : 10;
}

#game .screen.active {
    display : block;
}
```

The body rule simply cancels any default margin added around the body element by the browser. The #game rule styles the containing div with a dark gray background and makes it fill a 320x480 rectangle, which is a nice size for a game like this and also works well with, for example, the iPhone. The screen div elements all have the display property set to none. This ensures that the screens are hidden by default and appear only when you want them to. An active CSS class on a screen div element switches the display property to block.

Loading the scripts

In recent years, script loading has become an art in itself as the issue of loading scripts efficiently has received more and more attention. For this project, I show you the basics of dynamic script loading, but if you want something more advanced, I recommend looking at the Microjs website where you'll find several script loaders. One example is the Yepnope library, which is also incorporated into Modernizr. By using the feature detection of Modernizr and the conditional loading of Yepnope, it's easy to load only the right scripts and fallbacks.

You create the jewel.js script in a moment. Listing 2-5 shows the additions to the head element in index.html.

Listing 2-5   Adding the main script

```
...
<head>
    ...
    <script src="scripts/jewel.js"></script>
</head>
...
```

> **REMEMBER** Just as with link elements and style sheets, you no longer need to set the script type on script tags explicitly. If the type attribute is absent, a default value of text/javascript is used.

The main jewel.js script creates a jewel namespace object in which all the game modules will live. It also, among other things, provides the functionality necessary to load any other scripts that need to be loaded. To start with, add the empty load() and setup() functions. The load() function will be responsible for loading extra script files and will call the callback function when each script is done. Listing 2-6 shows the initial script.

Listing 2-6   The initial contents of jewel.js

```
var jewel = (function() {

    function load(src, callback) {
    }

    function setup() {
    }

    return {
        load: load,
        setup: setup
    };
})();
```

All game modules are properties of the jewel namespace and are basically just objects with some public methods. If you've ever used the so-called Module Pattern in your own code, you'll be familiar with this method. All functionality is defined inside an anonymous function that returns an object literal with references to the functions that should be exposed to the outside world. The anonymous function is immediately invoked, and the return value is assigned to a property on the jewel namespace object.

This modular approach is an easy way to keep the application code from polluting the global scope, thereby making integration with third-party scripts more difficult. The encapsulation in an anonymous function effectively hides, for good or bad, all variables and functions declared inside the module unless they're explicitly made public.

The load() function should load the file specified in the src parameter and put into an execution queue that operates on the first-in-first-out principle. This ensures that the scripts execute in the correct order. Because all the scripts are loaded in parallel, there's no guarantee that they finish loading in the order they were added. Listing 2-7 shows the load() function.

Listing 2-7   **The jewel.load() function**

```
var jewel = (function() {
    var scriptQueue = [],
        numResourcesLoaded = 0,
        numResources = 0,
        executeRunning = false;

    function executeScriptQueue() {
    }

    function load(src, callback) {
        var image, queueEntry;
        numResources++;

        // add this resource to the execution queue
        queueEntry = {
            src: src,
            callback: callback,
            loaded: false
        };
        scriptQueue.push(queueEntry);

        image = new Image();
        image.onload = image.onerror = function() {
            numResourcesLoaded++;
```

continued

Listing 2-7   **continued**
```
            queueEntry.loaded = true;
            if (!executeRunning) {
                executeScriptQueue();
            }
        };
        image.src = src;
    }
    ...
})();
```

First, the load() function adds the script to the scriptQueue array. It stores not only the name of the file but also the callback function and a Boolean flag indicating whether it has finished loading. After this, the file is loaded but not with a script element, as you might expect, but as an Image. Now, a JavaScript file is obviously not a valid image, but the browser will load the file just the same and trigger an onerror event when it's done loading. This lets you load the script without actually executing it, as would happen with a script element. Don't be alarmed if you see warnings related to MIME types in the console. These notices are harmless.

When the file has loaded, the onerror/onload handler changes the loaded flag and calls the executeScriptQueue() function shown in Listing 2-8.

Listing 2-8   **Executing scripts in the queue**
```
var jewel = (function() {
    var scriptQueue = [],
        numResourcesLoaded = 0,
        numResources = 0,
        executeRunning = false;

    function executeScriptQueue() {
        var next = scriptQueue[0],
            first, script;
        if (next && next.loaded) {
            executeRunning = true;
            // remove the first element in the queue
            scriptQueue.shift();
            first = document.getElementsByTagName("script")[0];
            script = document.createElement("script");
            script.onload = function() {
                if (next.callback) {
                    next.callback();
                }
                // try to execute more scripts
```

```
                    executeScriptQueue();
                };
                script.src = next.src;
                first.parentNode.insertBefore(script, first);
            } else {
                executeRunning = false;
            }
        }
        ...
})();
```

The `executeScriptQueue()` function checks whether the first script in the queue has finished loading and, if so, removes it from the queue and adds it to the page by creating a `script` element and inserting it before the very first `script` element on the page. You could also add it to the `head` element. However, that solution is less robust because a document isn't guaranteed to have a `head`, whereas you know it has least one `script` element—the one currently running. The `executeRunning` flag is set to true to stop the image `onload` handlers from calling `executeScriptQueue()` again.

You will know when the script has been executed by adding a handler for the `onload` event on the `script` element. This handler must should the `callback` function, if one was provided, and it should also call `executeScriptQueue()` again to try to execute the next script in the queue.

If the first script in the queue has not finished loading yet, `executeScriptQueue()` simply sets `executeRunning` to false. This will allow the image `onload` handler from Listing 2-7 to kick off the script execution again once the next script finishes loading.

Creating a DOM helper module

To ease the task of working with the DOM, you can often create a few helper functions for manipulating DOM elements. That is what the `dom.js` module provides. Listing 2-9 shows the `dom.js` module with the first batch of helper functions.

Listing 2-9 The DOM helper module

```
jewel.dom = (function() {

    function $(path, parent) {
        parent = parent || document;
        return parent.querySelectorAll(path);
    }
```

continued

Listing 2-9   **continued**

```
function hasClass(el, clsName) {
    var regex = new RegExp("(^|\\s)" + clsName + "(\\s|$)");
    return regex.test(el.className);
}

function addClass(el, clsName) {
    if (!hasClass(el, clsName)) {
        el.className += " " + clsName;
    }
}

function removeClass(el, clsName) {
    var regex = new RegExp("(^|\\s)" + clsName + "(\\s|$)");
    el.className = el.className.replace(regex, " ");
}

return {
    $ : $,
    hasClass : hasClass,
    addClass : addClass,
    removeClass : removeClass
};
})();
```

The `jewel.dom` module initially has only a few functions for manipulating CSS classes. The module also exposes a `$()` function, which is just a wrapper for the `querySelectorAll()` function. This function lets you use CSS selectors to easily select DOM elements, similar to the `$()` function in jQuery.

The `hasClass()` function examines the `className` attribute on a given element and returns `true` if the specified class is found. It does this using a regular expression with three parts. The first part (`^|\\s`) matches either the beginning of the string or a blank space, the second part is just the class name, and third part, (`\\s|$`), matches the end of a string or a blank space. The functions `addClass()` and `removeClass()` do what they advertise: They add or remove a specified CSS class from an element.

Finally, use `jewel.load()` to load the new module in `index.html`, as shown in Listing 2-10.

Listing 2-10   **Loading the jewel.dom module**

```
...
<head>
    ...
    <script src="scripts/jewel.js"></script>
    <script>
        window.addEventListener("load", function() {
            jewel.load("scripts/dom.js", jewel.setup);
        });
    </script>
</head>
...
```

Pass the `setup()` function as the callback parameter to have that function called when the DOM module is loaded and executed. If you load `index.html` in a browser now, you should see the game's dark gray background. If you want to test whether the files are loaded correctly, try adding an `alert()` or `console.log()` call to the `setup()` function in `jewel.js`:

```
var jewel = (function() {
    ...
    function setup() {
        console.log("Success!");
    }
    ...
})();
```

Debugging web applications

I assume you're somewhat familiar with the debugging tools available in modern browsers. Firefox, Chrome, and Internet Explorer 9+ all have very nice console and inspection tools, usually available by pressing F12. Most browsers today support the now almost standard console output API, allowing you to output debugging messages to the console by adding lines such as these:

```
console.log("Your log message here");
console.warn("Your warning here");
console.error("Your error here");
```

This is much less obtrusive than the `alert()` debugging that web developers had to resort to years ago. This book doesn't make a big deal out of adding debugging mechanisms or error handling in the code, focusing instead on getting to know the new features and technologies available today. However, I encourage you to add as many debug messages in the code as you want.

Adding functionality to the main module

Now it's time to move ahead and add some basic application logic such as switching between game states to the main module. Listing 2-11 shows the `showScreen()` function added to `jewel.js`.

Listing 2-11   **Switching screens**

```
jewel = (function() {
    ...
    // hide the active screen (if any) and show the screen
    // with the specified id
    function showScreen(screenId) {
        var dom = jewel.dom,
            $ = dom.$,
            activeScreen = $("#game .screen.active")[0],
            screen = $("#" + screenId)[0];
        if (activeScreen) {
            dom.removeClass(activeScreen, "active");
        }
        dom.addClass(screen, "active");
    }

    // expose public methods
    return {
        ...
        showScreen : showScreen
    };
})();
```

The `showScreen()` function simply displays the screen element with the specified ID attribute by giving it the `active` CSS class. If another screen is already active and visible, it's automatically hidden before the new screen is displayed.

REMEMBER   The `querySelectorAll()` function always returns a list of elements, even when only one or no elements at all are present. When you want to select just a single element, you therefore need to use the first element of this array rather than the array itself. Alternatively, you can use the `querySelector()` function.

Even if Jewel Warrior doesn't use a very deep namespace hierarchy, having to type the full module path to get to a function can still be annoying. To save on typing, you can easily make shortcut references to modules, as shown in Listing 2-11, where the showScreen() function has shorter, local references to the jewel.dom module and its $() function. Local references like these even improve JavaScript performance because the JavaScript engine doesn't need to traverse the namespace object structure to get to the variable every time it's needed.

Activating the splash screen

Now that you're able to switch between game screens, modify the jewel.setup() function to show the splash screen, as shown in Listing 2-12.

Listing 2-12 **Toggling the splash screen**

```
var jewel = (function() {
    ...
    function setup() {
        jewel.showScreen("splash-screen");
    }
    ...
})();
```

That takes care of toggling the visibility of the splash screen element, but of course your screen has no content yet. In the next part, I show you how to use web fonts to put a nice game logo on the splash screen.

Creating the Splash Screen

The splash screen is a simple screen that displays the game logo and text telling the user to click to continue. The Jewel Warrior logo is just the name of the game, set in an interesting typeface. Embedded web fonts now make logos like that easy to create using just HTML and CSS. Listing 2-13 shows the markup added to the splash screen div.

Listing 2-13   **Adding the splash screen markup**

```
...
    <div id="game">
        <div class="screen" id="splash-screen">
            <h1 class="logo">Jewel <br/>Warrior</h1>
            <span class="continue">Click to continue</span>
        </div>
        ...
    </div>
...
```

Working with web fonts

Until recently, the list of typefaces you could safely use on the web was short enough to memorize. Now, there are efforts to bring better types to the web converged on a common standard. By using CSS @font-face rules, you can embed fonts in a way that works in most browsers. The W3C recently published a new, standardized font format, Web Open Font Format (WOFF), and all modern desktop browsers already support it. However, if you want the highest level of browser compatibility, you must have the font available in several different formats. While Apple devices like the iPhone and the iPad all support the WOFF format provided they're running on iOS 5 or later, Android devices don't support WOFF in any versions older than the recently released Android 4.4.

> **NOTE** The WOFF web font format isn't part of HTML5, but has its own specification that reached final recommendation status in December 2012.

I chose two fonts for Jewel Warrior, Slackey Regular by Sideshow and Geo Regular by Ben Weiner. Both are available under free licenses from the Google Fonts directory (www.google. com/fonts). On the Google Fonts site, pick the fonts you want to use and select Add to Collection. When you're done, click the Use button in the bottom-right corner, and you'll be directed to a page where you can download a ZIP archive containing the selected TTF files. You can also find CSS links if you want to embed the fonts directly from the Google server, but be aware that your game will then require access to the Internet to use the font files.

If you want to use different typefaces in this or other web projects, I recommend just looking around the web. The Google Fonts site is only one of many font collections that target web fonts specifically. At FontSquirrel (www.fontsquirrel.com/), you can find many free fonts pre-packaged in kits that contain all the necessary font files and CSS. They even have an easy-to-use, online generator that lets you upload, for example, a TTF file and have a @font-face kit generated for you. I used this feature to convert the TTF files from Google Fonts to WOFF files.

Copy the font files from the Chapter 2 code archive and place them in a new folder called `fonts` in the project folder. The CSS font declarations go in a new CSS file, `fontfaces.css`, in the `styles` folder. Listing 2-14 shows the content of this style sheet.

Listing 2-14   **The custom @font-face rules**

```
@font-face {
    font-family: "Slackey";
    font-weight: normal;
    font-style: normal;
    src: url("../fonts/slackey.woff") format("woff"),
         url("../fonts/slackey.ttf") format("truetype");
}
@font-face {
    font-family: "Geo";
    font-weight: normal;
    font-style: normal;
    src: url("../fonts/geo.woff") format("woff"),
         url("../fonts/geo.ttf") format("truetype");
}
```

Setting up `@font-face` rules is quite simple. The `font-family` value is the name you use to refer to the font when using the font in the rest of the CSS. The `font-weight` and `font-style` properties let you embed font files for different weights and styles (bold, italic, and so on). I included only the regular fonts. When the browser encounters a `@font-face` rule, it reads the list of source files and downloads the first format it supports. Because Android devices don't support WOFF files yet, they simply ignore that entry and download the TrueType file instead.

WOFF and TTF font files are enough to get support from recent versions of Chrome, Opera, Firefox, Safari, as well as Internet Explorer 9+. If you want to support older browsers, you need more formats and the `@font-face` declaration gets a bit more complicated. For a solid cross-browser solution, I recommend reading the great article "Bulletproof @font-face Syntax" by Paul Irish at `http://paulirish.com/2009/bulletproof-font-face-implementation-syntax`.

TECHNICAL STUFF

Styling the splash screen

Throughout the game, I use Geo as the main font, so go ahead and set the font on the game container in `main.css`. This way, all the screen elements automatically inherit these values. Listing 2-15 shows the game container rule with the new font properties.

Listing 2-15   Adding a reference to the embedded font

```
#game {
    ...
    font-family : Geo;
    color : rgb(200,200,100);
}
```

Remember to also put a link reference to fontfaces.css in the head element in index.html:

```
<head>
    ...
    <link rel="stylesheet" href="styles/fontfaces.css" />
</head>
```

Now you can use the embedded fonts to make the splash screen look a bit nicer. The text on the splash screen already inherits the Geo font, but for this project, I want the logo to use Slackey. Listing 2-16 shows the CSS rules added to main.css.

Listing 2-16   Styling the splash screen

```
#splash-screen {
    text-align : center;
    padding-top : 100px;
}
#splash-screen .continue {
    cursor : pointer;
    font-size : 30px;
}
.logo {
    font-family : Slackey;
    font-size : 60px;
    line-height : 60px;
    margin : 0;
    text-align : center;
    color : rgb(70,120,20);
    text-shadow : 1px 1px 2px rgb(255,255,0),
                  -1px -1px 2px rgb(255,255,0),
                  5px 8px 8px rgb(0,0,0);
}
```

The logo is now set in Slackey, the text is colored green, and everything is placed in the center. The `text-shadow` declaration serves two purposes. A bright yellow outline is added using two thin shadows in opposite directions. The third shadow adds a soft drop shadow to the text.

Finally, spice up the bland, gray background with a CSS pattern, but add this to the main `#game` rule so that it applies to all screens. Listing 2-17 shows the additions to `main.css`.

Be aware, however, that the syntax for CSS gradients can vary a bit depending on which browsers you're targeting and the fact that vendor-prefixed versions are required to support older browsers. For the sake of brevity, Listing 2-17 only shows the non-prefixed version. You can find the vendor-specific versions for WebKit, Firefox, and IE in the sample code for this chapter.

Listing 2-17   Adding a background pattern

```
#game {
    ...
    background-color: rgb(60,60,40);
    background-size : 10px 10px;
    background-image:
        linear-gradient(
            45deg, transparent 0%, rgb(20,20,20) 25%,
            transparent 50%, rgb(20,20,20) 75%, transparent 100%
        ),
        linear-gradient(
            -45deg, transparent 0%, rgb(20,20,20) 25%,
            transparent 50%, rgb(20,20,20) 75%, transparent 100%
        );
}
```

This adds two linear gradients to the background that, when combined, create a cross-hatching effect.

Not many years ago, background patterns required the use of repeating image files, but the CSS features available today give you plenty of options for creating interesting patterns and backgrounds. I highly recommend checking out Lea Verou's gallery of CSS3 patterns (`http://lea.verou.me/css3patterns`) for inspiration.

Now, open `index.html` in a browser. After the page loads, the loader script should automatically switch to the splash screen. Figure 2-5 shows the splash screen.

FIGURE 2-5: Here is the splash screen in its current state.

Summary

In this chapter, I laid out the concepts of the Jewel Warrior game. I discussed the rules of the game, the jewel swapping mechanics, and how the player scores points by matching sets of identical jewels. I then described the various stages of the game, starting with the splash screen that is shown when the game first loads, through the menu to the actual game, and the high score list that displays when the game ends.

I then showed you how the foundation of the game is set up using a simple HTML skeleton and a bit of CSS. You found out how to add dynamic script loading, and I introduced a basic framework for setting up game stages and switching between the various game screens.

Near the end of the chapter, you discovered how web fonts and CSS `@font-face` declarations enable embedded fonts, and you used them to create a game logo for the splash screen.

Chapter 3
Going Mobile

In This Chapter

- Designing for mobile devices
- Supporting different screen resolutions
- Creating the main menu
- Making web applications for iOS

THIS CHAPTER COVERS some of the advantages and challenges you face when taking your web application to the mobile platform. It briefly discusses how user interaction on mobile devices differs from interaction on the desktop before explaining the concept of the viewport and how to make the game scale correctly on small screens.

The chapter then moves on to CSS media queries and shows how you can use them to create views of your game that adapt to and look good on both low- and high-resolution devices, regardless of their orientation.

In this chapter, you also find out how to make your applications and games feel like native applications by toggling the iOS web application mode and disabling some default browser behavior.

Finally, you discover a few tricks that can help you debug your iOS and Android web applications.

Developing Mobile Web Applications

Today hundreds of millions of devices, smartphones, and tablets run on software such as Apple's iOS and the Google-backed Android system. These devices can run most advanced applications and games built with HTML5.

Games have been particularly successful on platforms like iOS and Android. If you look through lists of the most downloaded iPhone and Android applications, you're bound to find several games, some at the top spots. Since the days of Snake on Nokia phones, playing games on mobile phones has become more and more common. With the recent generations of high-resolution, touch-enabled smartphones and tablets, the gaming experience has improved immensely.

Not all games are a natural fit for the small screen, however. Complex strategy games and fast-paced first-person shooters, for example, rely on big displays and ample control options. Similar games certainly exist on mobile platforms. However, the games that really succeed appear to be the ones that take advantage of the small and touch-enabled screen and that cater to the more casual pick-up-and-play mentality of mobile users. If users just need to kill a few minutes on the bus, they don't want to sit through a long introduction. Match Three games like Jewel Warrior fit this profile nicely. The gameplay is sufficiently simple that most people can pick it up and play with little or no instruction, and games can be as short or as long as needed. The game controls are also simple enough that the lack of keyboard and mouse isn't a problem. The jewel-swapping mechanics of the game fit the small touch screens nicely because the user can select and swap jewels simply by tapping them on the screen.

Write once, read many

One of the biggest advantages to developing mobile applications and games with HTML, CSS, and JavaScript is that, if you build it properly, your application can run on many different platforms and devices with little or no modification. In light of the challenges that native application developers face, this is a huge win for web applications. For example, in order to port a native iPhone game to Android, you need knowledge of the Objective-C language used on iOS devices and the Java used on Android, as well as their respective Software Development Kits (SDK). By using open web technologies, the tools and code stay the same no matter what platform or device you're developing for. This saves time in the development phase and later when you're doing post-release maintenance.

Another nice thing about web applications is that they get around the restrictive rules of distribution channels like Apple's App Store. Getting your app accepted for the App Store means subjecting it to a closed and somewhat obscure approval process. Web applications don't suffer from that. You can host and distribute your application anywhere you want.

The challenges of mobile platforms

Developing your application or game with web technology presents numerous challenges. Not being tied to a single distribution channel can be a drawback. Getting new apps from the App Store or from the Android Market is easy, and many users never venture any further than the built-in app delivery system they're familiar with, which means that making your potential users aware of your application can be a problem. Fortunately, more and more alternative channels are emerging, making it easier to get your apps out there.

Handling User Input on Mobile Devices

Developing for smartphones and tablets involves technical challenges as well. One of the most apparent challenges is how the interaction between user and application changes. On a desktop computer or laptop, users are accustomed to having both keyboard and mouse available. Smartphones and tablets primarily use the touch-enabled screen, which is very intuitive but also quite limited.

Some devices, like the iPhone and many Android devices, provide a few additional methods that allow users to interact with their environment. Cameras and microphones have been on cell phones for a long time, but the smartphones of today also come equipped with hardware sensors such as accelerometers and gyroscopes. These are all very interesting tools that you can use to create innovative game experiences. Motion-based input has been quite successful already. Several hit mobile games rely on nothing but tilting the device the right way at the right time, with goals as diverse as steering a vehicle (Shrek Kart), jumping on clouds (Doodle Jump), and guiding a ball through a maze (Labyrinth). These motion-based features can now be accessed with JavaScript in many modern browsers.

Keyboard input

When developing for mobile versus desktop, the biggest loss in terms of user input is probably the keyboard. Many types of games simply don't work as well without the detailed controls that come with the keyboard. Some mobile games opt for virtual buttons displayed on the screen, and in some cases, that will do just fine. In other cases, the lack of real buttons can make it hard to control the game. This is especially true for fast-paced games where the player often relies on the physical feeling of buttons to switch quickly between functions. Many devices offer tactile feedback in the form of vibrations, but without looking directly at the buttons, it's still hard to pick out the right ones to touch.

Android and iOS devices both have a virtual keyboard that slides up when needed. Because the keyboard is triggered only on elements that allow text input, it's difficult to use for much more than its intended purpose. Besides, on most regular-sized smartphones and iPod touch devices, it takes up a significant portion of the screen (see Figure 3-1).

FIGURE 3-1: The virtual keyboard on the iPod touch and iPhone lets users input data.

Mouse versus touch

Mobile devices also lack a mouse, of course, but at least the function of the touch screen is somewhat analogous to the computer mouse. Tapping the screen works the same as clicking the mouse, so for many purposes, you can use the touch screen in place of the mouse, and vice versa. You can even offer double taps to simulate a double-click on the mouse. That's about as far as the similarities go, however.

Computers rarely have more than one mouse, but most people have ten fingers. It would be a shame not to take advantage of them, so the latest touch-enabled devices expose so-called *multi-touch events*. This opens up a completely new world of possibilities. You probably already know the ubiquitous *pinch-to-zoom* found in mobile browsers and map applications, but multi-touch features are also used to implement multi-player games on the same screen.

Touch screens have limitations as well. For example, the concept of hovering the mouse pointer over an element has no counterpart in the world of touch. The screen can't tell where your finger is until you actually touch it, and when you do, it's no longer hovering. Computer mice usually have at least two buttons, and most people are used to the right mouse button as a shortcut to context menus or other alternative actions. On touch screens, it's difficult to differentiate between types of touches. We have only one type of finger. The workaround most often used is to differentiate between short and long taps, with a long press bringing up the context menu or whatever other action you would assign to the right mouse button.

With all these elaborate control mechanisms missing, you might think that the diversity in the mobile game market would suffer. However, constraints often fuel creativity. Sure, the App Store and Android Market do have problems with repetitive copycat applications and games, but many of these games use gameplay and game mechanics that are unique. Games like Fruit Ninja and Cut the Rope have shown that simple, well-timed swipes on the screen can provide perfect casual game experiences. Game types that never made sense before are now blockbusters.

Adapting to Small Screen Resolutions

Perhaps the most apparent difference when switching to handheld devices is the small form factor compared to full-size computers. Smaller screens usually have lower resolutions and often different aspect ratios. If you want your game to work well on most devices, you need to make sure it can handle a wide variety of display sizes. Table 3-1 shows a selection of smartphones and their resolutions. You can find more data like this on the MyDevice website (http://www.mydevice.io/devices/).

The display resolution varies greatly among devices. You need to pay particular attention to the device resolution. Whereas the display resolution is the number of physical pixels on the display, the device resolution represents the logical resolution used in, for example, CSS. Therefore, even though the iPhone 4 has a display resolution twice that of the iPhone 3, websites look the same on both displays. The iPhone 4 just renders the page in much crisper detail. Because the device resolutions are much more in line with each other, it's fairly easy to target these displays, which you will see later in this chapter, where I show you how to use media queries.

Table 3-1 **Smartphone displays**

Device	Display Resolution	Device Resolution	Pixel Ratio	Aspect Ratio
iPhone 3	480x320	480x320	1.0	3:2
Nokia Lumia	800x480	480x320	1.5	15:9
iPhone 4	960x640	480x320	2.0	3:2
iPhone 5	1136x640	568x320	2.0	16:9
Samsung Galaxy S3	1280x720	640x360	2.0	16:9
Google Nexus 4	1280x768	640x360	2.0	15:9
Samsung Galaxy S4	1920x1080	640x360	3.0	16:9
Sony Xperia Z	1920x1080	640x360	3.0	16:9
HTC One	1920x1080	640x360	3.0	16:9

This also goes for tablet displays. Some tablets have display resolutions similar to smartphones, whereas others can compete with desktop monitors. Still, the device resolutions are similar. Table 3-2 shows a small selection of display resolutions on various tablets.

Table 3-2   **Tablet displays**

Device	Display Resolution	Device Resolution	Pixel Ratio	Aspect Ratio
iPad 2	1024x768	1024x768	1.0	4:3
iPad Mini	1024x768	1024x768	1.0	4:3
Samsung Galaxy Tab 2 7"	1024x600	1024x600	1.0	4:3
Samsung Galaxy Tab 2 10"	1280x800	1280x800	1.0	16:10
iPad 4	2048x1536	1024x768	2.0	4:3
Google Nexus 10	2560x1600	1280x800	2.0	16:10

REMEMBER   With all of these different display sizes and resolutions available, the challenge of making the layout and graphics of the game scale appropriately for as many devices as possible is anything but trivial.

Creating scalable layouts

You can solve many of the problems caused by multiple display resolutions by using an elastic layout based on relative units instead of absolute values. CSS supports several different units that you can use when setting positions, dimensions, margins, and so on, and they each have their strengths and weaknesses. Some of these units are absolute and fixed-size. For example, setting the width and height properties using px values makes that element use the same amount of pixels no matter where you place it and how much space is available.

Other units are relative to other values. These units include the em and percent (%) units. Percentage values are relatively easy to understand; setting the width property to 25% makes the element use 25% of the width made available to it by its parent element. If you make the parent element bigger, the child element automatically adjusts itself so that it still uses 25% of the space. That makes percentage values much more suitable for multi-device development than fixed-size pixel values.

The em unit is another powerful tool for creating scalable layouts. It has its roots in traditional typography, where one em was equal to the width of a capital M in the typeface and size being used. Because the actual size of one em varies when you change the typeface or the point size, the unit is a relative unit. The em unit has transferred over to the digital world and web typography, albeit with the slight modification that one em is now equal to the height of the font.

This way, the computer can safely use kerning to adjust the space between letters to improve readability. It also allows the em unit to be used in other alphabets that have no letter M.

You can also use the em unit to define a few special characters. The width of the em dash (—) is equal to one em, as is the width of its cousin, the em space. HTML gives you both of these special characters through the entities — and .   **NOTE**

Use units like em and percentages to make the layout of the application more suitable for varying display sizes. The main font-size that all the content inherits is defined on the #game element in main.css. Choosing a base font-size can be tricky, but you can usually find a size that divides the page in a nice grid. Jewel Warrior uses an 8x8 board in the game, and the game width is set to 320 pixels. If the game takes up all of the width, a font-size value of 40 pixels means that each cell on the board is a 1x1 em block.

Listing 3-1 shows the changed #game element CSS in main.css.

Listing 3-1   **Setting the base font size**

```
#game {
    ...
    font-size : 40px;
    width : 8em;
    height : 12em;
    ...
}
```

The width and height of the #game element are also defined using em units. These absolute dimensions are used only when running the game in desktop browsers. In the next section, I show you how to make the game fit any available space on mobile devices.

There are even better units than em available in the most recent browser versions. The vw and vh units are relative to the size of the viewport, which makes it even easier to make things scale nicely across different display sizes. These units are scaled so that 1 vw is equal to 1% of the viewport width and 1 vh is equal to 1% of the viewport height. The related vmin and vmax units are equal to 1% of the smallest and largest dimension of the viewport, respectively. Unfortunately, Android supports these units only in the very recently released Android 4.4, so I have not used these units in this book. Similarly, Internet Explorer only supports the units in IE11.   **TIP**

Now that the #game element sets the base size, you can use em units to scale the rest of the content. In Listing 3-2, you can see the changes to the logo styles.

Listing 3-2   **Using relative units in logo Styles**

```
.logo {
    font-size : 1.5em;
    line-height : 0.9em;
    text-shadow : 0.03em  0.03em  0.03em rgb(255,255,0),
                 -0.03em -0.03em  0.03em rgb(255,255,0),
                  0.10em  0.15em  0.15em rgb(0,0,0);
    ...
```

Note that, because the .logo class has its own font-size value, the rest of the values specified in ems are now relative to that font-size value. Listing 3-3 shows the changes to the splash screen styles.

Listing 3-3   **Using relative units in the splash screen styles**

```
#splash-screen {
    ...
    padding-top : 2.5em;
}
#splash-screen .continue {
    cursor : pointer;
    font-size : 0.75em;
}
```

All the content on the splash screen is now based on the single font-size value specified in the game element CSS rule. Change that value and everything else changes as well.

Controlling the viewport

To really understand how mobile devices display web content, you need to understand what the viewport is and how it relates to the page. You can think of the *viewport* as the area on which the browser renders the page. You might think that this is simply the area of the browser window. In some cases, that is correct. The dimensions of the viewport and the dimensions of the "hole" through which the page is viewed are not the same thing, however. In desktop browsers, the width of the viewport is generally equal to the width of the browser window, but on mobile devices, this isn't necessarily true. For example, the mobile Safari browser on third-generation iPhones has a default viewport width of 980 pixels even if the actual display is only 320 pixels wide. The viewport can be controlled with a meta tag.

```
<meta name="viewport" content="...">
```

The content attribute takes a number of optional parameters that describe the viewport. Table 3-3 lists all the valid parameters for the viewport meta tag.

Table 3-3   **Viewport meta tag parameters**

Directive	Description
width	A numeric value in pixels that specifies the width of the viewport that the device should use to display the page. The special value device-width sets the width to the `device width.`
height	A numeric value in pixels that specifies the height of the viewport that the device should use to display the page. The special value `device-height` sets the height to device height.
user-scalable	Possible values for this parameter are `yes` and `no`. If set to `no`, the native pinch-zoom feature is disabled. The default is `yes`.
initial-scale	Determines the level of scaling applied to the page when it loads initially.
maximum-scale	A numeric value that determines the maximum level of scaling that the user can apply. This parameter has no effect if `user-scalable` is set to `no`.
minimum-scale	A numeric value that determines the minimum level of scaling that the user can apply. This parameter has no effect if `user-scalable` is set to `no`.

The default values for most of these directives depend on the device and the browser. Usually, you want to use the special `device-width` and `device-height` values instead of constant values. That way, the device can automatically scale the content to fill the screen. The viewport `meta` tag goes in the `head` section of the HTML page. Listing 3-4 shows the `meta` tag added to `index.html`.

Listing 3-4   **Setting the viewport**

```
<head>
    ...
    <meta name="viewport" content="width=device-width">
    ...
</head>
```

Disabling user scaling

Having the native user-zoom feature enabled in a game is, in most cases, a bad idea. If you leave it enabled, you risk accidental zooming by the user, which could break the game experience. Set the `user-scalable` parameter to `no`. The browser should display the content without further scaling, so the `initial-scale` value should be set to `1.0`. However, because `width` is set to `device-width`, the browser automatically infers a value of `1.0` for `initial-scale`, so you don't even need to set the scaling explicitly. This works the other way around as well; an `initial-scale` value of `1.0` automatically infers that `width` is equal to `device-width`, unless you explicitly set another value for the `width` parameter. The `maximum-scale` and `minimum-scale` parameters are irrelevant because the user zoom is disabled. Listing 3-5 shows the modified `viewport` `meta` tag.

Listing 3-5 **Disabling user scaling**

```
<head>
    ...
    <meta name="viewport"
          content="width=device-width, user-scalable=no">
    ...
</head>
```

If you load the game now on, for example, an iPad, the game area doesn't fill the entire screen, but you'll notice that, no matter how much users pinch the screen, they can't accidentally zoom and mess up the rendering of the game.

Creating Different Views

When users click on the splash screen, they're taken to the main menu. To ensure that the menu looks all right on both small and large screens, in this section, I show you how to load different style sheets depending on the screen size, as well as how to differentiate between portrait and landscape modes. First, however, you have to build the menu.

Creating the main menu

The menu is a simple, unordered list of buttons. Each button has a name attribute that indicates which screen should be loaded when the button is clicked. The menu also features a smaller version of the game logo, positioned above the menu items. Listing 3-6 shows the markup for the main menu added to index.html.

Listing 3-6 **Adding the menu HTML**

```
<div id="game">
    ...
    <div class="screen" id="main-menu">
        <h2 class="logo">Jewel <br/>Warrior</h2>
        <ul class="menu">
            <li><button name="game-screen">Play</button>
            <li><button name="high-scores">Highscore</button>
            <li><button name="about">About</button>
            <li><button name="exit-screen">Exit</button>
        </ul>
    </div>
</div>
```

Now add some CSS rules to the main.css style sheet. Listing 3-7 shows all the menu-related rules.

Listing 3-7 Adding menu CSS rules

```
/* Main menu styles */
#main-menu {
    padding-top : 1em;
}

ul.menu {
    text-align : center;
    padding : 0;
    margin : 0;
    list-style : none;
}
ul.menu li {
    margin : 0.8em 0;
}
ul.menu li button {
    font-family : Slackey, sans-serif;
    font-size : 0.6em;
    color : rgb(100,120,0);
    width : 10em;
    height : 1.5em;
    background : rgb(10,20,0);
    border : 0.1em solid rgb(255,255,0);
    border-radius : 0.5em;
    -webkit-box-shadow : 0.2em 0.2em 0.3em rgb(0,0,0);
    -moz-box-shadow : 0.2em 0.2em 0.3em rgb(0,0,0);
    box-shadow : 0.2em 0.2em 0.3em rgb(0,0,0);
}
ul.menu li button:hover {
    background : rgb(30,40,0);
}
ul.menu li button:active {
    color : rgb(255,255,0);
    background : rgb(30,40,0);
}
```

Note the extra `box-shadow` declarations in the button style. Many CSS3 features aren't fully supported across all browsers, and many are available only via vendor-specific prefixes such as `-webkit` for WebKit browsers and `-moz` for Firefox.

Remember that values specified in em units are relative to the `font-size` of the element. Because the button elements have a `font-size` value of their own, all the other CSS values of the button elements are now relative to this `font-size`. Furthermore, this `font-size` is itself specified in em units, so the actual, calculated `font-size` value for the buttons is equal to the inherited `font-size` value multiplied by its own `font-size` value.

Adding screen modules

Most of the game screens contain some form of activity or user interaction. I use discrete modules to encapsulate this functionality. The first screen module you need is the splash screen module. Instead of placing the screen modules directly on the top-level `jewel` namespace, you can keep them together by adding another level to the namespace. Modify the main `jewel` module in `jewel.js` as follows to add a container object for the screen modules:

```
var jewel = (function() {
    ...
    return {
        ...
        screens: {}
    };
})();
```

The splash screen module should listen for `click` events and, when the user clicks or taps anywhere on the screen, switch to the main menu screen. Screen modules are built the same way as the rest of the game modules. For now, you need to expose one method that sets up any initial behavior. Listing 3-8 shows the splash screen module. Put the code in a new file called `screen.splash.js` in the `scripts` folder.

Listing 3-8   **The splash screen module**

```
jewel.screens["splash-screen"] = (function() {
    var firstRun = true;

    function setup() {
        jewel.dom.bind("#splash-screen", "click", function() {
            jewel.showScreen("main-menu");
        });
    }

    function run() {
        if (firstRun) {
            setup();
            firstRun = false;
```

```
        }
    }

    return {
        run : run
    };
}) ();
```

The first time it's called, the public `run()` method calls the `setup()` function. This function sets up an event handler on the screen element that switches screens when the user clicks or taps the screen. As demonstrated in Listing 3-8, the `setup()` function uses a new helper function from the dom module. The `dom.bind()` function takes a selector string, finds the element, and attaches the handler function to the specified event. Listing 3-9 shows the `bind()` function added to the dom module in dom.js.

Listing 3-9   Adding the event binding helper function

```
jewel.dom = (function() {

    ...

    function bind(element, event, handler) {
        if (typeof element == "string") {
            element = $(element) [0];
        }
        element.addEventListener(event, handler, false);
    }
    return {
        ...
        bind : bind
    };
}) ();
```

Before attaching the event listener, the `dom.bind()` function tests the type of the `element` argument. If a string is passed, it's used as a selector string; otherwise, it's assumed that `element` is an actual DOM element.

Now you just need to make sure the `run()` function is called whenever the screen is displayed. Modify the `showScreen()` function in `jewel.js`, as shown in Listing 3-10. I have also added a helpful `alert()` that notifies you if the screen module doesn't exist.

Listing 3-10   **Calling the run method**

```
jewel = (function() {
    ...
    function showScreen(screenId) {
        var dom = jewel.dom,
            $ = dom.$,
            activeScreen = $("#game .screen.active")[0],
            screen = $("#" + screenId)[0];
        if (!jewel.screens[screenId]) {
            alert("This module is not implemented yet!");
            return;
        }
        if (activeScreen) {
            dom.removeClass(activeScreen, "active");
        }
        dom.addClass(screen, "active");
        // run the screen module
        jewel.screens[screenId].run();
    }
    ...
})();
```

When the splash screen is displayed for the first time, a `click` event handler is attached to the screen so that a click or tap takes the user to the main menu. Of course, you haven't created a main menu module yet. The function of the main menu module is mainly to take care of what happens when the user clicks or taps on a menu item. Listing 3-11 shows the module. Put the code in a file called `screen.main-menu.js` in the `scripts` folder.

Listing 3-11   **The main menu module**

```
jewel.screens["main-menu"] = (function() {
    var dom = jewel.dom,
        firstRun = true;

    function setup() {
        dom.bind("#main-menu ul.menu", "click", function(e) {
            if (e.target.nodeName.toLowerCase() === "button") {
                var action = e.target.getAttribute("name");
                jewel.showScreen(action);
            }
        });
    }
```

```
function run() {
    if (firstRun) {
        setup();
        firstRun = false;
    }
}

return {
    run : run
};
})();
```

The first time the main menu is displayed, the event handling is set up so that clicking the menu items takes the user to the appropriate screens. I used event delegation rather than attaching event handlers to every single menu button. A single `click` event handler is added to the menu `ul` element. When the event fires, the handler function examines the target element and determines whether the `click` event came from a `button` element. If it did, the event handler switches the game to the correct screen using the `name` attribute on the `button` element. Not only does event delegation usually save you some repetitive typing, but also it comes with a cool bonus: The parent event handler automatically covers any new items that are added dynamically with JavaScript.

> **TIP**
>
> The main menu currently uses the `click` event to handle the menu interaction. On touch-enabled devices, you can also use touch events that are sometimes better suited for those devices. However, because a tap on the screen is also translated into a click event, an old-fashioned `click` event handler often does the trick. In Chapter 8, I dive further into event handling, user input, and touch-based interaction.

Finally, load the new files to the `index.html`:

```
window.addEventListener("load", function() {
    jewel.load("scripts/dom.js");
    jewel.load("scripts/screen.splash.js");
    jewel.load("scripts/screen.main-menu.js", jewel.setup);
});
```

You can now click the splash screen to go to the main menu. The event handlers on the menu are in place, but the menu items lead nowhere until more screens are added further along in the process. Figure 3-2 shows the menu.

FIGURE 3-2: The main menu offers the user an array of game options.

Using CSS media queries

No matter how hard you try, sometimes you just can't make a single set of CSS rules behave properly across all devices and resolutions. Sometimes, the best solution is to make separate style sheets for different display sizes and load the appropriate ones when needed. CSS3 media queries provide a great solution for this problem. Media queries extend the media type functionality of CSS2 with additional conditions. Whereas CSS2 lets you use different style sheets depending on the media type (`print`, `screen`, `handheld`, and so on), media queries set conditions based on features of the media. Data such as resolution, display dimensions, and orientation can now be used to select the appropriate styles. This snippet shows an example of a style sheet with a media query:

```
<link rel="stylesheet"
     media="print and resolution > 150dpi"
     href="print150.css">
```

This query applies the `print150.css` style sheet to the content only when it's printed on a device with a resolution higher than 150 dots per inch (dpi).

You can also use media queries in the actual CSS:

```
@media screen and (min-width : 480px) {
    body {
        font-size : 150%;
    }
}
```

This example scales the font-size to 150%, but only when the content is displayed on a screen and only if the width of the display is at least 480 pixels. By using queries such as these, you can easily target different resolutions and screen sizes to ensure that the layout of the game behaves nicely when viewed on different devices. Table 3-4 shows a list of all the media features defined in CSS3.

Table 3-4 **Media features**

Feature	Values	Description
width	Non-negative length, for example, 980px	Describes the width of the viewport.
height	Non-negative length, for example, 800px	Describes the height of the viewport.
device-width	Non-negative length, for example, 320px	Describes the width of the output device.
device-height	Non-negative length, for example 480px	Describes the height of the output device.
orientation	landscape or portrait	Describes the orientation of the output device. If height is greater than width, the value of the orientation feature is portrait; otherwise, it is landscape.
aspect-ratio	Positive ratio, for example, ¾	The ratio of the width value to the height value.
device-aspect-ratio	Positive ratio, for example, ¾	The ratio of the device-width value to the device-height value.
color	Non-negative value, for example, 8	Describes the number of bits per color component (red, green, blue) used in the output device.
color-index	Non-negative value, for example, 64	Describes the number of entries in the color index of the output device. If the display isn't indexed, the value is 0.

continued

Table 3-4 **continued**

Feature	Values	Description
monochrome	Non-negative value, for example, 2	Describes the number of bits per pixel used in a monochrome output device. The value is 0 for non-monochrome displays.
resolution	Positive resolution, for example, 300dpi	
scan	progressive or interlace	Only applies to the tv media type.
grid	0 or 1	Indicates a grid-based output device, such as a computer terminal.

All media features except orientation, scan, and grid can also be used with min- and max- prefixes.

Detecting device orientation

You can use most smartphones and tablets in portrait or landscape mode with the device automatically rotating and adjusting the image. This capability is an interesting challenge for application developers because you need to make sure the application or game can handle this change. The three basic choices are

- Do nothing. Let the device rotate the display and hope for the best.

- Don't rotate the display, making it usable in only one orientation.

- Adjust the application to look good in both orientations.

For most websites, it's usually fine to let the device figure out how to display the site properly. As long as you set the viewport, things usually work out fine. Games, on the other hand, often use the screen space in a very controlled manner. Leaving it up to the device to rearrange things can destroy the experience and usability. Some applications choose to fix the display in one orientation. This fix is easy if the layout of the application or game can't easily adapt to both orientations. However, it's not the most practical solution for web applications because you can't disable the native display reorientation. Therefore, you have to rotate the whole page back using, for example, CSS transforms. That leaves only the third option, making sure the game can handle both orientations.

Applying special CSS for different orientations is relatively easy with the help of media queries. The orientation media feature makes it a breeze to apply rules specifically to, for example, devices in landscape mode:

```
@media screen and (orientation: portrait) {
    #sidebar {
        display : none;
    }
}
@media screen and (orientation: landscape) {
    #sidebar {
        display : block;
    }
}
```

This example shows only the `#sidebar` element when the page is displayed in landscape mode.

Adding a landscape style sheet

Now take a look at how to use media queries to add a special style sheet for mobile devices. The query should match the largest possible device that the mobile style sheet could handle. The iPad has a resolution of 768x1024, so this will be the upper boundary for the media query. Because the device width changes depending on the orientation, you need two queries to detect both portrait and landscape mode. You can combine multiple queries to the same style sheet by separating them with commas. Listing 3-12 shows the `link` element that loads the mobile style sheet.

Listing 3-12   **Loading the mobile style sheet**

```
<head>
    ...
    <link rel="stylesheet"
          href="styles/mobile.css"
          media="screen and (max-device-width: 768px)
                        and (orientation: portrait),
                 screen and (max-device-width: 1024px)
                        and (orientation: landscape)"/>
    ...
</head>
```

The media query specifies that the `mobile.css` style sheet should be applied only to screen devices that are at most 768 pixels wide when in portrait mode and 1024 pixels wide in landscape mode.

In the `mobile.css` style sheet, you first make the game fill the entire display. In `main.css`, you gave the game element a fixed size of 320x480 pixels. That works fine for placing the game on a web page and displaying it on a computer monitor. A game like Jewel Warrior doesn't need the vast screen space available on laptops or desktop computers. On mobile devices, you want to grab as much space as possible. Listing 3-13 shows the first rule added to `mobile.css`.

Listing 3-13   Filling the entire screen

```
#game {
    width : 100%;
    height : 100%;
}
```

This small change is enough to make the current application look fine on medium devices like the iPhone or high-resolution Android smartphones. Remember that you can scale everything simply by changing the `font-size` value on the game element. You can use the `font-size` scaling with a media query to, for example, scale up the content on large-screen devices like the iPad. Listing 3-14 shows the targeted CSS rules in `mobile.css`.

Listing 3-14   Scaling content for large displays

```
/* use a smaller base size for small screens */
@media (max-device-width: 480px) and (orientation: portrait),
@media (max-device-width: 640px) and (orientation: landscape) {
    #game {
        font-size : 32px;
    }
}
/* use a bigger base size for ipad and tablets */
@media (min-device-width: 768px) and (orientation: portrait),
@media (min-device-width: 1024px) and (orientation: landscape) {
    #game {
        font-size : 64px;
    }
}
```

The `ul.menu` rule scales the entire menu structure a bit so that it fits regardless of the different aspect ratio. Note also the two queries used to target the iPad, one for each of the orientations.

The landscape mode is a more problematic issue. Cramming the tall menu into the limited vertical space in landscape mode leads to very small buttons. A better solution is to have them automatically adjust themselves in a 2x2 grid if the space permits. The styles in Listing 3-15 apply to devices of various sizes in landscape mode.

Listing 3-15 **Adding landscape styles**

```
/* smartphones landscape */
@media (orientation: landscape) {
    #splash-screen,
    #main-menu {
        font-size : 1.0em;
        padding-top : 0.75em;
    }
    ul.menu li {
        display : inline-block;
        margin : 0;
    }
    ul.menu li button {
        margin : 0.5em;
        font-size : 0.5em;
    }
}
/* small screens landscape */
@media (orientation: landscape) and (max-device-width : 480px) {
    ul.menu li button {
        font-size : 0.4em;
    }
}

/* tablets landscape */
@media (orientation: landscape) and (min-device-width : 768px) {
    #splash-screen,
    #main-menu {
        padding-top : 1.5em;
    }
}
```

Setting `display` to `inline-block` on the menu items positions them side by side, wrapping only if there's not enough space. Figure 3-3 shows the menu in landscape mode as rendered on an HTC Desire.

All applications have different layouts, and no silver bullet makes everything look good on all devices. In the end, it comes down to experimenting—trying to find solutions that look good on as many devices as possible without too many special cases in the CSS.

FIGURE 3-3: The main menu can display in landscape mode.

Developing for iOS and Android Devices

Apple sits heavily on the handheld device market: That's no secret. Android devices are gaining market share, but the ubiquity of iPod, iPhone, and iPad devices that all run the same tightly controlled software makes them good targets for mobile web developers. Apple's mobile Safari and iOS system provides a few extra goodies for web application developers. You can use some of these features to better control how the application appears and have it blend in with the native applications on the device.

Placing web applications on the home screen

When you run a web application in mobile Safari, the available screen space is reduced because of to the surrounding Safari UI (icons, address bar, and so on). This isn't a huge problem for devices like the iPad where plenty of screen real estate is generally available. However, for small-screen devices like the iPod Touch or the iPhone, it quickly becomes a problem. For example, the iPod Touch 3G has a resolution of 320x480 pixels, but because the status bar and the Safari UI elements take up a good chunk of that space, you can use an area of only 320x360 for your application.

In Safari, the user can choose to place a link to an application or website on the home screen by tapping the bookmark icon. This adds an icon to the home screen that acts like a shortcut to the web address. However, the application still runs inside Safari and behaves exactly like a regular website, so it really is just a bookmark. Fortunately, there's an easy fix to get you a long way toward the feel of a native application. By adding a special `meta` tag to `index.html`, as shown in Listing 3-16, you can indicate that the page is a web application and should not be treated as a simple link.

Listing 3-16　**Enabling web application mode**

```
<head>
    ...
    <meta name="apple-mobile-web-app-capable" content="yes" />
    ...
</head>
```

With `apple-mobile-web-app-capable` set to `yes`, iOS knows that when this page is bookmarked and subsequently launched from the home screen, it must do so in full-screen mode without the usual Safari user interface. Of course, this feature isn't worth much if the user doesn't know about it. In the next section, I show how you can display a message to users who have the option available.

> In older versions of the iOS system, the bookmark icon used a plus (+) symbol, but as of iOS 4.2, the icon changed to a curved arrow. In iOS 7, the icon changed yet again to fit the general UI redesign in this version.　**NOTE**

One important motivation for getting the game placed on the home screen is that it keeps it fresh in the memory of the user. If the game exists only via Safari and, at best, a bookmark, the users will probably forget about it the next time they need to kill a bit of time. If you put it on the home screen, users see a constant reminder that the game is there, waiting to be played.

Issues with iOS 7

At the time of this writing, iOS 7 has just been released to the public, and there are some unfortunate issues related to web applications that hopefully will be resolved in future updates.

Strange things, such as apps being replaced or cloned, can happen if you install more than four web applications on the home screen. You cannot use `alert()` and other standard JavaScript message boxes in web apps launched from the home screen, and you cannot open external web pages in, for example, Safari or the App Store. There are also issues with cookies and the Application Cache. I am hopeful that these will all be fixed in iOS updates.

Detecting standalone apps

Safari provides an easy way to determine whether the page is being viewed as a web application or as a regular web page. Using JavaScript, you can examine the `window.navigator` object for a property named `standalone`. If this property exists and is true, the page was launched from the home screen in web application mode. Listing 3-17 shows a basic example of how to detect whether the application is running as a standalone application or in a browser.

Listing 3-17 Testing for the standalone property

```
if (window.navigator.standalone) {
    alert("You are running the standalone app!");
} else if (window.navigator.standalone === false) {
    alert("You are using app in mobile Safari!");
} else {
    alert("You are using the app in another browser!");
}
```

The test has three cases: one for standalone iOS web applications, one for web pages running in the mobile Safari browser, and finally a catchall for everything else. Note that the detection code explicitly tests the `standalone` property for the Boolean `false` value—to distinguish between the value being `false` and the property not existing. Only iOS devices support the `standalone` property; for other browsers, this property is `undefined`, and these browsers therefore match only the third case.

Use this knowledge to add an `isStandalone()` function to the `jewel` module in `jewel.js`, and use it to toggle an install screen instead of the normal splash screen when appropriate. Listing 3-18 shows the new function and the modified `setup()` function.

Listing 3-18 Adding the isStandalone() function

```
var jewel = (function() {
    ...
    function isStandalone() {
        return (window.navigator.standalone !== false);
    }

    function setup() {
        if (isStandalone()) {
            showScreen("splash-screen");
        } else {
            showScreen("install-screen");
        }
    }

    return {
        ...
        isStandalone: isStandalone
    };
})();
```

The new test determines whether the standalone mode is enabled. Because the question doesn't make sense on non-iOS devices, you treat a nonexistent standalone property as though it's running in standalone mode. Besides, what you're really interested in is being able to tell when the user has the option of installing the application but hasn't used that option yet.

Making a special splash screen

Now modify the loading sequence in `index.html` to load a different splash screen if standalone mode is not active. Listing 3-19 shows the modified function.

Listing 3-19   Loading the right splash screen

```
...
window.addEventListener("load", function() {
    jewel.load("scripts/dom.js");
    if (jewel.isStandalone()) {
        jewel.load("scripts/screen.splash.js");
        jewel.load("scripts/screen.main-menu.js", jewel.setup);
    } else {
        jewel.load("scripts/screen.install.js", jewel.setup);
    }
});
...
```

This install screen module in `screen.splash-install.js` is just an empty module with no real functionality. Its function is merely to display a non-interactive message. Listing 3-20 shows this module.

Listing 3-20   The install screen module

```
jewel.screens["install-screen"] = (function() {
    return {
        run : function() {}
    };
})();
```

The markup for the install screen is similar to the splash screen, so to create the install screen, make a copy of the splash screen element and change the id attribute to `install-screen`. The message shown on this screen should ask the user to install the game to the home screen via the bookmark button. Listing 3-21 shows the new screen element added to `index.html`.

Listing 3-21   Adding the install screen markup

```
<div id="game">
    ...
    <div class="screen" id="install-screen">
        <h1 class="logo">Jewel <br/>Warrior</h1>
        <span>
            Click the <img src="images/install-icon.png"
                            alt="Install icon">
            button to install the game to your home screen.
        </span>
    </div>
</div>
```

The CSS for the install screen is also very similar to that of the splash screen. The only difference is that the install screen has less padding at the top. You can find the install-icon. png image file in the images folder in the code archive for this chapter. Remember that the mobile Safari browser takes a lot of the available space. Listing 3-22 shows the styles for the install screen added to main.css.

Listing 3-22   Styling the install screen

```
/* Install screen for iOS devices */
#install-screen {
    padding-top : 0.5em;
    text-align : center;
}
#install-screen span {
    font-size : 0.75em;
    display : inline-block;
    padding : 0 0.5em;
}
```

When the game loads in the mobile Safari browser, the user now sees the install notification rather than the normal splash screen. If you want to test it in a desktop browser, you can simply modify the isStandalone() function to always return false. Figure 3-4 shows the install screen.

Adding an application icon
By default, iOS uses a tiny screenshot of the application when it generates an icon. Naturally, that won't always produce good results. With a special link element, you can specify an icon file to use instead of the screenshot.

```
<link rel="apple-touch-icon" href="icon.png"/>
```

FIGURE 3-4: The mobile Safari install screen shows when the game loads.

On devices running iOS 6 or earlier, the icon is processed in a way that adds a shiny effect. By using `apple-touch-icon-precomposed` instead of `apple-touch-icon`, you can tell iOS to leave the icon alone and use it as-is:

```
<link rel="apple-touch-icon-precomposed"
      href="images/ios-icon.png"/>
```

You can provide icons of different sizes to match the displays of the various iOS devices. Icons on iOS 7 are slightly bigger than in earlier versions. Older generations of iPod Touch and iPhone devices use 57x57 icons on the home screen and can't run iOS 7. The Retina displays on the iPhone 4 and newer devices have twice the resolution of their predecessors and can therefore take advantage of more detailed 114x114 icons (120x120 for iOS 7). Non-Retina iPads use 72x72 icons (76x76 for iOS 7), whereas newer iPad tablets can use 144x144 icons (152x152 for iOS 7). If you don't provide all sizes, the device will pick the most suitable size.

If you create icons in these different sizes, you can point to them in the HTML by adding a `sizes` parameter to the `link` element and adding extra `link` elements for each resolution you want to support. Listing 3-23 shows the extra elements added to the `head` element in `index.html`.

Listing 3-23   Using icons for multiple resolutions

```
<head>
    ...
    <link rel="apple-touch-icon-precomposed"
          href="images/ios-icon.png"/>
    <link rel="apple-touch-icon-precomposed" sizes="72x72"
          href="images/ios-icon-ipad.png"/>
    <link rel="apple-touch-icon-precomposed" sizes="114x114"
          href="images/ios-icon-iphone-retina.png"/>
    <link rel="apple-touch-icon-precomposed" sizes="144x144"
          href="images/ios-icon-ipad-retina.png"/>
    ...
</head>
```

The device automatically picks the icon with the most appropriate size. If the exact size needed for its resolution isn't available, it picks either the smallest icon that's larger than the ideal size or the largest icon with a smaller size. If it doesn't find a suitable icon, it falls back to using the default icon with unspecified size. Figure 3-5 shows the game icon on an iPod home screen.

FIGURE 3-5: The Jewel Warrior icon shows on the home screen.

You can also use one set of icons for the entire website by leaving out the `link` elements and placing the icon images in the root directory of the website. The iOS system then searches the root for a suitable icon using a list of predefined filenames in the format `apple-touch-icon[-<w>x<h>][-precomposed].png`. Precomposed icons are chosen over regular icons, and icons with the specific size needed for that resolution are chosen over the default icon. A device that uses 57x57 icons looks for the following list of filenames:

- `apple-touch-icon-57x57-precomposed.png`

- `apple-touch-icon-57x57.png`

- `apple-touch-icon-precomposed.png`

- `apple-touch-icon.png`

If you want to provide all three icon sizes and use precomposed icons, you must put the following files in the website's root directory:

- `apple-touch-icon-114x114-precomposed.png`

- `apple-touch-icon-72x72-precomposed.png`

- `apple-touch-icon-precomposed.png`

In this case, the file with no size specified in the filename should be a 57x57 icon so that it serves as both the correct icon for older iPhones as well as the default fallback icon for future devices with different resolutions.

In many situations, it's better to explicitly point to the icons using `link` elements. Placing the application icons in the root means that every application running on that domain uses the same icons. This can cause problems if you ever want to serve other applications or games from that website.

REMEMBER

Adding a startup image

When the user launches the game in standalone mode and later exits the game, iOS saves a screenshot of the current state of the game. The next time the application is launched, this image is displayed until the page is loaded. It's not always appropriate to show only the last state of the game. The game won't pick up exactly where it left off, so the old image will appear as a brief flash. Fortunately, it's easy to specify your own image. A simple fix to get rid of the flash from the past is to use an image with a solid color. A good choice is the same color that's used as the background in the game.

All of the iOS devices need an image that takes up the full screen minus the top 20 pixels that are reserved for the native status bar. That means 320x460 for the iPhone and iPod Touch and 768x1004 for the iPad. On the iPad, you can add an extra startup image for landscape mode. This image must have the dimensions 748x1024, which means that the content needs to be rotated 90 degrees. I have created three startup images that display only the dimensions of the images so you can see when each one is loaded. You can find these images in the `images` folder in the code archive for this chapter. Listing 3-24 shows the extra `link` tags added to the `head` element in `index.html`.

Listing 3-24   **Specifying a startup image**

```
<head>
    ...
    <link rel="apple-touch-startup-image"
          href="images/ios-startup-748x1024.png"
          media="screen and (min-device-width: 768px)
                     and (orientation:landscape)" />
    <link rel="apple-touch-startup-image"
          href="images/ios-startup-768x1004.png"
          media="screen and (min-device-width: 768px)
                     and (orientation:portrait)" />
    <link rel="apple-touch-startup-image"
          href="images/ios-startup-320x460.png"
          media="screen and (max-device-width:320px)"/>
</head>
```

If you add multiple `link` elements, the last element overrides all the others unless you specify a media query to target the specific devices. In Listing 3-24, the two first `link` elements target only the iPad, whereas the third element targets the smaller screen of the iPhone and iPod Touch.

Styling the status bar

All mobile iOS devices use a standard 20-pixel status bar at the top of the screen. Even when the web application is running in full-screen mode, this status bar is still visible. Consequently, the actual available screen space on, for example, an iPad is 768x1004 in portrait mode, as opposed to the full 768x1024. Unfortunately, you can't hide the status bar completely, but iOS does give you a bit of control over its appearance. By adding a special `meta` tag to the page, you can choose between a few different styles. Listing 3-25 shows the `meta` tag needed to toggle a solid black background on the status bar in `index.html`.

Listing 3-25   **Making the status bar black**

```
<head>
    ...
    <meta name="apple-mobile-web-app-status-bar-style"
          content="black" />
    ...
</head>
```

The value of the content attribute must be one of default, black, and black-translucent. Unfortunately, this feature is currently broken in iOS 7, along with a number of other things as mentioned earlier. Instead of using the value you provide, iOS 7 uses the background color of the body element to tint the status bar.

Getting the browser out of the way

A web browser imposes a lot of extraneous behavior on your application. While some of it might be welcome, other functionality only detracts from the experience. Ideally, a game running as a web application and the same game in native form should have no apparent differences. In the next sections, I show you a few things you can do to disable some of the native browser behavior.

Disabling overscroll

When you scroll a web page in the Android browser or mobile Safari, you'll notice that you can scroll past the end of the page. When you let go, the page springs back to the end position. Preferably, the game won't scroll at all because no content is ever outside the visible area on the screen. You can disable this overscroll feature simply by disabling touch scrolling altogether. Do so by listening for the touchmove event on the document element and calling the event.preventDefault() method. You can do this in the jewel.setup() function jewel.js, as shown in Listing 3-26.

Listing 3-26 Adding a setup function to the game module

```
var jewel = (function() {
    ...
    function setup() {
        // disable native touchmove behavior to
        // prevent overscroll
        jewel.dom.bind(document, "touchmove", function(event) {
            event.preventDefault();
        });
        ...
    }
    ...
);
```

If you load the game in a mobile browser, you can't scroll outside the game area anymore.

Hiding the address bar

The Android browser doesn't have a feature like the apple-mobile-web-app-capable meta tag that mobile Safari provides. You can't make Android load the page as an application;

the best you can do is put a shortcut on the home screen that opens in the standard browser application. However, the Android browser gives you more space to work with than Safari does, and the only space that's reserved is the top status bar. When a page loads in the Android browser, it's usually displayed in such a way that the URL address bar is still visible. With a bit of JavaScript, shown in Listing 3-28, you can make the address bar disappear—or at least move it out of the way.

The issue also exists on iPod Touch and iPhones, but it doesn't matter as much on those devices because you simply ask the user to install the game to the home screen. Because you disabled touch scrolling, hiding the address bar can also cause problems on iOS because there's no other way for the user to leave the page. If the user launches the game from the home screen icon, the address bar problem disappears.

The trick to hiding the address bar is to force the browser to scroll to the top of the page. If there's enough content, it automatically pushes the address bar out of view. Because the height is set to 100%, the game takes up as much space as it can, so scrolling to the top has no effect. You can make sure the page is long enough by increasing the height of the html element to, say, 200%. Listing 3-27 shows the Android-targeted changes to the jewel.setup() function in jewel.js.

Listing 3-27   Hiding the address bar

```
var jewel = (function() {
    ...
    function setup() {
        // hide the address bar on Android devices
        if (/Android/.test(navigator.userAgent)) {
            $("html")[0].style.height = "200%";
            setTimeout(function() {
                window.scrollTo(0, 1);
            }, 0);
        }
        ...
    }
    ...
);
```

Disabling default browser behavior

Mobile Safari and the Android browser have a few behaviors that, although they make sense and generally improve the user experience on regular web pages, are best left disabled for games.

When you keep your finger pressed down for a second or two on, for example, an image or a link, a small callout appears, giving you the option to follow the link, save the image, and so on.

This feature has no place in a game. The user should be able to tap and press anything without interference from the native browser behavior. The following CSS property disables the callout:

```
-webkit-touch-callout: none;
```

Likewise, the ability to select text and images can be disabled with the following CSS property:

```
-webkit-user-select : none;
```

The Android browser highlights clickable elements when you tap them. Again, this is something that makes more sense in the context of links on web pages. Remove the highlighting by setting its color to transparent:

```
-webkit-tap-highlight-color: rgba(0,0,0,0);
```

Under some circumstances, such as orientation changes, the browser sometimes automatically adjusts the size of the text to account for the change in available size. It's best to keep as much control over the appearance as possible, so disable the automatic adjustment with the following rule:

```
-webkit-text-size-adjust: none;
```

These four properties must apply to all content in the game and thus should go on one of the topmost elements. Listing 3-28 shows the extra CSS rules added to the `body` element in `main.css`.

Listing 3-28 Modifying mobile browser behavior
```
body {
    ...
    -webkit-touch-callout: none;
    -webkit-tap-highlight-color: rgba(0,0,0,0);
    -webkit-text-size-adjust: none;
    -webkit-user-select : none;
}
```

Debugging Mobile Web Applications

Debugging web applications on mobile devices can be a bit of a pain. If you're used to tools like Firebug or the WebKit developer tools, you'll find that debugging web applications on mobile devices is a completely different experience. You cannot inspect the HTML, you have no console to test JavaScript in, and you often find yourself resorting to `alert()` debugging when things don't work out as expected. Although the mobile browsers aren't as feature-rich as their desktop counterparts, they do have options that come in handy for debugging JavaScript.

First, if you're using Safari on a Mac OS X computer, you can connect your iPad or iPhone to the computer and use the desktop Web Inspector to debug your iOS web applications. See the instructions at Apple's website (`http://bitly.com/ioswebinspector`) for how to set up iOS debugging with Safari.

Enabling the Safari debugger

If you don't have access to a Mac OS X computer, Apple's mobile Safari browser has a built-in debug console that's disabled by default. To turn it on, go to the iOS settings and find the Safari pane. Scroll down to the bottom and select the Developer menu item (Figure 3-6). On the developer screen, you can turn the Debug Console on and off (Figure 3-7).

FIGURE 3-6: The mobile Safari settings enable you to access the debugging features.

FIGURE 3-7: Use the mobile Safari developer settings for debugging.

When the console is enabled, you see an error bar just below the URL bar in Safari. The error bar reports the number of errors on the page. If any HTML, CSS, or JavaScript errors occur, you can click the error bar to get detailed information. See Figure 3-8 for an example of the error details.

You can also write your own debug messages by a `console` API similar to that found in most desktop browsers.

```
console.log("Hello World") // prints a message in the log
```

You can also use the related `console.error()`, `console.warn()`, and `console.info()` functions as well as the rest of the standard console API (see `https://developer.mozilla.org/en-US/docs/Web/API/console`).

Safari may not offer extensive inspection features like those in desktop browsers, but the ones it has are definitely better than nothing. There's one slightly annoying catch, though. Debug Console works only when running in the full Safari browser. When the application is launched in standalone mode from the home screen, enabling Debug Console has no effect.

FIGURE 3-8: Once enabled, the debugger provides you with detailed
error information in mobile Safari.

Debugging on Android

In Android 4.0 and higher, the stock browser also comes with a built-in console. Simply type
about:debug in the address bar to enable the console. You probably won't get feedback telling you that anything happened, but if your page generates errors or writes anything to the
console, Show JavaScript Console appears in a black bar at the top. Click this bar, and it
expands, showing you any errors and console output as well as letting you evaluate JavaScript
expressions. A number of extra debugging-related options are located in the Settings menu.

Goggle Chrome for Android doesn't have built-in debugging tools but can be remotely
debugged with an extension for the desktop Chrome browser. Please refer to the instructions   at   `https://developers.google.com/chrome-developer-tools/docs/`
`remote-debugging` to install the necessary drivers and set up your Chrome environment
for Android debugging.

Unlike some of their desktop counterparts, the JavaScript console functions in Android and iOS take only one argument. You can supply more than one argument to, for example, `console.log()`, but only the first one is used in the log message.

TIP

Building Native Web Applications

Being able to develop iOS and Android applications with the tools and techniques you already know is great, but by doing so, you miss some of the opportunities available to native application developers. Two key elements available only to native applications are access to the native APIs and the opportunity to publish through the App Store and Android Market. Fortunately, you can do some things that at least get you part of the way.

PhoneGap

One solution is Adobe's PhoneGap (`www.phonegap.com`). PhoneGap aims to bridge the gap between native and web by wrapping your web application in a native application. It does so by using the native web view control to render your game or application, which means that your game or application renders just as though it were running in the mobile browser, only without the browser's UI. In fact, no native UI is present at all. You must create all the interface controls you need in your application with HTML and CSS.

PhoneGap can build applications for several mobile platforms besides Android and iOS. Here is the full list of supported systems:

- iOS
- Android
- WebOS
- BlackBerry OS
- Symbian
- Bada
- Windows Phone 7 + 8

Depending on which platforms you want to use, you need to do a bit of work to set up your development environment. To build Android applications, you need the Android SDK (`http://developer.android.com/sdk`) and Eclipse Classic (`www.eclipse.org`). Eclipse runs on Windows, Linux, and Mac OS X. You don't get the same freedom if you want to build your game for iOS because you need a machine running Mac OS X and the Xcode development suite (`http://developer.apple.com/xcode`). To install your game on the actual devices and distribute it through the App Store, you also must enroll in the iOS Developer Program (`http://developer.apple.com/programs/ios`). Enrolling is easy but doing so costs $99 per year.

PhoneGap is free and open source. Adobe gave the code to the Apache Software Foundation, and it's licensed under the Apache License. Please see the documentation at `http://phonegap.com` for setting up PhoneGap.

When your web application is executed via PhoneGap, you can do most of the things that you can in a proper mobile browser. However, PhoneGap has one advantage over regular web applications in that it exposes several native APIs through a JavaScript interface. The exposed functionality includes

- Media API
- Accelerometer and compass
- Camera and AV capture
- Wi-Fi and cellular connection
- Geolocation and compass
- Native notifications
- File system access

You can find even more functionality in the plug-ins available from the PhoneGap GitHub repository (`http://github.com/phonegap/phonegap-plugins`).

Not all platforms support all the APIs, though. Check the documentation (`http://phonegap.com/about/feature`) to see where each feature is supported. To use these native features, you include the PhoneGap JavaScript file in your project. Of course, the functions won't work correctly until the application runs on the actual device. Listing 3-29 shows a basic example of how to use the PhoneGap camera API to take a picture. The code for this example can be found in the file `01-phonegap.html` in the `examples` folder.

Listing 3-29 **Taking a picture with PhoneGap**

```html
<!DOCTYPE HTML>
<html lang="en-US">
<head>
    <meta charset="UTF-8">
    <script src="phonegap.js"></script>
</head>
```

```
<body>
    <button id="snap">Take a picture!</button>
    <script>
        var button = document.getElementById("snap");
        button.addEventListener("click", function() {
            navigator.camera.getPicture(
                function(data) {
                    var img = new Image();
                    img.src = "data:image/jpeg;base64," + data;
                    document.body.appendChild(img);
                }, function(errMessage) {
                    alert("Camera error: " + errMessage);
                }, {
                    quality : 70
                }
            );
        }, false);
    </script>
</body>
</html>
```

Although PhoneGap is great in itself, what makes it really stand out in my mind is the PhoneGap Build service (`https://build.phonegap.com`). With PhoneGap Build, you can upload an archive file containing all your project files, and PhoneGap Build then automatically builds Android and iOS applications, ready to download. You can also set up a Git repository—for example—on GitHub, and have PhoneGap Build pull the files from there. That makes the whole process of creating native applications very smooth.

Developing applications locally for iOS and Android requires that you set up the necessary tools and, in the case of iOS, that you're using Mac OS X. PhoneGap Build lets you build native iOS and Android applications with as little hassle as possible at the price of some flexibility. If you want to have full control over the build process, you must install the development tools yourself.

The archive file that you upload to PhoneGap Build can contain an XML configuration file that specifies metadata about the application. Listing 3-30 shows an example of such a file.

Listing 3-30 **Sample config.xml file**

```
<?xml version="1.0" encoding="UTF-8"?>
<widget xmlns        = "http://www.w3.org/ns/widgets"
        xmlns:gap    = "http://phonegap.com/ns/1.0"
        id           = "com.phonegap.jewelwarrior"
```
continued

Listing 3-30   **continued**

```
        version       = "1.0.0">

<name>Jewel Warrior</name>

<description>
    A game of jewel swapping
</description>

<author href="http://nihilogic.dk"
        email="jseidelin@nihilogic.dk">
    Jacob Seidelin
</author>

<icon src="favicon128.png" gap:role="default" />

<gap:platforms>
    <gap:platform name="android" minVersion="2.1" />
</gap:platforms>

<feature name="http://api.phonegap.com/1.0/media"/>

</widget>
```

You can find this example in the file `05-config.xml`. You can add more elements and settings to the configuration file, but these are some of the most important. The `platform` nodes specify which platforms you want to build for. Note that you can specify the minimum version for the target OS if your application works only on newer versions. The `feature` nodes list all the extra privileges your game needs to be able to run. In this example, the application requests access to only the media API. Not all the PhoneGap APIs are available via the Build service, however. See the help pages on the PhoneGap Build site for an up-to-date list of the supported APIs.

Even if you don't take advantage of the extra features available from the PhoneGap API, the Build service is very useful and easy to work with.

TIP   As an alternative to PhoneGap, I recommend checking out CocoonJS by Ludei (`www.ludei.com`). Similar to PhoneGap, CocoonJS gives you a JavaScript API that enables a number of features that are usually not available to web applications. Their cloud-based compiler then packages everything into native apps, ready for the Apple App Store, Android Market, and other distribution channels.

Future Mobile Platforms

At the moment, Android and iOS take the lion's share of the mobile market, but new platforms are always emerging, and a few of them are very interesting for web development.

Mozilla is hard at work on Firefox OS (`www.mozilla.org/en-US/firefox/os`), a mobile operating system based on Linux and, of course, Firefox. Firefox OS is still under heavy development, but it's promising a mobile system that has HTML5 and open web technologies at its very core. No consumer devices are running on Firefox OS yet, although LG has recently announced its first Firefox OS phone. To help foster interest and development on the platform, Mozilla released a Firefox OS simulator as an add-on for its desktop browser.

Tizen (`www.tizen.org`), another Linux-based system, is also one to watch out for. A joint effort by Samsung, Intel, and The Linux Foundation, this system has its roots in a few other projects, most notably Samsung's Bada, which ceased development in early 2013. Much like Firefox OS, Tizen also puts HTML5 and its related technologies on the same level as native applications. The first devices running Tizen should be on the market in 2014.

Summary

In this chapter, you found out how to use a combination of scalable layouts, the viewport `meta` tag, and CSS media queries to make your game behave nicely on multiple devices with varying resolutions. You also saw how media queries can be used to tackle the issue of landscape versus portrait orientations.

I showed you how to use the iOS standalone mode for web applications to put a game icon on the home screen that launches the game in full-screen mode. You used conditional loading to load an install screen instead of the regular splash screen. By introducing a few more settings, you learned how to control the appearance of the iOS status bar and how to add a splash image.

To help you improve the experience on iOS and Android devices, I showed you how to get rid of some unwanted browser behavior, such as overscrolling, the address bar, and the long-press callout on images and links.

Finally, I showed how third-party tools such as PhoneGap can help you turn your HTML5-powered web applications into native applications on multiple mobile platforms.

Part II

Creating the Basic Game

Chapter 4
Building the Game

In This Chapter

- Creating a module for the game board
- Encapsulating the game state
- Setting up the jewel board
- Implementing the game rules
- Reacting to jewel swaps

IN THIS CHAPTER, I show you how to implement the rules and game mechanics that control the jewel board. I walk you through all the necessary game logic and create a representation of the game board with which the rest of the application can interact. I show you how to encapsulate the state of the board in an isolated module that allows modifications to the board only when all the game rules are followed. In addition, I show you how to make sure that the board automatically reacts to the swaps and rearranges the remaining jewels accordingly.

I also discuss some of the issues that arise when the game must be able to use two different sources that control the board. The single-player experience relies on the local, client-side game logic described in this chapter, but the game must also work with a server-side implementation of the same rules.

Creating the Game Board Module

The core of the game mechanics is isolated from the display and input elements of the game. The board module you walk through in this chapter is a data model of the game state, specifically the current layout of jewels. The module exposes methods that the other modules, mainly the game screen, can use to interact with the game state. Because the board serves as a backend to the game display, the code in this chapter doesn't add visual elements to the game. This means that, in this chapter, you will have to call the functions manually in the JavaScript console in order to test their functionality.

The board module is just a representation of the jewel board. The only real functionality it exposes to the outside world is a query function for accessing the jewels on the board and a function for swapping jewels. The swapping function attempts to swap only a pair of jewels because jewels are swappable only if certain conditions are met. Swapping jewels also has consequences: Jewels are removed, new ones fall down, and so on. The board module handles all these conditions and reactions automatically. The module lives in the JavaScript file board.js in the scripts folder. Listing 4-1 shows the initial module.

Listing 4-1 **The board module**

```
jewel.board = (function() {

    /* game functions go here */

    return {
        /* exposed functions go here */
    };

})();
```

Load the board.js file to in index.html as shown in Listing 4-2.

Listing 4-2 **Loading the board module**

```
...
    window.addEventListener("load", function() {
        jewel.load("scripts/dom.js");
        if (jewel.isStandalone()) {
            jewel.load("scripts/screen.splash.js");
            jewel.load("scripts/screen.main-menu.js");
        } else {
            jewel.load("scripts/screen.install.js");
        }
        jewel.load("scripts/board.js", jewel.setup);
    });
...
```

So far, the barebones `board` module has no functionality at all. In the following section, you move on to the first method and start fleshing out the module.

Initializing the game state

The board logic needs a few settings defined, such as the number of rows and columns, the number of different jewel types, and so on. Settings like these are best kept separate from the actual game code so it's easy to change the values without having to go through all the code. Listing 4-3 shows a new `settings` object added to the `jewel` module in `jewel.js`.

Listing 4-3 **Adding a settings object**
```
var jewel = (function() {
    var settings = {
        rows : 8,
        cols : 8,
        baseScore : 100,
        numJewelTypes : 7
    };
    ...
    return {
        ...
        settings : settings
    }
})();
```

The `rows` and `cols` settings define the size of the board in terms of rows and columns. Jewel Warrior uses an 8x8 grid, a size that works well on small screens. The `baseScore` setting determines the number of points awarded per jewel that takes part in a chain. As you'll see later, the score is also multiplied for chains involving more than three jewels. The base score is set to 100 points per jewel, but you can change this number if you want to inflate or deflate the scores. The last of the new settings, `numJewelTypes`, indicates the number of different jewel types. This number also corresponds to the number of jewel sprites.

The new settings are now accessible to the rest of the game and most importantly, at least for now, to the board module.

Initializing the board

To flesh out the module, you first need a function for setting up and initializing the game board. When the game starts, the board is already filled with random jewels. Listing 4-4 shows the `initialize()` function added to `board.js`.

Listing 4-4   The Initializing function

```javascript
jewel.board = (function() {
    var settings,
        jewels,
        cols,
        rows,
        baseScore,
        numJewelTypes;

    function initialize() {
        settings = jewel.settings;
        numJewelTypes = settings.numJewelTypes;
        baseScore = settings.baseScore;
        cols = settings.cols;
        rows = settings.rows;
        fillBoard();
    }

    function fillBoard() { }

    function getJewel() { }

    function print() {
        var str = "";
        for (var y = 0; y < rows; y++) {
            for (var x = 0; x < cols; x++) {
                str += getJewel(x, y) + " ";
            }
            str += "\r\n";
        }
        console.log(str);
    }

    return {
        initialize : initialize,
        print : print
    };
})();
```

The first thing you see in Listing 4-4 is a group of variable declarations. The first variable just imports the settings module because you need to access the settings in a bit. The second variable, `jewels`, is an array of arrays, essentially a two-dimensional array, representing the current state of the jewel board. In the `jewels` array, each jewel is represented by an integer value that indicates the type of the jewel. Using this array structure makes it easy to access the individual jewels by their coordinates. For example, the following snippet retrieves the jewel type found at position (x=3, y=2) on the board:

```
var type = jewels[3][2];
```

The listing also contains a number of variables whose values come from the settings module. (The values are described in the next section.) The `print()` function outputs the board data to the JavaScript console and is merely there to aid you in debugging. You initialize the board module by typing the following into the console:

```
jewel.board.initialize()
```

Throughout this chapter, whenever you want to inspect the board data, you simply enter the following command to print the data to the console:

```
jewel.board.print()
```

Using asynchronous functions

Before moving on to the next function, I want to share a small modification you can make to the `initialize()` function to prepare for the future. Chapter 5 shows you how to use Web Workers to move the board logic to a separate thread by creating a Web Worker–based board module that exposes the same methods as the one created in this chapter. Web Workers communicate with the rest of the application via an asynchronous messaging API, which means that all the methods exposed by the board modules must be able to function asynchronously.

Similarly, if you add a board module that uses a server-side backend to verify and validate the board data, you also need to send asynchronous Ajax requests to the server. Every function that modifies the game state would require a trip to the server and back before the caller receives the response. In other words, just because the function call returns, doesn't mean the result is ready.

You can solve this problem of deferred response in several ways, including using full-fledged custom event-dispatching systems or the concept of *promise* objects, as known from, for example, CommonJS and Node.js. The simplest solution, though, is just to provide a callback

function as an argument to the relevant method and have that method call the callback function when it is done. You probably already know this pattern from JavaScript functions such
as `window.setTimeout()` or the `addEventListener()` method on DOM elements.
These functions both take another function as one of the parameters and call that function
at some point in the future. Listing 4-5 shows the modified `initialize()` function in
`board.js`.

Listing 4-5   Initializing with the callback function

```
jewel.board = (function() {
    ...
    function initialize(callback) {
        ...
        if (callback) {
            callback();
        }
    }
    ....
})();
```

Now, all the action in the `initialize()` function happens immediately, so the result is
pretty much the same as it was without the callback function. The main difference is that
when you add the Web Worker module, it can use the same function signature, making the
integration of that module a lot easier.

Filling the initial board

The `fillBoard()` function used in Listing 4-5 must initialize a `cols` x `rows` grid and fill it
with random jewels. Listing 4-6 shows this function added to `board.js`.

Listing 4-6   Filling the jewel board

```
jewel.board = (function() {
    ...
    function fillBoard() {
        var x, y;

        jewels = [];
        for (x = 0; x < cols; x++) {
            jewels[x] = [];
            for (y = 0; y < rows; y++) {
                jewels[x][y] = randomJewel();
            }
```

```
        }
    }
    ...
})();
```

The jewel type is picked using the helper function `randomJewel()`, which simply returns an integer value between `0` and `(numJewelTypes - 1)`. Listing 4-7 shows the random-Jewel() function.

Listing 4-7 **Creating a random jewel**
```
jewel.board = (function() {
    ...
    function randomJewel() {
        return Math.floor(Math.random() * numJewelTypes);
    }
    ...
})();
```

The basic algorithm for randomly filling the board is now in place. The current solution is a bit simplistic, though, and doesn't guarantee that the resulting board is any good. Because the jewels are picked at random, there's a good chance that at least one or two chains are already on the board. The starting state of the game shouldn't have chains because that would lead to the player immediately getting points without lifting a finger. To ensure that this situation never occurs, the `fillBoard()` function must pick the jewels in a way that doesn't form chains of more than two identical jewels.

The fill algorithm fills the board starting from the top-left corner and finishing in the bottom-right corner, so there will only ever be jewels above and to the left of the position currently being filled. A chain takes at least three identical jewels, which means that, for there to be a chain, the randomly picked jewel must be the same type as either the two jewels to the left or the two jewels above. For a relatively small board like the one Jewel Warrior uses, a simple brute-force solution is good enough. Listing 4-8 shows the changes to the fill routine.

Listing 4-8 **Removing initial chains**
```
jewel.board = (function() {
    ...
    function fillBoard() {
        var x, y,
            type;
        jewels = [];
        for (x = 0; x < cols; x++) {
```

continued

Listing 4-8   **continued**

```
        jewels[x] = [];
        for (y = 0; y < rows; y++) {
            type = randomJewel();
            while ((type === getJewel(x-1, y) &&
                     type === getJewel(x-2, y)) ||
                    (type === getJewel(x, y-1) &&
                     type === getJewel(x, y-2))) {
                type = randomJewel();
            }
            jewels[x][y] = type;
        }
    }
    ...
})();
```

The algorithm now includes a loop that keeps picking a random jewel type until the chain condition is *not* met. In most cases, the randomly picked jewel cannot form a chain at all, and in the few cases in which it does, an alternative is quickly found.

Without some form of bounds checking, however, a loop like the one in Listing 4-7 would try to access positions outside the board, resulting in errors. Instead of accessing the `jewels` array directly, the `fillBoard()` routine uses a helper function, `getJewel()`, that guards against these out-of-bounds errors. Listing 4-9 shows this function.

Listing 4-9   **Getting jewel type from coordinates**

```
jewel.board = (function() {
    ...
    function getJewel(x, y) {
        if (x < 0 || x > cols-1 || y < 0 || y > rows-1) {
            return -1;
        } else {
            return jewels[x][y];
        }
    }
    ...
})();
```

The `getJewel()` function returns -1 if either of the coordinates is out of bounds, that is, if x or y is negative or greater than (`cols - 1`) or (`rows - 1`), respectively. To ensure that the return value is never equal to a real jewel type and therefore isn't able to take part in a chain valid jewel types are in the range [0, numTypes - 1].

You now have enough code to set up the board and fill it with random jewels. If you type the following into the JavaScript console, you should see the jewels printed out as numeric values

```
jewel.board.initialize()
jewel.board.print()
```

Implementing the Rules

Now that the initial board is ready, you can turn your attention to jewel swapping. The module exposes a `swap()` method that takes two sets of coordinates and tries to swap the jewels at those positions. Only valid swaps are allowed, and those that don't meet the requirements are rejected. You can start by implementing the validation mechanism.

Validating swaps

A swap is valid only if it results in at least one chain of three or more identical jewels. To perform this check, you use a function, `checkChain()`, that tests whether a jewel at a specified position is part of a chain. `checkChain()` determines this outcome by noting the jewel type at the specified position and then looking to the left and to the right and counting the number of jewels of the same type found in those directions. It then performs the same search for the up and down directions. If the sum of identical jewels in either the horizontal or vertical search is greater than two (or three if you include the center jewel), there is a chain. Listing 4-10 shows the `checkChain()` function in `board.js`.

Listing 4-10   **Checking for chains**

```
jewel.board = (function() {
    ...
    // returns the number jewels in the longest chain
    // that includes (x,y)
    function checkChain(x, y) {
        var type = getJewel(x, y),
            left = 0, right = 0,
            down = 0, up = 0;
        // look right
        while (type === getJewel(x + right + 1, y)) {
            right++;
        }
        // look left
        while (type === getJewel(x - left - 1, y)) {
            left++;
        }
```

continued

Listing 4-10   continued

```
        // look up
        while (type === getJewel(x, y + up + 1)) {
            up++;
        }
        // look down
        while (type === getJewel(x, y - down - 1)) {
            down++;
        }
        return Math.max(left + 1 + right, up + 1 + down);
    }
    ...
})();
```

Note that checkChain() doesn't return a Boolean value but instead returns the number of jewels found in the largest chain. This result gives a bit of extra information about the jewel that you can use later when the score is calculated. Now that you can detect chains at a given position, determining whether a swap is valid is relatively easy. The first condition is that the two positions must be adjacent. Only neighboring jewels can be swapped. If they are neighbors, assume that the swap is valid and switch the jewels types around. If the swap was actually good, checkChain() should return a number larger than 2 for one of the two positions. Swap the jewels back and return the result from the checkChain() calls. Listing 4-11 shows the canSwap() function in board.js that implements this validation.

Listing 4-11   **Validating a swap**

```
jewel.board = (function() {
    ...
    // returns true if (x1,y1) can be swapped with (x2,y2)
    // to form a new match
    function canSwap(x1, y1, x2, y2) {
        var type1 = getJewel(x1,y1),
            type2 = getJewel(x2,y2),
            chain;

        if (!isAdjacent(x1, y1, x2, y2)) {
            return false;
        }

        // temporarily swap jewels
        jewels[x1][y1] = type2;
        jewels[x2][y2] = type1;
```

```
        chain = (checkChain(x2, y2) > 2 ||
                 checkChain(x1, y1) > 2);

        // swap back
        jewels[x1][y1] = type1;
        jewels[x2][y2] = type2;

        return chain;
    }
    return {
        canSwap : canSwap,
        ...
    }
})();
```

Another helper function, isAdjacent(), is introduced in the canSwap() validation function. This function returns true if the two sets of coordinates are neighbors and false if they aren't. The function easily determines whether they're neighbors by looking at the distance between the positions along both axes, also called the *Manhattan distance*. The sum of the two distances must be exactly 1 if the positions are adjacent. Listing 4-12 shows the isAdjacent() function in board.js.

Listing 4-12 Testing adjacency

```
jewel.board = (function() {
    ...
    // returns true if (x1,y1) is adjacent to (x2,y2)
    function isAdjacent(x1, y1, x2, y2) {
        var dx = Math.abs(x1 - x2),
            dy = Math.abs(y1 - y2);
        return (dx + dy === 1);
    }
    ...
}
```

You can test the canSwap() function in the JavaScript console after you initialize the board module. Use the print() function to inspect the board data and then test different positions by entering, for example, jewel.board.canSwap(4,3,4,2).

Detecting chains

After performing a swap, the game must search the board for chains of jewels to remove. Immediately following a swap, relatively few jewels are candidates for removal. There can be only the chains involving the two swapped jewels. However, when those jewels are removed, other jewels fall down and more jewels enter the board from the top. This means that the board must be checked again, but this time the situation is not so simple. The only way to be sure all chains are detected is to be thorough and search the whole board. When you use the `checkChain()` function, this task is not so complicated. Listing 4-13 shows the `getChains()` function that loops across the board, looking for chains.

Listing 4-13   Searching the board for chains

```
jewel.board = (function() {
    ...
    // returns a two-dimensional map of chain-lengths
    function getChains() {
        var x, y,
            chains = [];

        for (x = 0; x < cols; x++) {
            chains[x] = [];
            for (y = 0; y < rows; y++) {
                chains[x][y] = checkChain(x, y);
            }
        }
        return chains;
    }
    ...
})();
```

The variable `chains` returned at the end of `getChains()` is a two-dimensional map of the board. Instead of jewel types, this map holds information about the chains in which the jewels take part. Each position on the board is checked by calling `checkChain()`, and the corresponding position in the `chains` map is assigned the return value.

Removing chained jewels

Identifying the chains is not enough, however. The game must also act on that information. Specifically, the chains must be removed, and the jewels above should fall down. The chain map is processed in the `check()` function shown in Listing 4-14.

Listing 4-14   Processing chains

```
jewel.board = (function() {
    ...
    function check() {
        var chains = getChains(),
            hadChains = false, score = 0,
            removed = [], moved = [], gaps = [];
```

```
        for (var x = 0; x < cols; x++) {
            gaps[x] = 0;
            for (var y = rows-1; y >= 0; y&#x2013;) {
                if (chains[x][y] > 2) {
                    hadChains = true;
                    gaps[x]++;
                    removed.push({
                        x : x, y : y,
                        type : getJewel(x, y)
                    });
                } else if (gaps[x] > 0) {
                    moved.push({
                        toX : x, toY : y + gaps[x],
                        fromX : x, fromY : y,
                        type : getJewel(x, y)
                    });
                    jewels[x][y + gaps[x]] = getJewel(x, y);
                }
            }
        }
    }
    ...
})();
```

This function removes jewels from the board and brings in new ones where necessary. Besides modifying the game board, the check() function also collects information about all the removed and repositioned jewels in two arrays, removed and moved. This data is important because you need it later for animating the changes on the screen, for example.

Using two nested loops, the check() function visits every position on the board. If the position is marked in a chains map with a value greater than two, information about the position and jewel type is recorded in the array removed using a simple object literal. Because a falling jewel simply overwrites this position later, you don't need to modify the actual jewels array yet.

Notice that the inner loop examines the rows from the bottom up instead of the usual top-down approach. This approach lets you immediately start moving the other jewels down. The algorithm also maintains a gaps array that contains a counter for each column. Before the algorithm processes a column, it sets the counter for that column to zero. Every time a jewel is removed, the counter is incremented. Whenever a jewel is allowed to stay, the gap counter determines whether the jewel should be moved down. If the counter is positive, the jewel must be moved down an equal number of rows. This information is recorded in a second array, moved, using a similar object literal, but this time recording both the start and end positions. You also need to update the jewels array now because this position is not touched again.

Creating new jewels

The check() function is not finished; it has a few loose ends. By moving existing jewels down, you fill the gaps below but leave new gaps at the top of the board. So, after processing all the jewels in a column, you need to create new jewels and have them come down from the top. Listing 4-15 shows this modification.

Listing 4-15   **Adding new jewels**

```
jewel.board = (function() {
    ...
    function check() {
        var x, y,
        ...
        // fill from top
        for (x = 0; x < cols; x++) {
            for (y = 0; y < gaps[x]; y++) {
                jewels[x][y] = randomJewel();
                moved.push({
                    toX : x, toY : y,
                    fromX : x, fromY : y - gaps[x],
                    type : jewels[x][y]
                });
            }
        }
    }
    ...
})();
```

The number of new jewels you need to create in a column is equal to the number of gaps found in that column. The positions they need to occupy are easy to calculate because new jewels always enter the board from the top. Information about the new jewels is also added to the moved array alongside any existing jewels that might have moved down. Because the new jewels don't have an actual starting position, an imaginary position outside the board is invented as though the jewels were already up there, waiting to fall down into the board.

Awarding points

In the initialize() function, I introduced a baseScore value for calculating the number of points given. Use that value to calculate the total rewarded across the board. Listing 4-16 shows the scoring added to the check() function.

Listing 4-16 **Awarding points for chains**

```
jewel.board = (function() {
    ...
    function check() {
        ...
        for (x = 0; x < cols; x++) {
            gaps[x] = 0;
            for (y = rows-1; y >= 0; y&#x2013;) {
                if (chains[x][y] > 2) {
                    hadChains = true;
                    gaps[x]++;
                    removed.push({
                        x : x, y : y,
                        type : getJewel(x, y)
                    });

                    // add points to score
                    score += baseScore *
                            Math.pow(2, (chains[x][y] - 3));

                } else if (gaps[x] > 0) {
                    ...
                }
                ...
            }
        }
    }
    ...
})();
```

For every jewel that is part of a chain, a specific number of points is added to score. The number of points depends on the length of the chain. For every extra jewel in the chain, the multiplier is doubled.

The score variable isn't the player's total score; it's just the score accumulated during this check() call. The board module has no concept of players; it simply calculates how many points should be awarded for a particular swap.

REMEMBER

The chains are now gone, and the gaps are filled with new jewels. However, it's possible for the new jewels to create new chains, so you're not done yet. The check() function must call itself again recursively until no chains are left at all. The function should also return the recorded changes. Listing 4-17 shows the changes to the check() function.

Listing 4-17   **Checking the board recursively**

```
jewel.board = (function() {
    ...
    function check(events) {
        ...

        events = events || [];

        if (hadChains) {
            events.push({
                type : "remove",
                data : removed
            }, {
                type : "score",
                data : score
            }, {
                type : "move",
                data : moved
            });
            return check(events);
        } else {
            return events;
        }
    }
    ...
}
```

You need to join the data collected in removed, moved, and score with whatever data the recursive calls collect. To do so, add an optional events argument to the check() function. This argument is used only in the recursive calls. If no value is passed in this argument, initialize events to an empty array. After the board is processed, add the accumulated score, and the board changes to the events array using the simple event object format shown in Listing 4.17. Each event object has just a type and a data property. If no chains are found, the board is not modified, and you don't need to call check() again. Just return the events array that will then bubble up to the first call and be returned to the caller. This way, the caller gets a complete list of every change that happened between the last swap and the final board.

Refilling the grid

If the game goes on long enough, the player inevitably faces a board that has no moves. The game needs to register this fact so the board can be refilled with fresh jewels and the game can continue. For this purpose, you need a function that can tell whether any moves are available. Listing 4-18 shows the hasMoves() function.

Listing 4-18   **Checking for available moves**

```
jewel.board = (function() {
    ...
    // returns true if at least one match can be made
    function hasMoves() {
        for (var x = 0; x < cols; x++) {
            for (var y = 0; y < rows; y++) {
                if (canJewelMove(x, y)) {
                    return true;
                }
            }
        }
        return false;
    }
    ...
})();
```

The hasMoves() function returns true if at least one jewel can be moved to form a chain; otherwise, it returns false. The canJewelMove() helper function, which does the actual task of checking a position for moves, is shown in Listing 4-19.

Listing 4-19   **Checking whether a jewel can move**

```
jewel.board = (function() {
    ...
    // returns true if (x,y) is a valid position and if
    // the jewel at (x,y) can be swapped with a neighbor
    function canJewelMove(x, y) {
        return ((x > 0 && canSwap(x, y, x-1 , y)) ||
                (x < cols-1 && canSwap(x, y, x+1 , y)) ||
                (y > 0 && canSwap(x, y, x , y-1)) ||
                (y < rows-1 && canSwap(x, y, x , y+1)));
    }
    ...
})();
```

To check whether a given jewel can be moved to form a new chain, the canJewelMove() function uses canSwap() to test whether the jewel can be swapped with one of its four neighbors. Each canSwap() call is performed only if the neighbor is within the bounds of the board; that is, canSwap() tries to swap the jewel with its left neighbor only if the jewel's x coordinate is at least 1 and less than (cols - 1), and so on.

If a time comes when the player cannot swap any jewels and `hasMoves()` therefore returns `false`, the board must be automatically refilled. The refill is triggered in the `check()` function. After the board is checked for chains, the jewels are removed, and new ones are brought in. Add a call to the `hasMoves()` function to test whether the new board allows for further swaps and, if necessary, refill the board. Listing 4-20 shows the changes.

Listing 4-20   Triggering a refill

```
jewel.board = (function() {
    ...
    function check(events) {
        ...

        if (hadChains) {
            ...

            // refill if no more moves
            if (!hasMoves()) {
                fillBoard();
                events.push({
                    type : "refill",
                    data : getBoard()
                });
            }
            return check(events);
        } else {
            return events;
        }
    }
})();
```

In addition to calling `fillBoard()`, this listing adds a `refill` event to the `events` array. This event carries with it a copy of the jewel board, created by the `getBoard()` function shown in Listing 4-21.

Listing 4-21   Copying the board data

```
jewel.board = (function() {
    ...

    // create a copy of the jewel board
    function getBoard() {
        var copy = [],
            x;
```

```
        for (x = 0; x < cols; x++) {
            copy[x] = jewels[x].slice(0);
        }
        return copy;
    }

    return {
        ...
        getBoard : getBoard
    };
})();
```

Simply calling `fillBoard()` doesn't guarantee that the new board has available moves, though. There's a slight chance that the randomly picked jewels just produce another locked board. A locked board, then, should trigger another, silent refill, without the player knowing. The best place to put this check is in the `fillBoard()` function itself. A call to `hasMoves()` can determine whether the board is usable, and if it isn't, `fillBoard()` calls itself recursively before returning. This way, the board keeps refilling until it has at least one pair of movable jewels. Listing 4-22 shows the refill check added to the `fillBoard()` function.

Listing 4-22 **Refilling the board recursively**

```
jewel.board = (function() {
    ...
    function fillBoard() {
        ...

        // try again if new board has no moves
        if (!hasMoves()) {
            fillBoard();
        }
    }
    ...
})();
```

This refill check also takes care of the special case in which the starting board has no jewels that can be swapped to form a chain. Just as probability dictates that the starting board sometimes has chains from the get-go, it's also possible that there are no moves at all, of course. The recursive call fixes that problem.

Swapping jewels

All the functions that govern the state of the board are now in place. The only thing missing is a function that actually swaps jewels. This task is relatively straightforward. You already have the canSwap() function that tells whether the player is allowed to swap a given pair of jewels, and the check() function that takes care of all the board modifications following the swap. Listing 4-23 shows the swap() function.

Listing 4-23   **The swap function**

```
jewel.board = (function() {
    . . .
    // if possible, swaps (x1,y1) and (x2,y2) and
    // calls the callback function with list of board events
    function swap(x1, y1, x2, y2, callback) {
        var tmp,
            events;

        if (canSwap(x1, y1, x2, y2)) {

            // swap the jewels
            tmp = getJewel(x1, y1);
            jewels[x1][y1] = getJewel(x2, y2);
            jewels[x2][y2] = tmp;

            // check the board and get list of events
            events = check();

            callback(events);
        } else {
            callback(false);
        }
    }

    return {
        . . .
        swap : swap
    };
})();
```

Because the swap() function needs to be exposed to the rest of the game and because it potentially modifies the board, it must work in the same asynchronous fashion as the initialize() function. Besides the two sets of coordinates, swap() takes a callback function as its fifth argument. Depending on whether the swap succeeds, this callback function is called with either a list of events that happened after the swap or, in case of an invalid swap, with `false`. Listing 4-24 shows the functions that are now exposed via the `board` module.

Listing 4-24 **Returning the public methods**

```
jewel.board = (function() {
    ...

    return {
        initialize : initialize,
        swap : swap,
        canSwap : canSwap,
        getBoard : getBoard,
        print : print
    };
})();
```

That's it. With those functions exposed, the only way to alter the game state is to set up a fresh board or call the `swap()` method. All the rules of the game are enforced by the `swap()` method, so the integrity of the board is guaranteed. In addition, the only entry point to the jewel data is via the `getBoard()` function, which doesn't allow write access to the data, minimizing the risk that the rest of the code can inadvertently "break" the board.

You can test the `swap()` function by calling it directly from the JavaScript console. Initialize the board module by entering:

```
jewel.board.initialize(function(){})
```

Use `jewel.board.print()` to locate suitable positions and then enter, for example:

```
jewel.board.swap(4,3,4,2, function(e){console.log(e)})
```

Remember that the `swap()` functions need a callback function. Just give it a function that outputs the events array to the console.

Summary

This chapter showed you how to implement the core of the game mechanics. You walked through the implementation of all the basic game rules concerning jewel swapping, chains, and falling jewels. The game board is now neatly encapsulated in an isolated module and allows access to the data only through a few access points, ensuring that all modifications happen in accordance with the rules of the game.

This chapter also showed you how to prepare for future multiplayer functionality by shaping the module such that the game can use both the single-player, local game logic and the server-bound multiplayer module. Using callback functions for some of the key methods allows the two modules to share the same interface, making it easier to add an asynchronous, server-bound board module at a later time.

Chapter 5
Delegating Tasks to Web Workers

In This Chapter

- Introducing Web Workers
- Describing major API functions
- Looking at examples
- Creating a worker-based board module

IN THIS CHAPTER, I show you how to use Web Workers, a cool feature that came out of the Web Hypertext Application Technology Working Group (WHATWG; refer to Chapter 1 for more on this group). I begin by describing what workers can do, their limitations, and the functions and objects available to them.

I then move on to a few simple examples and show you how to move a CPU-intensive task to a worker to keep the browser responsive to user interaction.

Finally, I show you how to use Web Workers to create a worker-based version of the board module you implement in Chapter 4.

Working with Web Workers

JavaScript is single threaded by design. You cannot run multiple scripts in parallel; the browser processes any request you send it in a serial manner. When you use functions such as `setTimeout()` and `setInterval()`, you may think you're spawning separate threads that run independently from the main JavaScript thread, but in reality, the functions they call are pushed onto the same event loop that the main thread uses. One drawback is that you cannot have a function that blocks the execution and expect the browser to behave. For example, the XMLHttpRequest object used in Ajax has both synchronous and asynchronous modes. The asynchronous mode is used the most by far because synchronous requests tie up the thread, blocking any further execution until the request finishes. This includes any interaction with the page, which appears all but frozen.

Web Workers go a long way toward solving this problem by introducing functionality that resembles threads. With Web Workers, you can load scripts and make them run in the background, independent from the main thread. A script that runs in a worker cannot affect or lock up the main thread, which means you can now do CPU-intensive processing while still allowing the user to keep using the game or application.

NOTE In this book, I often refer to *worker threads*. The Web Workers specification defines the functionality of workers as being "thread-like" because implementations don't necessarily have to use actual OS-level threads. The implementation of Web Workers is up to the browser vendors.

Even though they're often mentioned in the same sentence as other HTML5 features, Web Workers aren't part of the HTML5 specification but instead have their own specification. The full Web Workers specification is available at the WHATWG website: `www.whatwg.org/specs/web-workers/current-work`.

Limitations in workers

You need to be aware of some important limitations on what a worker can do. In many cases, however, these constraints don't pose problems as long as your code is encapsulated well and you keep your data isolated.

No shared state

One of the first issues to be aware of is the separation of state and data. No data from the parent thread is accessible from the worker thread, and vice versa. All changes to the data of either thread must happen through the messaging API. Although this limitation may seem like a nuisance at first, it's a tremendous help in avoiding nasty concurrency problems. If workers could freely manipulate the variables in the parent thread, the risk of running into problems such as deadlocks and race conditions would make using workers much more complex. With the relatively low entry bar to the world of web development, the decision to limit flexibility in return for simplicity and security makes sense.

No DOM access

As you may have guessed, this separation of worker and parent thread also means that workers have no access to the DOM. The `window` and `document` objects simply don't exist in the scope of the worker, and any attempt to access them only results in errors.

This lack of DOM access doesn't mean that the worker cannot send messages to the main thread that are then used to change the DOM. The messaging API doesn't restrict you from defining your own message protocol for updating certain DOM elements or exchanging information about the elements in the document. However, if you plan to do heavy DOM manipulation, perhaps reconsidering whether the functionality really belongs in a worker is better.

Because Microsoft added support for Web Workers in Internet Explorer 10, Web Workers are now available in all modern desktop browsers. The stock browser in earlier versions of Android doesn't support Web Workers, but as of Android 4.4, the stock browser will be based on Chrome for Android, which does include support. Mobile Safari in iOS 5.0+ and IE Mobile in Windows Phone 8 also support Web Workers.

NOTE

What workers can do

In general, you can do anything with workers you'd otherwise do with JavaScript. Creating a worker simply loads a script and executes it in a background thread. You aren't limited in terms of JavaScript capability. In addition to pure JavaScript, you have access to a few nice extras.

First, there's a new function called `importScripts()`. You provide this function with a list of paths that point to scripts that you want to load. The function is *variadic*, which means that you must specify the paths as individual arguments:

```
importScripts("script1.js", "script2.js", "script3.js", ...);
```

Because the files are loaded synchronously, `importScripts()` doesn't return until all the scripts finish loading. After each script is done loading, it's executed within the same scope as the calling worker, which means that the script can use all variables and functions declared in the worker and that the worker can subsequently use all variables and functions introduced by the imported script. Overall, this approach enables you to separate your worker code easily into discrete modules.

The script that created the worker can terminate the worker when it's no longer needed, but the worker itself can also choose to exit. A worker can self-terminate by calling the global `close()` function.

Timeouts and intervals

The timer functions that you know from the `window` object are all available in worker threads, which means that you're free to use the following functions:

- `setTimeout()`
- `clearTimeout()`
- `setInterval()`
- `clearInterval()`

If the worker is terminated, all timers are automatically cleared.

WebSockets and Ajax workers

You can also use the `XMLHttpRequest` object to create and process background Ajax requests. `XMLHttpRequest` are useful if you need, for example, a background worker that continuously pings the server for updates that are then relayed to the main thread via the messaging API. Because blocking in a worker thread doesn't affect the main UI thread, you can even do synchronous requests—something that's usually a bad idea in non-worker code.

WebSockets support in worker threads is a bit of a gray area. For example, Chrome supports this combination, whereas Firefox lets you use WebSockets only in the main JavaScript thread, thus limiting the number of users who can benefit from it. For now, therefore, it's better to leave WebSockets code to the main thread.

Using Workers

To create worker threads, you use the `Worker()` constructor:

```
var worker = new Worker("myworker.js");
```

You can create workers only from scripts that have the same origin as the creating script, which means you cannot refer to scripts on other domains. The script must also be loaded using the same scheme. That is, the script must not use `https:` if the HTML page uses the `http:` scheme, and so on. Additionally, you cannot create workers from a script running from a `file://` URL.

When you're done using the worker, make sure you call the `terminate()` method to free up memory and avoid old, lingering workers:

```
worker.terminate();
```

You can create more than one worker thread. You can even create more workers that use the same script. Some tasks are well suited for parallelization, and with computers sporting more and more CPU cores, dividing intensive tasks between a few workers can potentially produce a nice boost in performance. However, don't create workers in large numbers because of the cost of overhead in the setup process. Instead, try to keep the number of workers down to a handful or two.

Sending messages

Workers and their parent threads communicate through a common messaging API. Data is passed back and forth as strings, but that doesn't mean you can send only string messages. If you send a complex structure such as an array or object, it's automatically converted to JSON format. For this reason, you can build fairly advanced messages, but note that some things, such as DOM elements, cannot be converted to JSON.

In the creating thread, call the `postMessage()` method on the worker with the data that you want to send. Here are a few examples:

```
// send a string
worker.postMessage("Hello worker!");

// send an array
worker.postMessage([0, 1, 2, 3]);

// send an object literal
worker.postMessage({
    command : "pollServer",
    timeout : 1000
});
```

In the same way, simply call `postMessage()` to send messages from the worker thread to the main thread:

```
// send a string to main thread
postMessage("Hello, I'm ready to work!");
```

Receiving messages

Messages can be intercepted by listening for the message event. In the parent thread, the event is fired on the worker object, whereas in the worker object, it's fired on the global object.

To listen for messages from the worker, attach a handler to the message event:

```
worker.addEventListener("message", function(event) {
    // message received from worker thread
}, false);
```

Similarly, in the worker thread, listen for the message event on the global object:

```
addEventListener("message", function(event) {
    // message received from main thread
}, false);
```

In both cases, you can find the message data in the data property on the event object. It's automatically decoded from JSON, so the structure of the data is intact.

Catching errors

If an error occurs in a worker thread, you may want to know about it in the main thread so that you can display a message, create a log entry, and so forth. In addition to the message event, worker objects emit an error event, which is fired if an error happens that's not caught in the worker thread. When the event fires, it's too late to do anything about the error. The worker has already stopped whatever it was doing, but at least you're informed that the error occurred.

```
worker.addEventListener("error", function(error) {
    alert("Worker error: " + error);
}, false);
```

Shared workers

The type of worker I just described is called a *dedicated* worker. The Web Workers specification also defines another type: the *shared* worker. Shared workers differ from dedicated workers in that they can have multiple connections. They aren't bound to one HTML page. If you have multiple HTML pages from the same origin running in the same browser, these pages can all access shared workers created by one of the pages.

To create a shared worker, use the SharedWorker() constructor. In addition to the script path, this constructor takes a second, optional name parameter. If the name parameter isn't given, an empty string is used for the name. If you attempt to create a shared worker and one has already been created with the same script and name, a new connection to that worker is created instead of a brand new worker.

I don't go into depth about shared workers here, and they aren't used for the Jewel Warrior game. Let me just give you a short example to show how multiple pages can connect to and communicate with the same worker. Listing 5-1 shows the test HTML page that creates a shared worker.

Although Chrome and Safari support both types of workers, Firefox 25 and Internet Explorer 11 **NOTE** support only dedicated workers. Neither Chrome for Android or Safari on iOS currently support shared workers, although they have been available in some beta versions of mobile Safari, so it's likely that this feature will be enabled again in a future iOS update.

Listing 5-1   Shared worker test page

```
<!DOCTYPE HTML>
<html>
<textarea cols=80 rows=20 id="output"></textarea>
<script>
    var worker = new SharedWorker("shared-worker.js","worker");
    worker.port.addEventListener("message", function(event) {
        document.getElementById("output").value +=
            event.data + "\r\n";
    }, false);
    worker.port.start();
    worker.port.postMessage("Hello");
</script>
</html>
```

Whenever the page receives a message from the worker, the message is printed in the output `textarea`. The worker is greeted with a `"Hello"` when the connection is established. Listing 5-2 shows the worker script.

Listing 5-2   The shared-worker.js script

```
var c = 0;
addEventListener("connect", function(event) {
    var id = c++,
        port = event.ports[0];
    port.postMessage("You are now connected as #" + id);
    port.addEventListener("message", function(event) {
        if (event.data == "Hello") {
            port.postMessage("And hello to you, #" + id);
        }
    }, false);
    port.start();
}, false);
```

Shared workers don't have a global `message` event as dedicated workers do. Instead, they must listen for `connect` events that fire whenever a new page creates a connection to the worker. Communication between the worker and connecting threads happens via port objects that emit `message` events and expose the `postMessage()` method. Note also the `port.start()` function, which must be called before any messages can be received.

When the HTML page in Listing 5-1 is loaded, it connects to a worker. If you open another tab with the same or a similar page, it connects to the same worker, and you see the connection counter increasing.

A prime example

Let's move on to another example that's just slightly more useful. Here, I use a dedicated worker to do some CPU-intensive processing, thereby freeing up the main thread.

Consider the problem of determining whether a number is a prime number. A prime is a number that has only two (natural number) divisors, 1 and itself. For example, 9 isn't a prime because it can be divided by 3. On the other hand, 7 cannot be divided by any other number and is therefore a prime.

Listing 5-3 shows `prime.js`, a simple brute-force algorithm that returns a Boolean value indicating whether a number, n, is a prime.

Listing 5-3   **The prime-checking algorithm**
```
function isPrime(n) {
    if (n < 2) return false;
    for (var i=2,m=Math.sqrt(n);i<=m;i++) {
        if (n % i === 0) {
            return false;
        }
    }
    return true;
}
```

The smallest prime number is 2, so `isPrime()` returns `false` for anything less than 2. If a pair of divisors exists, one of the divisors must be smaller than or equal to the square root of n, so you need to test only numbers in the range `[2, sqrt(n)]` to determine the primality of n. So, for each number i from 2 to `sqrt(n)`, you use the remainder operator (`%`) to test whether i can divide n. If it can, n isn't a prime and `isPrime()` returns `false`. If the loop exits without finding a divisor, n is a prime, and the function returns `true`.

Creating the test page

Because the loop must run to the end if the n is a prime, any sufficiently large prime number makes isPrime() hog the CPU for a while, effectively locking down the main UI thread for that page.

To see that this is actually the case, create the prime-no-worker.html test page shown in Listing 5-4.

Listing 5-4 **The non-worker test page**

```html
<!DOCTYPE HTML>
<html lang="en-US">
<head>
    <meta charset="UTF-8">
    <title>Prime Number</title>
    <script src="prime.js"></script>
</head>
<body>

Number (n): <input id="number" value="1125899839733759">

<button id="check">Is n prime?</button><br/><br/>
<button id="click-test">Try to click me!</button>

<script>
    var button = document.getElementById("check");
    button.addEventListener("click", function() {
        var input = document.getElementById("number"),
            n = parseInt(input.value, 10),
            res = isPrime(n);
        if (res) {
            alert(n + " is a prime number");
        } else {
            alert(n + " is NOT a prime number");
        }
    }, false);

    var buttonHello = document.getElementById("click-test");
    buttonHello.addEventListener("click", function() {
        alert("Hello!");
    }, false);
</script>

</body>
</html>
```

This simple test page features an input field with a button. When you click the check button, the value of the number field is passed to isPrime(), and the result is displayed in a message box. The default number I specified in the input field is a prime and should take a while to check, but if it's too fast, just add some more isPrime(n) calls.

The second button, click-test, is there to test whether the UI responds. Try clicking this button while isPrime() is running. Nothing happens until after the isPrime() call finishes and the results are displayed.

Moving the task to a worker

If, instead, you move the isPrime() function to a worker thread, the main UI thread is kept free, and the UI remains as responsive as ever. Listing 5-5 shows the prime-worker.js script.

Listing 5-5 **The worker script**

```
importScripts("prime.js");

addEventListener("message", function(event) {
    var res = isPrime(event.data);
    postMessage(res);
}, false);
```

Notice how the prime.js file is reused by importing it with the importScripts() function. The message event handler simply passes along data it receives to isPrime() and posts back the result to the main thread when it's done. The worker thread may be busy, but the main thread isn't. Now change the click event handler in the HTML page as shown in Listing 5-6.

Listing 5-6 **Communicating with the worker**

```
button.addEventListener("click", function() {
    var input = document.getElementById("number"),
        n = parseInt(input.value, 10),
        worker = new Worker("prime-worker.js");

    worker.addEventListener("message", function(event) {
        if (event.data) {
            alert(n + " is a prime number");
        } else {
            alert(n + " is NOT a prime number");
        }
```

```
    }, false);

    worker.postMessage(n);

}, false);
```

When the check button is clicked, a new worker is created from the `prime-worker.js` script. The value of the number input field is converted to a number and posted to the worker using the `postMessage()` method. The `message` event handler waits for a response from the worker and pops up a message box with the result.

If you try clicking the test button now, you see that the UI still responds and the `"Hello!"` alert appears as soon as you click. All the intensive processing happens independently in the background and doesn't affect the page.

Using Web Workers in Games

You have now seen some basic examples of how to use Web Workers, but how do they relate to games? When deciding what elements to delegate to worker threads, you must ask yourself a few questions.

First, do you need to move the game element to a separate worker thread? Does the game element do anything that could benefit from running independently?

Second, does the game element depend on having access to the DOM? Remember that worker threads cannot access the document, so tasks that depend on the DOM must be done in the main thread.

Good candidates for workers include elements such as artificial intelligence (AI). Many games have entities that the player doesn't control but instead react to player actions or the environment in general. Processing the behavior of enemies and other entities is potentially a rather intensive task. This task doesn't need to manipulate the page and could therefore be a candidate for a worker thread. Physics simulation is another example. Like AI, physics simulation can be demanding on the CPU and doesn't necessarily need to run in the same thread as long as the data is kept synchronized.

Creating the worker module

In the case of Jewel Warrior, moving anything to a web worker is difficult to justify. Because of the relatively small 8x8 board, the board module that takes care of the game logic is fairly lightweight in terms of processing needs. It could easily run in a separate worker thread, though. Because the module was designed with multiplayer support in mind, it already has an asynchronous interface, which makes it easy to adapt to the asynchronous nature of worker messaging. It's pure logic; it manipulates only its own internal data and doesn't need DOM access. Listing 5-7 shows the beginnings of the `board.worker.js` script.

Listing 5-7   **Importing the board module**

```
var jewel = {};

importScripts("board.js");
```

The board worker imports the regular board module, which lets you reuse the functionality already present in the board module. Because the module is created in the `jewel` namespace, an empty `jewel` object is created prior to importing the script. If the object doesn't exist when the script is imported and executed, you get a runtime error.

When the board worker receives a message from the game, it needs to call the appropriate method on the imported board module and post back the results. The messages coming from the game to the worker use a custom message format described by the following object literal:

```
{
    id : <number>,
    command : <string>,
    data : <any>
}
```

Here, the `id` property is an ID number uniquely identifying this message. The `command` property is a string that determines what the worker should do, and the `data` property contains any data needed to perform that task. All messages posted to the worker trigger a response message with the following format:

```
{
    id : <number>,
    data : <any>,
    jewels : <array>
}
```

The `id` property is the ID number of the original message; `data` is the response data, if any. The `jewels` property contains a two-dimensional array that represents the current state of the jewel board. The board data is always attached, so the main thread can keep a local copy of the data for easy access. Listing 5-8 shows the `message` event handler in the `board.worker.js` script.

Listing 5-8   **The message handler**

```
addEventListener("message", function(event) {
    var board = jewel.board,
        message = event.data;

    switch (message.command) {
        case "initialize" :
            jewel.settings = message.data;
            board.initialize(callback);
            break;
        case "swap" :
            board.swap(
                message.data.x1,
                message.data.y1,
                message.data.x2,
                message.data.y2,
                callback
            );
            break;
    }

    function callback(data) {
        postMessage({
            id : message.id,
            data : data,
            jewels : board.getBoard()
        });
    }

}, false);
```

The worker supports two commands, `initialize` and `swap`, that are mapped to the corresponding methods on the board module. When the worker receives the `initialize` command, `data` must contain the `settings` object from the `jewel` namespace in the parent.

Remember that the `board.initialize()` function takes a callback function as its first and only argument. A special callback function is defined in the worker and passed to `board.initialize()` and any other asynchronous board methods. When the callback function is called, the data parameter is sent to the main thread as a message, and it's then up to the main thread to handle the callback message.

Keeping the same interface

Now you can put this new worker module to use. The game should be able to run with or without worker support, so ideally, you need a new worker-based board module that has the same interface as the non-worker board.js module. Any functions exposed in the board module must also exist in the worker board module with the same signatures—specifically, the functions initialize(), swap(), and getBoard(). The idea is that if those functions exist and follow the same logic, you can replace one module with the other, and the rest of the game is none the wiser. Listing 5-9 shows the initial worker-based board module with the initialize() function. Put the code in a new file called board.worker-interface.js.

Listing 5-9   **The worker board module**
```
jewel.board = (function() {
    var worker;

    function initialize(callback) {
        worker = new Worker("scripts/board.worker.js");
    }

})();
```

Currently, initialize() just sets up a new worker object from the worker script. Notice that the callback function isn't called from initialize(). The callback must not be called before the worker has done its job and posted the response message back to the board module.

Sending messages

The worker thread must be told to call the initialize() method on the real board module. To do so, you must send messages to the message event handler in Listing 5-8. The post() function in board.worker-interface.js that sends messages to the message event handler is shown in Listing 5-10.

Listing 5-10   **Posting messages to the worker**
```
jewel.board = (function() {
    var worker,
```

```
            messageCount,
            callbacks;

    function initialize(callback) {
        messageCount = 0;
        callbacks = [];
        worker = new Worker("scripts/board.worker.js");
    }

    function post(command, data, callback) {
        callbacks[messageCount] = callback;
        worker.postMessage({
            id : messageCount,
            command : command,
            data : data
        });
        messageCount++;
    }
})();
```

The post() function takes three arguments—a command, the data for the command, and a callback function—that must be called when the response is received. To handle callbacks, you need to keep track of the messages posted to the worker. Each message is given a unique id; in this case, I chose a simple incrementing counter. Whenever a message is posted to the worker, the callback is saved in the callbacks array using the message id as an index.

You can now use this post() function to create the swap() function. When swap() is called, it must post a "swap" message to the worker, providing it with the four coordinates. Listing 5-11 shows the worker-based swap() in board.worker-interface.js.

Listing 5-11   **The swap message**

```
jewel.board = (function() {
    ...

    function swap(x1, y1, x2, y2, callback) {
        post("swap", {
            x1 : x1,
            y1 : y1,
            x2 : x2,
            y2 : y2
        }, callback);
    }
})();
```

Handling responses

When the `callback` function is passed to `post()`, it's entered into the `callbacks` array so it can be fetched whenever the worker posts a response back to the main thread. The board module listens for responses by attaching a `message` event handler in `initialize()`, as shown in Listing 5-12.

Listing 5-12   The message handler

```
jewel.board = (function() {

    ...

    function messageHandler(event) {
        // uncomment to log worker messages
        // console.log(event.data);

        var message = event.data;
        jewels = message.jewels;

        if (callbacks[message.id]) {
            callbacks[message.id](message.data);
            delete callbacks[message.id];
        }
    }

    function initialize(callback) {
        rows = jewel.settings.rows;
        cols = jewel.settings.cols;
        messageCount = 0;
        callbacks = [];
        worker = new Worker("scripts/board.worker.js");
        jewel.dom.bind(worker, "message", messageHandler);
        post("initialize", jewel.settings, callback);
    }
})();
```

After the event handler is attached, the `"initialize"` message is sent to the worker. When the worker finishes setting up the board, it calls its own callback function, which posts a message back to the board module, which then calls the callback function originally passed to `initialize()`.

The only function missing now is `getBoard()`, which you can copy verbatim from the `board.js` module to the worker-based module in `board.worker-interface.js`. You can also copy the `print()` and `getJewel()` functions if you want to inspect the board data. The final step is to expose the methods at the end of the module, as Listing 5-13 shows.

Listing 5-13 **Exposing the public methods**

```
jewel.board = (function() {
    ...
    return {
        initialize : initialize,
        swap : swap,
        getBoard : getBoard,
        print : print
    };
})();
```

Loading the right module

Now you have two board modules: the one from Chapter 4 and the new one that delegates the work to a worker thread. Because workers are supported in only some browsers, the new board module must be loaded only if workers are available. If they aren't, the game must fall back to the regular board module. Listing 5-14 shows the modifications to the loading sequence in index.html.

Listing 5-14 **Loading the worker-based board module**

```
window.addEventListener("load", function() {
    jewel.load("scripts/dom.js");
    if (jewel.isStandalone()) {
        jewel.load("scripts/screen.splash.js");
        jewel.load("scripts/screen.main-menu.js");
        if (jewel.hasWebWorkers()) {
            jewel.load("scripts/board.worker-interface.js",
                    jewel.setup);
        } else {
            jewel.load("scripts/board.js", jewel.setup);
        }
    } else {
        jewel.load("scripts/screen.install.js", jewel.setup);
    }
});
```

Now you're using feature detection to load the correct board module, allowing users with modern browsers to take advantage of Web Workers while automatically falling back to a non-worker–based solution for users with older browsers. Actually detecting support for workers is as simple as testing whether the `Worker()` constructor exists on the `window` object. Add the `hasWebWorkers()` function to `jewel.js`, as shown in Listing 5-15.

Listing 5-15   Detecting support for Web Workers

```
jewel = (function() {

    ...

    function hasWebWorkers() {
        return ("Worker" in window);
    }

    return {
        hasWebWorkers: hasWebWorkers,
        ...
    };
})();
```

Preloading the worker module

When you use the `Worker()` constructor to create a new worker, the `board.worker.js` script is automatically pulled from the server. It would be nice if the file were already in the cache so the user didn't have to wait for the additional HTTP request before the game could begin. You could use the `jewel.load()` function, but doing so will also execute the script, which can cause problems as the script is intended to run only in a worker context. Instead, add a `preload()` function to `jewel.js` that loads only the script using the `Image` object trick and nothing else. This approach puts the loaded script in the cache without executing so that it won't interfere with or slow down the execution of the other scripts. Listing 5-16 shows the new function.

Listing 5-16   Preloading scripts without executing them

```
var jewel = (function() {
    ...
    function preload(src) {
        var image = new Image();
        image.src = src;
    }

    return {
        preload: preload,
        ...
    }
})();
```

Now simply preload `board.worker.js` when you load the `board.worker-interface.js` script. Listing 5-17 shows the worker script added to the loading sequence in `index.html`.

Listing 5-17 **Preloading the worker module**

```
window.addEventListener("load", function() {
    jewel.load("scripts/dom.js");
    if (jewel.isStandalone()) {
        jewel.load("scripts/screen.splash.js");
        jewel.load("scripts/screen.main-menu.js");
        if (jewel.hasWebWorkers()) {
            jewel.preload("scripts/board.worker.js");
            jewel.load("scripts/board.worker-interface.js",
                    jewel.setup);
        } else {
            jewel.load("scripts/board.js", jewel.setup);
        }
    } else {
        jewel.load("scripts/screen.install.js", jewel.setup);
    }
});
```

Summary

In this chapter, you saw how to use Web Workers to free up the main UI thread by delegating any CPU-intensive tasks to workers running in the background. You learned how to create worker objects and how to use the messaging API to send messages back and forth between the worker and parent script.

You also used that knowledge to implement a worker-based board module that uses the existing board logic but runs in a separate worker thread. I hope you gained a better understanding of the possibilities that lie in Web Workers and how they can potentially change the way web applications are written as well as the amount of processing you can do in the browser.

Chapter 6
Creating Graphics with Canvas

In This Chapter

- Using canvas versus other methods
- Drawing with the canvas element
- Drawing paths and shapes
- Applying transformations to the canvas
- Modifying image data

THIS CHAPTER SHOWS you how to create dynamic graphics with the canvas element. It starts by giving you an overview of the ways in which you can display graphics and graphics on the web before diving into the canvas drawing API.

The meat of this chapter is all about how to use the canvas API. First, you walk through the basics of drawing simple shapes and paths and applying various styles to the content. You learn how to use the canvas state stack to your advantage and see how to mix images and text content with graphics on the canvas.

Then you learn how to use transformations to modify the way things are drawn and how to apply different compositing operations. Finally, the chapter rounds off the canvas tour by looking at how to use low-level pixel access to create some really interesting effects.

Ways to Display Graphics on the Web

In the past, all graphics on the web had to be represented by bitmap images in formats such as GIF or JPEG. More options for displaying graphics on the web are available today.

Bitmap images

Bitmaps are images defined by a rectangular grid of pixels. The traditional formats used on the web—JPEG, PNG, and GIF—are all bitmap formats. Bitmaps are perfectly adequate for many purposes. In some cases, such as displaying photos, they are the only sensible choice. The img tag has been around since forever and has full support in all browsers.

The main disadvantages of bitmap images are that the images don't scale well and that the content is static and non-interactive. Sure, animated image formats exist, but you cannot dynamically change the content of the images. Bitmap images don't have much in terms of interactivity either. You can attach event handlers to the images, but the content is static and therefore doesn't produce visual results to user actions.

If you scale a bitmap image to a size that's larger than the original, some degradation in the quality of the image inevitably occurs. You have only so many pixels to work with, and the computer cannot intelligently decide what it should use to fill the voids. Computers typically employ one of two basic strategies when it comes to image rescaling. One is the nearest-neighbor strategy, which is fast but makes the image appear pixelated. The other is interpolation using, for instance, bilinear or bicubic algorithms. This is the default resampling method for all modern browsers, and it has a softening effect.

SVG graphics

Scalable Vector Graphics (SVG) is an alternative to bitmap graphics that is useful for displaying vector-based art. Because this format is based on XML, you can edit the files by hand, although many graphics applications also export directly to the SVG format. The insides of an SVG file look something like this:

```
<svg xmlns="http://www.w3.org/2000/svg" viewBox="0 0 512 512">
  <path fill="#E34F26" d="M71,460 L30,0 481,0 440,460 255,512"/>
  <path fill="#EF652A" d="M256,472 L405,431 440,37 256,37"/>
</svg>
```

You can also add images, text, and various shapes to an SVG file, but you have to declare all content in this XML format. In addition to graphical elements, you can declare basic animations and event handlers.

The SVG format is not brand new; the development of the SVG specification began in 1999. However, only recently have all major browser vendors added native support for it. Although you're able to modify the SVG content using DOM functions, there's no nice API such as what the `canvas` element provides. This brings me to the main topic of this chapter: the `canvas` element.

The canvas element

One of the major, early features of the HTML5 specification was the `canvas` element. Web developers had long been looking for ways to create dynamic graphics, and `canvas` finally solved that problem. The `canvas` element provides a two-dimensional drawing surface with a rich JavaScript API for drawing all sorts of shapes, paths, and objects on that surface. The API is so full-featured, actually, that a project such as canvg (`http://code.google.com/p/canvg`) is able to provide a near-complete canvas-based SVG renderer.

A major difference between canvas and SVG is that the canvas API does what is known as *immediate mode* rendering in contrast to SVG's *retained mode*. Immediate mode means that any content drawn on the canvas is immediately rasterized and rendered to the surface. The canvas doesn't maintain any sort of internal structure of the shapes and paths that have been drawn. As soon as you tell the canvas to draw, for example, a square, it does the job and then forgets all about what those pixels represent. An SVG image, on the other hand, always has an XML structure that describes exactly which elements make up the image.

Another feature that really sets canvas apart from SVG is the low-level access to pixel data. Because you can access and modify individual pixels, there's really no limit to what you can do with a `canvas` element. This is evidenced by the existence of ray tracers, imaging applications, as well as numerous experiments displaying amazing effects inspired by the demoscene (`http://en.wikipedia.org/wiki/Demoscene`).

When to choose canvas

When to use canvas and when to opt for some other technology isn't always clear. In many cases, there's no right answer, either. Regular bitmap images are still relevant, and if the content doesn't rely on any dynamic data and is otherwise static, you're often better off just using old-fashioned images.

If the content can be described by sufficiently simple elements, SVG can be a good alternative. The vector-based format makes it a good choice for graphics that need to scale to different sizes. The added bonus of being able to attach events and simple animations to elements makes SVG a nice option for both UI and game graphics. However, if the contents get too complicated with too many elements that are continuously added, modified, and removed, performance can be a problem.

The canvas element really shines when you need fine-grained control over the output. With pixel-level data access, you can do things that aren't possible with any other technology. One disadvantage of using canvas is that, even if many of its drawing functions are vector-based, the output is a bitmap, subject to the same scaling issues as regular images. If you make the element bigger using CSS, the content still appears pixelated. However, because all the canvas-based graphics are created programmatically, you have the option of creating them in the best resolution at runtime.

An advantage of having bitmap-based output is that you don't need to worry about how many times you add content to the canvas element. No matter how many shapes and images you add, the resulting canvas is always just a bitmap. You don't need to worry about filling the canvas element with too much content that could slow things down.

Drawing with canvas

Let's get started with the canvas element. You can create a new canvas element with JavaScript like any other DOM element:

```
var canvas = document.createElement("canvas");
document.body.appendChild(canvas);
```

Alternatively, you can declare it in the markup using the appropriate HTML tags:

```
<canvas id="mycanvas"></canvas>
```

This approach creates a canvas element with the default dimensions 300x150 pixels. When created, the canvas is fully transparent. You can provide alternative fallback content by adding it as children of the canvas element:

```
<canvas id="mycanvas">
    <h3>Sorry, this page requires a modern browser!</h3>
</canvas>
```

The browser renders only whatever you put inside the canvas tags if it has no canvas support, much the same way the contents of noscript tags are displayed only when JavaScript is disabled. This is an easy way to show a helpful message or, if possible, show a static image in place of the otherwise interactive or animated canvas content.

An important concept to understand when using `canvas` is the context object. The `canvas` element doesn't provide graphics functionality by itself. It merely defines a two-dimensional surface and exposes a few properties for setting the dimensions:

```
canvas.width = 400;
canvas.height = 300; // the canvas is now 400x300 pixels
```

The dimensions of the canvas aren't necessarily equal to its CSS dimensions. You can scale a `canvas` element to any width and height using CSS without any effect to the actual dimensions of the canvas. The content is simply stretched. In this regard, the canvas behaves very much like a bitmap image.

When you want to add graphics to this surface, you must do so via a context object created using the `getContext()` method on the `canvas` element:

```
var ctx = canvas.getContext("2d"); // create a 2D context object
```

Note the parameter passed to the `getContext()` method. The `canvas` element allows for any number of context types with different interfaces to create graphics on the canvas surface. Currently, the only other context is the WebGL context, which you can use to create 3D graphics. I show you more about WebGL in Chapter 9. In this chapter, you use only the 2D context, which is also the only context documented in the canvas specification. The specification is always evolving, so please refer to the W3C specification (`www.w3.org/TR/2dcontext`) for the most up-to-date information.

Drawing shapes and paths

Many of the canvas drawing functions use the same path API to define paths of points that make up the shape you want to draw. You initiate a new path by calling the `ctx.beginPath()` method on the context object. Invoking this method also clears any previously added path data.

Several different functions are available for adding path segments. The most basic path function simply adds a line segment. Listing 6-1 shows an example of how to begin a new path and create a rectangle.

Listing 6-1   **Adding a rectangle path**

```
ctx.beginPath();
ctx.moveTo(150, 200);
ctx.lineTo(250, 200);
ctx.lineTo(250, 230);
ctx.lineTo(150, 230);
ctx.closePath();
```

A path is always made up of a number of subpaths. The first path function called in Listing 6-1 is ctx.moveTo(), which creates a new subpath with a single point at the specified coordinates. The ctx.lineTo() method moves the position, adds a new point, and connects it to the previous position with a line.

NOTE If you don't call moveTo() to create the subpath, it's automatically created when, for example, lineTo() is called. However, because no starting position is defined, that lineTo() call moves only the position and doesn't actually add a line.

When you're done adding segments to the path, you can close the path using the ctx.closePath() method of the context object. Adding this method creates a final line segment from the current position to the position of the first point. The example in Listing 6-1 uses this feature to add the fourth and final edge of the rectangle. The ctx.closePath() call is optional because you may not always want to close the path.

You should not use the ctx.beginPath() method to create additional subpaths because that function clears all path data before creating the new path. If you want to add more subpaths to the current path, you can do so by calling the ctx.moveTo() method.

Fills and strokes

Now that the path is defined, you can draw it to the canvas surface. The canvas path API has two different methods for converting the path to graphics: ctx.fill() and ctx.stroke(). As you may have guessed, ctx.fill() fills the inside of the path with a color, and ctx.stroke() draws only the edges. The color used for each of these methods is set using the ctx.fillStyle and ctx.strokeStyle properties of the context object:

```
ctx.fillStyle = "#aaeeaa"; // light green fill color
ctx.strokeStyle = "#111155"; // dark blue stroke color
```

You can specify colors using any valid CSS color, meaning that hexadecimal format, color keywords, rgb(. . .), hsl(. . .), and so on are accepted. Aside from the color, you can also set the width of the stroke with the `ctx.lineWidth` property:

```
ctx.lineWidth = 5.0; // thicker stroke
```

When you're done setting up the path and have defined the fill and stroke styles, finish the job by calling `ctx.fill()` and/or `ctx.stroke()`. Listing 6-2 shows a basic example.

Listing 6-2 **Drawing a triangle**

```
<canvas id="canvas" width="250" height="250"></canvas>
<script>
    var canvas = document.getElementById("canvas"),
        ctx = canvas.getContext("2d");
    ctx.beginPath();
    ctx.moveTo(125, 50);
    ctx.lineTo(200, 200);
    ctx.lineTo(50, 125);
    ctx.closePath();

    ctx.fillStyle = "rgba(255,150,50,0.5)";
    ctx.fill();

    ctx.strokeStyle = "red";
    ctx.lineWidth = 2.0;
    ctx.stroke();
</script>
```

The resulting triangle is shown in Figure 6-1. You can find this example in the file `01-triangle.html`.

Mind the transparency if you're using both the `ctx.stroke()` and `ctx.fill()` methods on the same path. When you stroke the path, the line is drawn with the path in the center of the line. This means that half the stroke is drawn on the inside and the other half is drawn on the outside. If either the fill or stroke color isn't opaque, it's usually a good idea to draw the transparent part first to avoid unwanted blending near the edge. In the example in Listing 6-2, the `ctx.stroke()` method is called after `ctx.fill()` to avoid just this pitfall.

There's a small gotcha regarding horizontal and vertical line segments. Because strokes are drawn with the path in the *center* of the stroke, a 1-pixel-wide vertical line would have half a

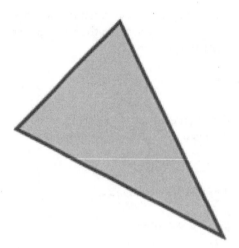

FIGURE 6-1: Draw a simple triangle.

pixel on the left side and half a pixel on the right side. Now, that doesn't work because there's no such thing as half a pixel. The result is that a semitransparent 2-pixel-wide line is used instead. This result may or may not be what you want, but an easy fix is to add 0.5 to both the x and y coordinates of the points, thereby making the line centered on the center of the pixel.

Rectangles

Drawing something like a rectangle is pretty easy using just `ctx.moveTo()` and `ctx.lineTo()` calls, but it would be a bit tedious to go through that procedure every time you need something trivial like that. Fortunately, you can do the same job with less typing when you use the `ctx.rect()` method:

```
ctx.beginPath();
ctx.rect(150, 200, 100, 30);
ctx.fillStyle = "rgba(255,150,50,0.5)";
ctx.fill();
```

Rectangles are fairly common, and if you just want to draw a single rectangle, there's an even simpler way. The `ctx.fillRect()` method takes four parameters that define a rectangle that should be filled using the current `ctx.fillStyle`:

```
ctx.fillStyle = "rgba(255,150,50,0.5)";
ctx.fillRect(150, 200, 100, 30);
```

A similar shortcut exists for stroking rectangles:

```
ctx.strokeStyle = "red";
ctx.strokeRect(150, 200, 100, 30);
```

A third variant of the rectangle function, `ctx.clearRect()`, takes the same four parameters, but instead of drawing, it clears the area. All pixels in the specified rectangle are set to black with the alpha channel set to 0—that is, fully transparent:

```
ctx.clearRect(150, 200, 100, 30);
```

If you want to clear the entire canvas, you can just set either the `width` or `height` property on the `canvas` element. Even setting the value to itself triggers a canvas reset:

```
canvas.width = canvas.width; // canvas is now cleared
```

Any time you write to one of these properties, the contents of the canvas are cleared back to the initial transparent state. Be careful, though. Resetting the canvas this way also clears fill and stroke styles, for example, as well as transformations and clipping paths, which you hear more about later.

Note that `ctx.fillRect()`, `ctx.strokeRect()`, and `ctx.clearRect()` are independent from the path API and don't require you to set up a path before using them. They also don't interfere with any current path data, so it's safe to call them while setting up and drawing other paths.

Arcs and circles
Straight lines and rectangles get you only so far. You also can add arc segments with the aptly named `arc()` function:

```
ctx.arc(x, y, radius, startAngle, endAngle, ccw)
```

This function adds a circular arc segment to the current subpath. It does so by using an imaginary circle with the specified radius and a center in the point (x, y). A segment of the circumference of this circle is then added to the subpath. The `startAngle` and `endAngle` parameters define which segment of the circumference to add. The last parameter, `ccw`, is a Boolean value that indicates which direction around the imaginary circle the rasterizer should travel to get from `startAngle` to `endAngle`. If it's set to `true`, the counterclockwise direction is used; otherwise, it travels clockwise.

Both `startAngle` and `endAngle` are measured in radians. The number of radians in a full circle is equal to 2π. If you're more comfortable working with degrees, you can convert degrees to radians by multiplying by 180 divided by π.

Listing 6-3 shows an example of how to draw arc segments.

Listing 6-3 **Drawing arcs**

```
<canvas id="canvas" width="400" height="400"></canvas>
<script>
    var canvas = document.getElementById("canvas"),
        ctx = canvas.getContext("2d");

    ctx.fillStyle = "rgba(100,150,200,0.5)";
    ctx.beginPath();
    ctx.arc(180, 240, 80, 0.25 * Math.PI,
        1.25 * Math.PI, false);
    ctx.arc(220, 160, 80, 0.25 * Math.PI,
        1.25 * Math.PI, true);
    ctx.closePath();
    ctx.fill();

    ctx.lineWidth = 32;
    ctx.strokeStyle = "#664422";
    ctx.stroke();
</script>
```

When adding an arc segment to an existing subpath, you must once again mind the position of the last-used point. Unless you move the position to the beginning of the arc, the arc is connected to the last point by a straight line.

To draw a full circle, simply set `startAngle` to 0 and `endAngle` to (2 * Math.PI). The ccw parameter is irrelevant in this case because both directions give the same result. An example of full circles is shown in Listing 6-4.

Listing 6-4 **Drawing a full circle**

```
<canvas id="canvas" width="400" height="400"></canvas>
<script>
    var canvas = document.getElementById("canvas"),
        ctx = canvas.getContext("2d");
```

```
    ctx.beginPath();
    ctx.arc(200, 200, 160, 0, 2 * Math.PI, false);
    ctx.moveTo(200 + 180, 200);
    ctx.arc(200, 200, 180, 0, 2 * Math.PI, false);

    ctx.lineWidth = 2;
    ctx.strokeStyle = "black";
    ctx.stroke();
</script>
```

Figure 6-2 shows the arcs and circles. You can find these examples in the file `02-arcs.html`.

FIGURE 6-2: Draw arcs and circles.

Bézier curves

Arcs are great, but they're just one type of curved path you can draw. The canvas context offers two methods for drawing Bézier curves. You may know these curves from the path tools in graphics applications such as Adobe Illustrator and Photoshop. Bézier curves are a powerful tool and can be generalized to higher dimensions to form Bézier surfaces and can be used in both engineering and advanced 3D computer graphics. I don't go into the math behind Bézier curves here; you just need to know that they're a type of parametric curve that uses a number of control points to describe a curved path from one point to another.

The first method, ctx.quadraticCurveTo(), adds a quadratic Bézier curve. In addition to the end point, this type of curve uses a single control point:

```
ctx.quadraticCurveTo(cx, cy, x, y);
```

This example adds a quadratic Bézier curve from the current position to (x, y), using the control point (cx, cy). Listing 6-5 shows a simple example of how to draw a quadratic curve. You can also find this example in the file 03-quadraticCurve.html.

Listing 6-5   **Drawing a quadratic curve**
```
<canvas id="canvas" width="500" height="300"></canvas>
<script>
    var canvas = document.getElementById("canvas"),
        ctx = canvas.getContext("2d");
    // draw quadratic Bézier curve
    ctx.beginPath();
    ctx.moveTo(50,200);
    ctx.quadraticCurveTo(425,25,450,200);
    ctx.fillStyle = "rgba(150,50,100,0.5)";
    ctx.fill();
    ctx.stroke();

    // draw control point
    ctx.strokeStyle = ctx.fillStyle = "rgba(0,0,0,0.5)";
    ctx.beginPath();
    ctx.moveTo(450,200);
    ctx.lineTo(425,25);
    ctx.lineTo(50,200);
    ctx.stroke();
    ctx.fillRect(450-2,25-2,4,4);
</script>
```

Figure 6-3 shows the resulting drawing. I drew this example to help you understand how the method affects the curve.

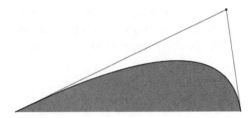

FIGURE 6-3: In this quadratic Bézier curve, it's as though the control point pulls toward the curve.

The second curve method is called `ctx.bezierCurveTo()`. This method might as well have been named `ctx.cubicCurveTo()` because it creates a cubic Bézier curve. Cubic curves use two control points. Listing 6-6 shows an example of such a curve.

Listing 6-6   **Drawing a cubic curve**

```
<canvas id="canvas" width="450" height="400"></canvas>
<script>
var canvas = document.getElementById("canvas"),
    ctx = canvas.getContext("2d");

    // draw cubic Bézier curve
    ctx.beginPath();
    ctx.moveTo(50,200);
    ctx.bezierCurveTo(150,25,350,350,400,200);
    ctx.fillStyle = "rgba(150,50,100,0.5)";
    ctx.fill();
    ctx.stroke();

    // draw control points
    ctx.strokeStyle = ctx.fillStyle = "rgba(0,0,0,0.5)";
    ctx.beginPath();
    ctx.moveTo(50,200);
    ctx.lineTo(150,25);
    ctx.lineTo(350,350);
    ctx.lineTo(400,200);
    ctx.stroke();
    ctx.fillRect(150-2,25-2,4,4);
    ctx.fillRect(350-2,350-2,4,4);
</script>
```

Figure 6-4 shows the resulting drawing. Again, I drew the control points for this figure. As you might imagine, the cubic curve gives you a lot more flexibility and can even create self-intersecting curves. This example is found in the file 04-cubicCurve.html.

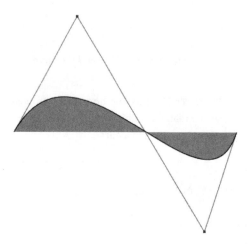

FIGURE 6-4: A cubic Bézier curve uses two control points.

A nice feature of cubic Bézier curves is that you can easily add one after the other to form longer and more detailed curves. Just put the first control point of the following curve segment in the opposite direction of the last control point of the previous segment. The curve segments then join smoothly without any abrupt breaks.

Clipping paths

Aside from filling and stroking, you can do one other thing with paths. You can use the `ctx.clip()` method to use the path as a clipping path. This makes the current path act as a mask that is applied to all subsequent drawing functions. As long as the clipping path is active, only the area within that region is modified. Listing 6-7 shows a simple example of a clipping path.

Listing 6-7   **Applying a clipping path**

```
<canvas id="canvas" width="400" height="400"></canvas>
<script>
    var canvas = document.getElementById("canvas"),
        ctx = canvas.getContext("2d");

    function makeClippingPath() {
        // make a star-shaped clipping path
```

```
        ctx.beginPath();
        ctx.moveTo(270,200);
        for (var i=0;i<=20;i++) {
            ctx.lineTo(
                200 + Math.cos(i/10 * Math.PI) * 70 * (i%2 + 1),
                200 + Math.sin(i/10 * Math.PI) * 70 * (i%2 + 1)
            );
        }
        ctx.clip();
    }

    // fill the entire canvas
    ctx.fillStyle = "sienna";
    ctx.fillRect(0,0,400,400);

    makeClippingPath();

    // try to fill the canvas again
    ctx.fillStyle = "lightsalmon";
    ctx.fillRect(0,0,400,400);
</script>
```

The resulting drawing is shown in Figure 6-5. This example can be found in the file
`05-clipping-path.html`.

FIGURE 6-5: In this clipping path example, even though the second `ctx.fillRect()` fills the entire
canvas, only the star-shaped region defined by the clipping path is actually modified.

If you want to reset the clipping path, you need to use the `ctx.save()` and `ctx.restore()` methods. These are covered later in this chapter. A `resetClip()` function has been added to the specification but is not yet implemented in any browser.

Path objects

A recent addition to the 2D context specification are the so-called path objects. Path objects are meant to encapsulate reusable paths, meaning that you can use them on context objects again and again without having to redefine the path each time. This feature has not yet been implemented in any official browser versions but it can be enabled in Chrome Canary (`www.google.com/intl/en/chrome/browser/canary.html`), the cutting-edge build of Chrome aimed at developers. Enter **chrome://flags** in the address bar and enable the Experimental Canvas Features option.

Because of the experimental nature of this feature, it might change in the future or be scrapped completely, so I won't go into details of how to use these objects. However, in their current state, they're very easy to use. You create a path object with the `Path()` constructor:

```
var path = new Path();
```

The path object implements path methods similar to those on the context object, such as `moveTo()`, `lineTo()`, `rect()`, `arc()`, and so on. To draw the path, you pass the path object as an argument to, for example, the `ctx.fill()` or `ctx.stroke()` method.

Using advanced strokes and fill styles

So far, you've seen how to control the stroke color as well as the line width. You can use a few additional parameters to control the appearance of the stroke.

Line caps

First up is the `ctx.lineCap` property. This property controls how the ends of open paths appear. There are three values:

- butt
- round
- square

The default value, `butt`, looks like a clean, perpendicular cut at the end of the stroke. The last point in the path is positioned in the center of the line cap. The `round` value rounds the end of the stroke by drawing a semicircle with the center positioned at the last point. Finally, the `square` value looks a bit like the `butt` line cap, but instead of cutting off right at the last point, the line is extended so the last point is positioned at the center of a square whose sides are equal to the line width. Figure 6-6 shows how the three different `ctx.lineCap` values alter the end of a stroke.

butt   round   square

FIGURE 6-6: Line caps come in three flavors.

Line joints

The `ctx.lineJoin` property is similar to `ctx.lineCap` but describes what to do whenever two consecutive path segments share the same point. As with `ctx.lineCap`, this property has three possible values:

- `bevel`
- `round`
- `miter`

All three values use the same, basic starting condition. Consider two lines that share a point in a path. Imagine that the lines terminate at the point using the `butt` method from the `ctx.lineCap` property. The strokes of these lines then have two edges each, an inner edge and an outer edge. These outer edges, together with the perpendicular line endings, define two outer corners of the joint.

The `bevel` value is the most basic of the three joints. This joint type simply fills the triangle defined by the meeting point and the two outer corners.

The `round` joint builds on the `bevel` and smooths out the joint by rendering an arc connecting the outer corners.

The third value, `miter`, is the default value and is slightly more complicated. This value creates a miter joint at the meeting point. This is the type of joint used in, for example, picture frames where the ends of the four sides are cut at an angle to form the corner of the frame when connected. In the real world, these joints are often used to form 90-degree corners, but in the context of canvas, any angle works.

Extend the outer edges beyond the meeting point until the outer edges intersect. Fill the triangle defined by this miter point and the two corner points. Now, as you might imagine, path segments that meet at very acute angles could cause miter joints that extend far out from the meeting point. You can use the `ctx.miterLimit` property to control this issue. The miter limit determines the maximum allowed distance from the meeting point to the miter point. The value of the `ctx.miterLimit` property is specified in multiples of half line widths. For example, if the `lineWidth` is 3.0, a `ctx.miterLimit` value of 5.0 is equal to 7.5. That's nice because you can change the line width without worrying about having to adjust the miter limit as well. If the distance to the miter point is greater than the limit, the joint falls back to using the `bevel` method. Initially, `ctx.miterLimit` is set to 10. Figure 6-7 shows examples of how the different join values appear.

FIGURE 6-7: You have three options for joining lines.

Dashed and dotted lines

The first editions of the canvas specification only specified solid lines so if you wanted to draw a dashed line, you had to do it the hard way by drawing every little dash as a separate line. Fortunately, dashed lines have now been added to the specification. Chrome, Opera, and Internet Explorer 11 already support the new functions and Firefox and Safari are expected to follow soon.

The new `ctx.setLineDash()` method takes an array of segment lengths to use when stroking a path.

```
ctx.setLineDash([16,8]);
```

Any following `ctx.stroke()` calls draw the line with 16 pixel dashes and 8 pixel spaces. You can provide more than two values to create more interesting dash patterns, such as alternating between long and short dashes.

The related `ctx.getLineDash()` method returns the current segment list.

Using gradients

Fills and stroke styles need not be plain, solid colors. Canvas supports both linear and radial gradients. To use a gradient, you need to create a gradient object:

```
var gradient = ctx.createLinearGradient(
    50, 50, 250, 400
);
```

This example creates a linear gradient along the line from (50, 50) to (250, 400). You can also create radial gradients:

```
var gradient = ctx.createRadialGradient(
    100, 100, 10,
    100, 100, 175
);
```

This example creates a radial gradient with an inner circle centered at (100, 100), a radius of 10, and an outer circle in the same spot but with a radius of 175. Both gradient objects expose an addColorStop() method that you can use to assign colors to the gradient:

```
gradient.addColorStop(0, "red");
gradient.addColorStop(0.5, "green");
gradient.addColorStop(1, "blue");
```

This example sets three colors on the gradient: red at the start, green in the middle, and blue at the end. To use the gradient, you need to assign it to either the ctx.fillStyle or ctx.strokeStyle property. A full example of how to use gradients is shown in Listing 6-8.

Listing 6-8 **Using gradients**

```
<canvas id="canvas" width="400" height="400"></canvas>
<script>
    var canvas = document.getElementById("canvas"),
        ctx = canvas.getContext("2d");

    var linGrad = ctx.createLinearGradient(
        50, 0, 250, 400
    );
    linGrad.addColorStop(0, "aquamarine");
    linGrad.addColorStop(1, "darkolivegreen");
```

continued

Listing 6-8   **continued**

```
    ctx.fillStyle = linGrad;
    ctx.fillRect(0, 0, 400, 400);

    var radGrad = ctx.createRadialGradient(
        200, 200, 25, 200, 200, 150
    );
    radGrad.addColorStop(0, "white");
    radGrad.addColorStop(0.7, "yellow");
    radGrad.addColorStop(1, "orange");
    ctx.fillStyle = radGrad;
    ctx.beginPath();
    ctx.arc(230, 230, 150, 0, Math.PI * 2, false);
    ctx.fill();
</script>
```

The example is available in the file `06-gradient.html`. See Figure 6-8 for the result.

FIGURE 6-8: Using gradients can give your drawing object some depth.

TIP   If you change the gradient after assigning it, you don't need to reassign it. All fill styles or stroke styles that use the gradient are automatically updated.

Using patterns

The last type of fill and stroke styles I discuss is patterns. You can use an existing image instead of a solid color or gradient. The image can be a regular image, a `canvas` element, or a `video` element. Start by creating a pattern object:

```
var gradient = ctx.createPattern (
    document.getElementById("myImage"),
    "repeat"
);
```

The second argument specifies how the pattern should repeat. The possible values are

- `repeat`

- `repeat-x`

- `repeat-y`

- `no-repeat`

The default value is `repeat`, which makes the pattern repeat in both directions. The `repeat-x` and `repeat-y` values make the pattern repeat in only one direction, and if you choose `no-repeat`, no repetition is applied at all. The pattern is anchored at the origin of the coordinate space and isn't affected by where you use it. This means that a pattern created from a small image with no repetition may not be visible in, for example, the bottom-right corner of the canvas.

The `ctx.createPattern()` method returns a pattern object that has no properties or methods. Just assign it to the `ctx.strokeStyle` or `ctx.fillStyle`, and you're done.

Using transformations

When you create a new `canvas` element, the coordinate space used to draw content on it corresponds to the dimensions of the `canvas` element. That is, the pixel in the upper-left corner of the canvas is position (0, 0), and the pixel in the bottom-right corner is at position (w - 1, h - 1), where w and h are the width and height of the element. You can apply a number of different transformations such as scaling and rotation to this coordinate space to make certain operations easier.

Understanding the transformation matrix

At the heart of these transformations is a transformation matrix. Every point used by the canvas is multiplied by this matrix before it's used for rendering. Don't worry if your linear algebra is a bit rusty; I don't spend much time dwelling on the math.

Initially, the matrix is set to the identity matrix:

```
1 0 0
0 1 0
0 0 1
```

If you're comfortable with matrices, you can modify the transformation matrix directly using the `ctx.transform()` method:

```
ctx.transform(a, b, c, d, e, f);
```

This method multiplies the current matrix with the matrix:

```
a c e
b d f
0 0 1
```

You can also use the `ctx.setTransform()` method to completely overwrite the current matrix:

```
ctx.setTransform(a, b, c, d, e, f);
```

This method essentially resets the transformation matrix to the identity matrix and uses `ctx.transform()` with the specified matrix parameters.

If you want to reset the transformation, you have to set it manually to the identity matrix. A simpler `ctx.resetTransform()` method has recently been added to the 2D context specification along with the `ctx.currentTransform` property, which will allow access to the current transformation matrix in the form of an SVGMatrix object. Neither of these features have been implemented in any official browser versions yet, although both are available in Chrome Canary.

Translating

The `ctx.translate()` method of the context object adds a translation matrix to the transformation:

```
ctx.translate(x, y);
```

This method basically adds the x and y values to the coordinates of any points you draw. This means that

```
ctx.translate(50, 100);
ctx.fillRect(120, 130, 200, 200);
```

actually draws the rectangle with the upper-left corner in position (170, 230) on the canvas.

Scaling
You can also scale the coordinate space using the `ctx.scale()` method. This method takes two arguments, one for each axis. These values are used to scale the points drawn on the canvas. For example, changing the scale with

```
ctx.scale(2, 0.5);
```

stretches any subsequent drawing to twice the width and half the height. You can achieve the same effect by applying this transformation:

```
ctx.transform(
    2, 0,
    0, 0.5,
    0, 0
);
```

One neat trick that I sometimes use is to scale the coordinate space so that the entire canvas surface lies within 1 unit in the coordinate space. You can do that by scaling the coordinates using the dimensions of the canvas:

```
ctx.scale(1 / canvas.width, 1 / canvas.height);
```

All coordinates are now relative to the dimensions, and all visible points on the canvas lie between 0 and 1 on both axes. Drawing, for example, a rectangle that fills the upper-right quarter is now as easy as this:

```
ctx.fillRect(0.5, 0, 0.5, 0.5);
```

Rotating
The `ctx.rotate()` method adds a rotation operation to the transformation matrix. The angle is measured in radians and is a clockwise rotation:

```
ctx.rotate(t);
```

Using this method is essentially the same as applying the following transformation:

```
ctx.transform(
        Math.cos(t), Math.sin(t),
     - Math.sin(t), Math.cos(t),
        0, 0
);
```

One issue you should be aware of is that the rotation always happens around the origin. If you want to rotate around a specific point, you should first translate the coordinate space so that point is placed at the origin. Then you can perform the rotation and reverse the translation, if necessary.

In general, you need to be careful when combining transformations. The order in which you apply the transformations can sometimes change the result. For example, performing a translation followed by a rotation doesn't produce the same result as doing it the other way around.

Drawing ellipses

Currently, none of the common desktop browsers provide a way to draw ellipses on a canvas. However, a recent revision of the canvas specification added an `ellipse()` method to the 2D context that will eventually be available as the browser makers implement the new changes. Until then, you can roll your own function using a few transformations and the `arc()` function. Listing 6-9 shows the `ellipse()` method added to the prototype of `CanvasRenderingContext2D`.

Listing 6-9 **Adding a polyfill for the ellipse function**

```
if (!CanvasRenderingContext2D.prototype.ellipse) {
    CanvasRenderingContext2D.prototype.ellipse =
        function(x, y, radiusX, radiusY, rotation,
                startAngle, endAngle, anticlockwise) {
            this.translate(x, y);
            this.rotate(rotation);
            this.scale(radiusX, radiusY);
            this.arc(
                0, 0, 1, startAngle, endAngle, anticlockwise
            );
            this.scale(1/radiusX, 1/radiusY);
            this.rotate(-rotation);
            this.translate(-x, -y);
        };
}
```

The ellipse() method is similar to the arc() method but takes a radius parameter for both the x- and y-axes as well as a rotation parameter. Before calling arc(), the coordinate system is translated to the center of the ellipse (x, y) and rotated. The next step scales the coordinate system by the radius parameters, effectively squishing the coordinates so the resulting arc takes the form of an ellipse rather than a circle. All that's left to do then is draw an arc with radius 1 and of course revert the transformations to not interfere with any following drawing. You can find an example of this function in use in the file 07-ellipse.html.

Adding text, images, and shadows

Apart from shapes and paths, you also can add both text and images to a canvas. You can draw images to the canvas using the ctx.drawImage() method on the context:

```
ctx.drawImage(image, dx, dy, dw, dh);
```

This method draws an img element, image, to the canvas. The dx, dy, dw, and dh arguments define the rectangle where the image should go. The upper-left corner is at (dx, dy), and the lower-right corner is at (dx + dw, dy + dh). The dw and dh arguments are optional and, if left out, default to the dimensions of the image. The ctx.drawImage() method can also take both a source and a destination rectangle:

```
ctx.drawImage(image, sx, xy, sw, sh, dx, dy, dw, dh);
```

You can use this argument pattern to draw only a subregion of an image to the canvas. The rectangle defined by sx, sy, sw, and sh is taken from the source image and drawn in the rectangle defined by dx, dy, dw, and dh on the destination canvas. If the dimensions of the two regions don't match, the copied area is stretched and scaled to fit the destination.

The image argument doesn't have to be an img element. Both canvas elements and video elements are valid sources. If you use a video element, the current frame is drawn to the canvas.

Before drawing an image, make sure that the image is completely loaded. Trying to draw an image that's not ready triggers an error. You can ensure that the image is loaded either by checking the complete property on the image object or by only drawing from a load event handler attached to the image before setting the src property.

Adding text

The canvas element also lets you add text content to the canvas. However, you should always make sure that it's actually appropriate to use canvas to render the text. Because the canvas element behaves essentially like an image on the page, you can apply much of the same logic to text on the canvas as you would to text in images. If it's possible to get the same or a similar result using CSS, perhaps you should reconsider going for a canvas-based approach. For example, regular HTML and CSS are often better suited for elements such as headings and buttons.

As with paths, you can draw text in two ways: one for filled text and one for drawing the outline or stroke of the text. First, however, you should specify the font with which you want to draw the text. You do so by setting the `ctx.font` property on the context. The value can be any font value as you know them from CSS. For example:

```
ctx.font = "italic 12px Arial, sans-serif";
```

This line specifies a 12px Arial in italic style. If Arial is not present, the default sans serif typeface is used.

> **NOTE** If you use embedded fonts, make sure that the font files are completely loaded before attempting to use them for canvas text. If the font file is not ready, the canvas uses a default font instead.

You can now draw the text using one of two methods:

```
ctx.fillText("Hello World!", 100, 50);
ctx.strokeText("Hello World!", 100, 50);
```

The `ctx.fillText()` method fills the specified text using the active `ctx.fillStyle` value, and `ctx.strokeText()` strokes the outline of the text using the active `ctx.strokeStyle` value. The second and third arguments specify the x and y coordinates where you want the text to go. You can change the text alignment using the `ctx.textAlign` property:

```
ctx.textAlign = "center";
```

Possible values for `ctx.textAlign` are

- `start`
- `end`
- `left`
- `center`
- `right`

The `left`, `center`, and `right` values are trivial. The meaning of the `start` and `end` values depends on standard text direction of the current locale. For left-to-right locales, `start` is the same as `left`, and `end` is the same as `right`. For right-to-left locales, the situation is reversed. The default value for `ctx.textAlign` is `start`, so if you don't want the text to adapt to the locale automatically, you should manually set the alignment.

The vertical position of the text is determined by the y coordinate in `ctx.fillText()` and `ctx.strokeText()`, but it's also affected by the baseline of the text. You can control the baseline by setting the `ctx.textBaseline` property on the context:

```
ctx.textBaseline = "middle";
```

Possible values for `ctx.textBaseline` are

- `top`
- `middle`
- `bottom`
- `hanging`
- `alphabetic`
- `ideographic`

Only the `top`, `middle`, `bottom`, and `alphabetic` values are fully supported in today's browsers. See Figure 6-9 for an illustration of how the values affect the position of the text.

FIGURE 6-9: In these baseline examples, the horizontal line is drawn at the same y coordinate as the text.

The `ctx.fillText()` and `ctx.strokeText()` methods both have an optional fourth argument, `maxWidth`—a numeric value that, if specified, constrains the text to a maximum width. If the rendered text would extend beyond that width in the specified font, the browser automatically shrinks the text so it fits. It's up to the browser to see whether a more condensed font is available or whether the text can be scaled horizontally to fit.

One final method exists on the context related to text. The `ctx.measureText()` method takes one parameter, a string, and returns a text metrics object. This object has one property, `width`, which is the width of text if it were to be drawn on the canvas using the current font value.

```
var textWidth = ctx.measureText("Hello World!").width;
```

The `ctx.measureText()` method can be really useful if, for example, you have other content that depends on the size of the text or if you need to scale the `canvas` element to fit the rendered text.

Text drawn on a canvas has a few drawbacks compared to regular text on web pages. The browser doesn't know that the pixels represent text, so the user can't just select the text with the mouse. However, you can provide the text as fallback content for the canvas. This makes it possible for screen readers, for instance, to pick up the text. If the canvas content is interactive in some way, you can even put links in the fallback content. These links are then focusable when navigating the page with the keyboard:

```
<canvas id="intro" width=400 height=400>
    This is a fancy intro image.
    <a href="page2.html">Click to go to page 2</a>
</canvas>
```

Unfortunately, using this approach does mean that you need to maintain the text content in both the canvas code as well as in the fallback content. Canvas accessibility is still being actively worked on, so in the future, I hope this issue will be handled better.

Using shadow effects

You can use shadow effects to create a sense of depth in the image. The context object has four shadow-related properties. First, it has the shadow color:

```
ctx.shadowColor = "rgb(100,120,30)";
```

The color value can be any valid CSS color. The offset of the shadow is controlled by two properties, one for each axis:

```
ctx.shadowOffsetX = 8;
ctx.shadowOffsetY = 8;
```

This example puts the shadow below and to the right of the content. Note that these are coordinate space units, so all transformations are also applied to these values. Finally, you can control the softness of the shadow with the ctx.shadowBlur property:

```
ctx.shadowBlur = 10;
```

If you set a blur value of 0, you get a clean, sharp border rather than a soft shadow. Listing 6-10 shows an example of how shadows are used. You can find this example in the file 08-shadows.html.

Listing 6-10   Applying shadow effects

```
<canvas id="canvas" width="400" height="350"></canvas>
<script>
    var canvas = document.getElementById("canvas"),
        ctx = canvas.getContext("2d");

    ctx.shadowColor = "black";
    ctx.shadowOffsetX = 15;
    ctx.shadowOffsetY = 15;
    ctx.shadowBlur = 8;

    ctx.lineWidth = 6;
    ctx.strokeStyle = "darkorange";
    ctx.fillStyle = "sienna";
    ctx.fillRect(100,50,200,250);
    ctx.strokeRect(100, 50, 200, 250);

    ctx.fillStyle = "aquamarine";
    ctx.fillRect(50, 100, 150, 100);
    ctx.shadowColor = "transparent";
    ctx.strokeRect(50, 100, 150, 100);
</script>
```

The resulting drawing is shown in Figure 6-10. As you can see on the sienna-colored rectangle, shadows can cause a bit of trouble if you use both strokes and fills on the same path. One solution is to disable the shadow while stroking, for example, by setting the shadow color to transparent.

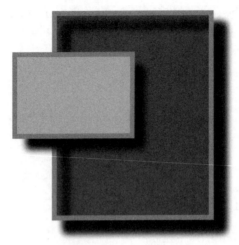

FIGURE 6-10: Applying the shadow effect can create a three-dimensional image.

Managing the state stack

With so many different properties and values that affect how content is rendered on the canvas, keeping track of old values can be hard if you need to revert to a previous state after performing some task. Fortunately, the canvas has a built-in state stack that makes it easy to save all current values, do some drawing, and then revert to the previous values.

Almost all properties such as fill colors and text properties are part of the canvas state, so you don't have to worry about overwriting old values as long as you save the state and restore it when you're done. The components that make up the canvas state are

- The transformation matrix
- The clipping path
- strokeStyle, fillStyle
- lineWidth, lineCap, lineJoin, miterLimit
- globalAlpha, globalCompositeOperation
- shadowOffsetX, shadowOffsetY, shadowColor, shadowBlur
- font, textAlign, textBaseline

The current state is saved by called the ctx.save() method on the context object:

```
ctx.fillStyle = "black";
...
ctx.save(); // save state with fill style
```

This example pushes the current state onto the stack, allowing you to safely modify any of the properties mentioned earlier. When you're done messing around with the canvas state, you can go back to the way things were before by calling the `ctx.restore()` method:

```
...
ctx.fillStyle = "white";
...
ctx.restore(); // restore state, fill style is black again
```

The `ctx.restore()` method replaces the current state with the last saved state and removes that one from the stack. This capability can be useful when you don't know the current value of all the properties. For example, when writing subroutines that need to change one or more properties, you can simply call `ctx.save()` at the beginning of the function and `ctx.restore()` before returning, thereby preserving the integrity of the canvas state.

Drawing the HTML5 logo

In this section, I show you a more complete example of how to draw using the `canvas` element. The target of this exercise is drawing the HTML5 logo. Before starting, take a look at Figure 6-11 to get a sense of what you will create in this section. You can find the complete example in the file `09-html5logo.html`.

First, make a nice background. Listing 6-11 shows the background function.

Listing 6-11 **Drawing a background**

```
function drawBackground(canvas) {
    var ctx = canvas.getContext("2d"),
        grad,
        i;

    ctx.save();
    // scale coordinates to unit
    ctx.scale(canvas.width, canvas.height);

    grad = ctx.createRadialGradient(
        0.5, 0.5, 0.125, 0.5, 0.5, 0.75
    );
    grad.addColorStop(0.1, "rgb(170,180,190)");
    grad.addColorStop(0.9, "rgb(50,60,70)");
    ctx.fillStyle = grad;
    ctx.fillRect(0,0,1,1);
```

FIGURE 6-11: The HTML5 logo created in this section.

```
// draw a star shape by adding horizontal lines
// while rotating the coordinate space
ctx.beginPath();
ctx.translate(0.5,0.5);
for (i=0;i<60;i++) {
    ctx.rotate(1 / 60 * Math.PI * 2);
    ctx.lineTo(i % 2 ? 0.15 : 0.75, 0);
}
ctx.fillStyle = "rgba(255,255,255,0.1)";
ctx.fill();
ctx.restore();
}
```

Note how the state is saved at the beginning and restored at the end. No matter what you do to the state in the rest of the function, the state is returned to its original form. Also note that the coordinate space is scaled using the full dimensions of the canvas. The upper-left corner is still (0, 0), but the lower-right corner is now (1, 1). That makes it much easier to work with coordinates without having to know the actual dimensions.

On to the actual logo. The logo is defined by a number of different shapes. The `drawLogo()` function in Listing 6-12 declares these shapes as lists of points at the beginning.

Listing 6-12   **Path data for the logo drawing function**

```
function drawLogo(canvas) {
        var logo = [
                [40,460], [0,0], [450,0], [410,460], [225,512]
            ],
            five0 = [
                [225,208], [225,265], [295,265], [288,338],
                [225,355], [225,414], [341,382], [357,208]
            ],
            five1 = [
                [225,94], [225,150], [362,150], [367,94],
            ],
            five2 = [
                [225,208], [151,208], [146,150], [225,150],
                [225,94], [84,94], [85,109], [99,265], [225,265]
            ],
            five3 = [
                [225,355], [162,338], [158,293], [128,293],
                [102,293], [109,382], [225,414]
            ];


}
```

In a situation such as this, in which you have many different paths, having a helper function or two to save on the typing can be nice. Listing 6-13 shows a helper function that you can use to add a list of points to a path.

```
function makePath(ctx, points) {
    ctx.moveTo(points[0][0], points[0][1]);
    for (var i=1,len=points.length;i<len;i++) {
        ctx.lineTo(points[i][0], points[i][1]);
    }
}
```

The makePath() function just moves the position to the first point and then iterates through the rest of the list, adding line segments along the way. It doesn't begin or close any paths, so you can create multiple subpaths in the same path. Now you can use that function and the path data to draw the logo. Listing 6-14 shows the logo function.

```
function drawLogo(ctx) {
    ...
    // save original state
    ctx.save();

    // translate the coordinate space to center of logo
    ctx.translate(-225,-256);
    // fill background of logo
    ctx.beginPath();
    makePath(ctx, logo);
    ctx.fillStyle = "#e34c26";
    ctx.fill();

    // add down-scaling at the center of the logo
    ctx.save();
    ctx.translate(225,256);
    ctx.scale(0.8, 0.8);
    ctx.translate(-225,-256);
    // clip the right half of the logo
    ctx.beginPath();
    ctx.rect(225,0,225,512);
    ctx.clip();
    // paint a lighter, down-scaled logo on the right half
    ctx.beginPath();
    makePath(ctx, logo);
    ctx.fillStyle = "#f06529";
    ctx.fill();
```

```
    // restore scaling and clipping region
    ctx.restore();

    // restore original state
    ctx.restore();
}
```

The `drawLogo()` function first translates the coordinates to place the origin in the center of the logo. This point is found by examining the path data. The rightmost point is at x = 450, and the bottommost point is at y = 512, which puts the center at (225, 256). Then the orange background part of the HTML5 logo is drawn using the `makePath()` function.

The inner part of the logo is a lighter shade of orange that fills only the right half, slightly downscaled. You can reuse the path from the first part by scaling the coordinate space and applying a clipping region to the canvas. To scale the coordinates correctly, the code translates the coordinates back before the scaling is applied. The coordinate space is once again translated to the center of the logo before a path spanning the entire right half of the canvas is clipped. When the logo path is filled again with a lighter shade, only the right half is actually drawn, creating the desired effect. It would arguably have been simpler to define the extra path data and just draw that as it is. Doing it this way demonstrates transformations, clipping regions, as well as how to use the state stack.

The white 5 in the middle of the logo is still missing. Drawing that part is just a matter of filling the relevant paths. Listing 6-15 shows the added paths.

Listing 6-15   Drawing the rest of the logo

```
function drawLogo(canvas) {
    ...
    // restore scaling and clipping region
    ctx.restore();


    // fill white part of "5"
    ctx.beginPath();
    makePath(ctx, five0);
    makePath(ctx, five1);
    ctx.fillStyle = "#ffffff";
    ctx.fill();
```

continued

Listing 6-15   **continued**
```
    // fill light grey part of "5"
    ctx.beginPath();
    makePath(ctx, five2);
    makePath(ctx, five3);
    ctx.fillStyle = "#ebebeb";
    ctx.fill();
    // restore original state
    ctx.restore();
}
```

You can now put all these pieces together and draw the full logo on a canvas element. Listing 6-16 shows how.

Listing 6-16   **Putting the pieces together**
```
<canvas id="canvas" width="400" height="400"></canvas>
<script>
    function makePath(ctx, points) {...}

    function drawBackground(canvas) {...}

    function drawLogo(canvas) {...}

    var canvas = document.getElementById("canvas"),
        ctx = canvas.getContext("2d");

    drawBackground(canvas);

    ctx.translate(200, 200);
    ctx.scale(0.5, 0.5);

    drawLogo(canvas);

</script>
```

Note that the coordinate space is scaled and translated before drawLogo() is called. The reason is that drawLogo() doesn't know where on the canvas it should draw the logo or how big it should be. By performing these transformations outside the function, you can control how and where the function places the logo. You could even rotate it or draw a whole bunch of logos on the same canvas. Listing 6-17 shows an example of how to draw multiple instances of the logo.

Listing 6-17   **Drawing multiple logos**

```
<canvas id="canvas" width="400" height="400"></canvas>
<script>
    ...
    var canvas = document.getElementById("canvas"),
        ctx = canvas.getContext("2d");

    drawBackground(canvas);

    // draw 20 logos
    for (var i=0;i<20;i++) {
        ctx.save();

        // calculate random rotation and scale
        var x = Math.random() * canvas.width,
            y = Math.random() * canvas.height,
            angle = (Math.random() - 0.5) * Math.PI,
            scale = 0.05 + Math.random() * 0.1;

        // transform the coordinate space
        ctx.translate(x, y);
        ctx.scale(scale, scale);
        ctx.rotate(angle);

        drawLogo(ctx);

        ctx.restore();
    }
</script>
```

This example draws 20 instances of the HTML5 logo in random places on the canvas. Each logo has its own scaling and rotation. Because the state is saved and restored in each iteration of the loop, all instances are drawn independently. Figure 6-12 shows the resulting drawing.

FIGURE 6-12: Here the HTML5 logos appear in random places.

Compositing

You've already seen how you can use paths to define clipping regions that mask whatever you draw on the canvas. That is not the only way you can control how content is added to the canvas.

You can use the `ctx.globalAlpha` property, for example, to set a global alpha channel value. Any content that you draw on the canvas has its own transparency value multiplied by the `ctx.globalAlpha` value. For example, setting `ctx.globalAlpha` to 0.5 and then filling a path with the color `rgba(20, 85, 45, 0.7)` results in a combined alpha value of 0.35. The `ctx.globalAlpha` setting can be useful when you want to draw shapes and images and make them semitransparent regardless of their own alpha channels.

In addition to `ctx.globalAlpha`, you can use the `ctx.globalCompositeOperation` property. This property provides a number of different operations that alter the way the new source content is combined with the existing destination canvas. Table 6-1 shows a list of the possible values for `ctx.globalCompositeOperation`. In the descriptions, A refers to the source content, and B refers to the destination.

Table 6-1   Composite operations

Value	Description
source-atop	Renders A on top of B but only where B is not transparent.
source-in	Renders only A and only where B is not transparent.
source-out	Renders only A and only where B is transparent.
source-over	Renders A on top of B where A is not transparent.
destination-atop	Renders B on top of A but only where B is not transparent.
destination-in	Renders only B and only where A is not transparent.
destination-out	Renders only B and only where A is transparent.
destination-over	Renders B on top of A where A is not transparent.
lighter	Renders the sum of A and B.
copy	Disregards B and renders only A.
xor	Renders A where B is transparent and B where A is transparent. Renders transparent where neither A nor B is transparent.

> **NOTE**
>
> If you're familiar with computer graphics and image processing, you might recognize most of these as Porter-Duff operations. Except for the trivial copy operation, Porter and Duff describe all the composite operators in their 1984 paper, "Compositing Digital Images," available at `http://keithp.com/~keithp/porterduff/p253-porter.pdf`.

The default operation is `source-over`, which paints the source content over the old, leaving the destination visible in only the transparent parts of the new. If the source content has parts that are semitransparent, the results for some of the operations can sometimes be difficult to imagine. For example, the `destination-in` operation renders the destination in the non-transparent parts of the source, but it also uses the alpha value of the source content. This means that filling a rectangle that spans the entire canvas with a fully transparent color would essentially clear the canvas. See Figure 6-13 for examples of all the composite operations as they should appear.

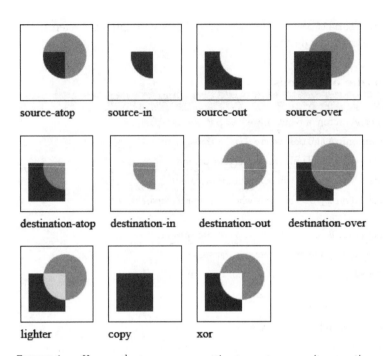

source-atop   source-in   source-out   source-over

destination-atop   destination-in   destination-out   destination-over

lighter   copy   xor

FIGURE 6-13: You use the transparency setting to create composite operations.

In addition to these basic composite operations, you can also set `ctx.globalComposite-Operation` to one of the following blend modes:

- `normal`
- `multiply`
- `screen`
- `overlay`
- `lighten`
- `color-dodge`
- `color-burn`
- `hard-light`
- `soft-light`
- `difference`
- `exclusion`

- hue

- saturation

- color

- luminosity

If you've ever used Adobe Photoshop or a similar photo editing application, you probably already know some or all of these blend modes from the layer compositing feature in such applications. The blend modes are a recent addition and therefore only some browsers implement them. At the time of this writing, the latest versions of Chrome, Firefox, Opera, and Safari all support the new modes. Internet Explorer 11 only supports the basic composite operations from Table 6-1.

While the canvas specification covers the Porter-Duff operations, a separate W3C specification called "Compositing and Blending" (`http://dev.w3.org/fxtf/compositing-1/`) has been created to cover both the Porter-Duff operations and the new blend modes in sufficient detail.

Accessing Image Data

Perhaps the most powerful feature of the `canvas` element is the ability to access and modify raw RGBA pixel values from the canvas. This low-level data access lets you modify the image in ways that are otherwise very difficult or even impossible to achieve.

Retrieving pixel values

The 2D context object provides a method called `ctx.getImageData()`. You can use this method to retrieve the data for a rectangular area of the image:

```
var imageData = ctx.getImageData(50, 75, 100, 200);
```

This example extracts the pixel data from a 100x200 rectangular region with the upper-left corner in position (50, 75). The `ctx.getImageData()` method returns an image data object that has the following properties:

- width

- height

- data

The width and height properties specify the dimensions of the data contained in the data object. These values might not be the same as the dimensions of the region specified in the ctx.getImageData() call. Depending on the device and display, the actual number of pixels used behind the scenes could differ from what is apparent from the element's dimensions.

The data property is an array of RGBA color data. The length of the array depends on the dimensions of the data. Because each pixel requires four values—one for each of the red, green, and blue channels and one for the alpha channel—the length of the data array is equal to (width * height * 4). Each RGBA value is an integer in the range [0,255].

When iterating over the image data, you should use the width and height properties of the image data object and not those of the canvas element. Otherwise, you can't be certain that you're actually modifying all the data because of the difference between device pixels and CSS pixels.

Updating pixel values

Modifying the pixel data and saving it back to the canvas is easy. The ctx.putImageData() method takes an image data object and a set of coordinates indicating where the data should be placed. Usually, you just want to save the data back to where it came from, in which case the coordinates should be the upper-left corner of the rectangular area used in the ctx.getImageData() call. Listing 6-18 shows a basic example of how to modify the pixel data.

Listing 6-18 **Creating a pixel-based pattern**

```
<canvas id="canvas" width="400" height="400"></canvas>
<script>
var canvas = document.getElementById("canvas"),
    ctx = canvas.getContext("2d"),
    imageData = ctx.getImageData(
                    0,0,canvas.width,canvas.height),
    w = imageData.width, h = imageData.height,
    x, y, index;

for (y = 0; y < h; y++) {
    for (x = 0; x < w; x++) {
        index = (y * w + x) * 4;
        var r = x / w * 255,
            g = y / h * 255,
            b = 128,
            block = (56 * (1 - x*y/w/h));
```

```
        imageData.data[index] = r - r % block;
        imageData.data[index+1] = g - g % block;
        imageData.data[index+2] = b - b % block;
        imageData.data[index+3] = 255;
    }
}
ctx.putImageData(imageData, 0, 0);
</script>
```

You can find this example in the file 10-imageData.html. Figure 6-14 shows the resulting canvas pattern.

FIGURE 6-14: Use a simple pixel-based canvas effect to create this iterative pattern.

The pattern algorithm itself is not that interesting and is just an example. However, note that the alpha channel (index+3) is set to the constant value 255. When you create a new canvas element, it's initially transparent black. That means all pixel values have the value 0.

If you don't alter the alpha value, the content you put back on the canvas with `ctx.putIm-ageData()` is transparent as well, which is probably not what you want.

The image data methods aren't affected by any compositing, clipping, or transformation settings. Pixels are accessed and updated directly, independent of the canvas state.

Exporting image file data

Sometimes you may need to convert the graphics on the `canvas` element to a real bitmap image. One way to do so is to grab all the pixel data and write your own functions for turning that into file data. Some image formats, such as BMP files, are relatively easy to implement, but others, such as JPEG and PNG, are more complicated. The `canvas` element has a method called `canvas.toDataURL()` that actually gives you the entire canvas as a PNG file in the form of a base64-encoded string. The content of the string looks something like this:

```
data:image/png;base64,...image data here...
```

The string is formatted as a `data:` URI, so you can use it as the source for a regular image element:

```
var data = canvas.toDataURL();
document.getElementById("myImage").src = data;
```

Other possible use cases include posting the data to a server-side script for further processing or storing it locally using Web Storage.

The `canvas.toDataURL()` method takes an optional argument that specifies the type of image that should be returned. The default value for this argument is `image/png`. PNG is the only format required by the specification, but some browsers also support, for example, JPEG images. Any relevant parameters for the specific encoder are passed after the image type:

```
var jpeg = canvas.toDataURL("image/jpeg", 0.7);
```

In browsers that support exporting JPEG files, this line would create a string with JPEG data using a quality level of 0.7. Realistically, you can expect only that PNG files work. The only way to test whether a given format is supported is to try calling `canvas.toData-URL()` and checking whether the beginning of the string includes the image type you expected.

Understanding security restrictions

When it comes to image data and pixel-level access, the `canvas` element comes with a few security-related restrictions. Just as the `XMLHttpRequest` object can't access documents on other servers, the `canvas` element doesn't let you read pixel values if it contains data that originates in a location other than where the document is located. The `ctx.drawImage()` method doesn't stop you from drawing external images, but from that moment on, the canvas is marked as tainted. This means that the image data becomes write-only and any attempt to access the data with `ctx.getImageData()` will throw a security exception. Using patterns with external data triggers the same situation as does using fonts from other origins.

The restrictions apply to any methods that could potentially leak information from external sources. The affected methods are `ctx.measureText()` if it uses an external font and `canvas.toDataURL()` and `ctx.getImageData()` if any external content has been drawn on the canvas.

If you control the server that hosts the images you want to use, you can set the server to serve the files with cross-origin resource sharing (CORS), making the files available to JavaScript as though they were hosted on the same domain. Read more about CORS at `http://enable-cors.org`.

> **TIP** If you absolutely need to use content from other domains, you can get around this limitation by writing a small proxy script in your favorite server-side language. If you can make the server download the file and relay it to the browser, it will appear to the `canvas` element as though the file is from its own origin. The downside is that this approach puts extra load on your web server.

You also can't access data from the user's own local files. This applies even if you open the document locally as well, so you can't use these features when running from a `file://` URI.

Creating pixel-based effects

Let's look at another effect that uses the image data methods. This time, I used image data to create a twirl effect on an image file. The image is a bitmap version of the HTML5 logo you created earlier in this chapter. Listing 6-19 shows the code for the effect.

Listing 6-19   **A twirl effect**
```
<canvas id="canvas" width="400" height="400"></canvas>
<script>
    var canvas = document.getElementById("canvas"),
        ctx = canvas.getContext("2d"),
```
continued

Listing 6-19   **continued**

```
        image = new Image();

    image.addEventListener("load", function() {
        ctx.drawImage(this, 0, 0);
        var cw = canvas.width, ch = canvas.height,
            imgData = ctx.getImageData(0,0,cw,ch),
            newData = ctx.getImageData(0,0,cw,ch),
            w = imgData.width, h = imgData.height,
            x, y, sx, sy,
            dist, angle,
            idx1, idx2,
            amount = 20;

        for (y = 0; y < h; y++) {
            for (x = 0; x < w; x++) {
                sx = x - w / 2;
                sy = y - h / 2;
                dist = Math.sqrt(sx * sx + sy * sy);
                angle = Math.atan2(sy, sx) + dist / w * amount;
                sx = Math.cos(angle) * dist;
                sy = Math.sin(angle) * dist;
                sx = Math.floor(sx + w / 2);
                sy = Math.floor(sy + h / 2);
                sx = Math.min(w-1, Math.max(0, sx));
                sy = Math.min(h-1, Math.max(0, sy));

                idx1 = (x + y * w) * 4;
                idx2 = (sx + sy * w) * 4;

                newData.data[idx1] = imgData.data[idx2];
                newData.data[idx1+1] = imgData.data[idx2+1];
                newData.data[idx1+2] = imgData.data[idx2+2];
            }
        }
        ctx.putImageData(newData, 0, 0);
    }, false);

    // load the image
    image.src = "html5.png";
</script>
```

First, an image element is created, and the canvas drawing function is attached to its load event. When the image is ready, it's immediately drawn to the canvas so the image data can be accessed. In this example, you create two independent image data objects, each containing data of the entire canvas. Changing data in one image data object doesn't affect any other objects, even if they are created from the same canvas. The `newData` object holds the modified content. The `imgData` object is not modified at all and is used only to read data. The nested loops access each pixel in the `newData` data and use a bit of math to calculate from where in `imgData` it should pick the pixel values. Working with two image data objects protects you from accidentally overwriting pixel values that you might need later in the algorithm. You can find this example in the file `10-twirl.html`. Figure 6-15 shows the result.

FIGURE 6-15: Here the twirl effect is applied to the HTML5 logo.

For this example to work, you need to load the file from a web server. Drawing the image from a local file makes the canvas write-only. The image file must also reside on the same domain as the script because of the same-origin restrictions.

REMEMBER

Summary

In this chapter, you got the grand tour of the `canvas` element. You saw pretty much all the features that the 2D drawing API has to offer, from drawing simple paths, shapes, and curves to creating advanced fills and strokes.

You also saw how the image data methods let you access pixels on an individual basis and saw examples of how to use that data to create complex effects and interesting patterns as well as how to use it to modify data from bitmap images.

Chapter 7
Creating the Game Display

NOW THAT YOU'RE familiar with the `canvas` element, it's time to put that knowledge to work. The game is sorely missing some visuals, and you can now begin putting things on the screen.

The graphics you create in this chapter aren't complex. Rather, I focus on how to get the basic jewel board up and running. Before getting to that, though, I show you how you can modify the loader to preload game assets. You use that functionality to freshen up the splash screen with a progress bar as well as a new background.

I also show you the first of two different approaches to creating the graphics for the jewel board. In this chapter, you create the game graphics using the 2D canvas context; in Chapter 11, you find out how to use WebGL to create a similar display module with 3D graphics.

Tracking Load Progress

As the game evolves, more and more modules are added, so it's a good idea to provide feedback to users while the resources are loading. Currently, nothing happens until all scripts are loaded and executed. Only then is the `jewel.setup()` function called and the splash screen shown. If you call `jewel.setup()` as soon as the splash screen loads, a progress bar indicates how much has loaded. Listing 7-1 shows the changes to the loading sequence in `index.html`.

Listing 7-1   Calling setup earlier in the loading process

```
window.addEventListener("load", function() {
    jewel.load("scripts/dom.js");
    if (jewel.isStandalone()) {
        jewel.load("scripts/screen.splash.js", jewel.setup);
        jewel.load("scripts/screen.main-menu.js");
        if (jewel.hasWebWorkers()) {
            jewel.preload("scripts/board.worker.js");
            jewel.load("scripts/board.worker-interface.js");
        } else {
            jewel.load("scripts/board.js");
        }
    } else {
        jewel.load("scripts/screen.install.js", jewel.setup);
    }
});
```

The `jewel.setup()` function is now called as soon as the splash screen can be shown and while the rest of scripts continue to load.

You also need a way to determine how much has loaded at any given time, so add a `getLoadProgress()` function to `jewel.js`, as shown in Listing 7-2.

Listing 7-2   Calculating the loading progress

```
var jewel = (function() {
    ...
    function getLoadProgress() {
        return numResourcesLoaded / numResources;
    }

    return {
        getLoadProgress: getLoadProgress,
        ...
    };
})();
```

This function returns the current loading progress as a value between 0 and 1.

Adding a progress bar

Now that the splash screen can access the progress value, you can also add a visual cue on the splash screen that lets the user know what's going on. A simple progress bar goes a long way with users. First, add a few `div` elements to the splash screen HTML in `index.html`. Listing 7-3 shows the new tags.

Listing 7-3   **The Splash screen HTML with progress bar**

```
<div id="game">
    . . .
    <div class="screen" id="splash-screen">
        <h1 class="logo">Jewel <br/>Warrior</h1>
        <div class="progress">
            <div class="indicator"></div>
        </div>
        <span class="continue">Click to continue</span>
    </div>
    . . .
</div>
```

HTML5 actually introduces a new `progress` tag but support isn't ubiquitous yet. Most desktop browsers support it, but only the very latest versions of Android and iOS include support for this new element. If you use this element instead, the HTML may look like the following:

```
<progress class="loader" value="0" max="100" />
```

Changing the `value` attribute automatically changes the appearance of the `progress` element as well. You can easily make your own progress bar, though. Create two nested elements like the ones in Listing 7-3 and let the outer element define the overall dimensions and border of the progress bar. You can then simply scale the CSS `width` of the inner element progressively from 0% to 100% to indicate the progress. Listing 7-4 shows the new CSS rules in `main.css`.

Listing 7-4   **Styling the progress bar**

```
#splash-screen .continue {
    cursor : pointer;
    font-size : 0.75em;
    display : none;
```

continued

Listing 7-4   **continued**

```
}

...
/* Progress bar */
.progress {
    margin : 0 auto;
    width : 6em;
    height : 0.5em;
    border-radius : 0.5em;
    overflow : hidden;
    border : 1px solid rgb(200,200,100);
}

.progress .indicator {
    background-color : rgb(200,200,100);
    height : 100%;
    width : 0%;
}
```

The CSS modifications in Listing 7-4 also hide the `continue` text. It shouldn't be visible until the splash screen determines that it's safe to continue. The `.progress` styles just center the progress bar and give it some rounded corners and the same color as the game text. If you load the splash screen now, the empty progress bar displays beneath the game logo. You can test the progress bar by manually setting the width of the `.indicator` element. You can do so in the browser's JavaScript console by entering, for example:

```
jewel.dom.$(".progress .indicator")[0].style.width = "25%";
```

Next move on to the splash screen module and modify it so it checks the loading progress and updates the progress bar. Listing 7-5 shows the revised `screen.splash.js`.

Listing 7-5   **Updating the progress bar**

```
jewel.screens["splash-screen"] = (function() {
    var firstRun = true;

    function checkProgress() {
        var $ = jewel.dom.$,
            p = jewel.getLoadProgress() * 100;
```

```
        $("#splash-screen .indicator")[0].style.width = p + "%";
        if (p == 100) {
            setup();
        } else {
            setTimeout(checkProgress, 30);
        }
    }

    function setup() {
        var dom = jewel.dom,
            $ = dom.$,
            screen = $("#splash-screen")[0];
        $(".continue",screen)[0].style.display = "block";
        dom.bind(screen, "click", function() {
            jewel.showScreen("main-menu");
        });
    }

    function run() {
        if (firstRun) {
            checkProgress();
            firstRun = false;
        }
    }

    return {
        run : run
    };
})();
```

The `run()` method now calls `checkProgress()` instead of `setup()`. The check-Progress() function queries the `jewel.getLoadProgress()` function you just added and adjusts the width of the inner `div` of the progress bar accordingly. If the progress has reached 100%, it then calls `setup()`; otherwise, it uses `setTimeout()` to schedule another check in 30 milliseconds. This way, the Click to Continue link isn't shown until everything finishes loading.

Try loading the game now. You should see the progress bar on the splash screen filling up as the files load. If the files are on your local drive, the loading might happen so fast that you can barely see it. At the very least, there should a brief flash.

Building the Game Screen

Finally, you reach the actual game screen. Start by adding the game screen element to `index.html`, as shown in Listing 7-6.

Listing 7-6   The game screen HTML

```
<div id="game">

    ...

    <div class="screen" id="game-screen">
        <div class="game-board ">
        </div>
    </div>
</div>
```

Just one element appears on the game screen for now, the `game-board` element, and it's just a container for the actual jewel board. Give the element the correct dimensions in `main.css`, as shown in Listing 7-7.

Listing 7-7   The game board CSS

```
#game-screen .game-board {

    position : relative;
    width : 8em;
    height : 8em;

}
```

Now you can create a new screen module for the game screen. Listing 7-8 shows the initial code in `screen.game.js`.

Listing 7-8   The game screen module

```
jewel.screens["game-screen"] = (function() {
    var firstRun = true;

    function startGame() {
        var board = jewel.board,
            display = jewel.display;
        board.initialize(function() {
            display.initialize(function() {
                // start the game
            });
```

```
        });
    }

    function setup() {
        // do nothing for now
    }

    function run() {
        if (firstRun) {
            setup();
            firstRun = false;
        }
        startGame();
    }

    return {
        run : run
    };

})();
```

The first time the game screen module runs, it will call the `setup()` function, which doesn't do anything yet. The `startGame()` function uses the asynchronous `initialize()` function on the board module from the previous chapters. The callback function tries to initialize the display module, but fails because the module doesn't exist yet. Remember to load the new file in `index.html` to make sure it loads after the splash screen.

Drawing the board with canvas

Now you can move on quickly to the display module. I show you two different takes on how to create the first round of graphics for this game. The first approach is based on drawing 2D graphics on a `canvas` element. Listing 7-9 shows the initial canvas display module, `display.canvas.js`.

Listing 7-9 **The canvas display module**
```
jewel.display = (function() {
    var canvas, ctx,
        cols, rows,
        jewelSize,
        firstRun = true;
```

continued

Listing 7-9 **continued**

```
function setup() {
    var $ = jewel.dom.$,
        boardElement = $("#game-screen .game-board")[0];

    cols = jewel.settings.cols;
    rows = jewel.settings.rows;

    canvas = document.createElement("canvas");
    ctx = canvas.getContext("2d");
    jewel.dom.addClass(canvas, "board");

    var rect = boardElement.getBoundingClientRect();
    canvas.width = rect.width;
    canvas.height = rect.height;
    jewelSize = rect.width / cols;

    boardElement.appendChild(canvas);
}

function initialize(callback) {
    if (firstRun) {
        setup();
        firstRun = false;
    }
    callback();
}

return {
    initialize : initialize
};
})();
```

The first time the module is initialized, the setup() function is called. This function creates a canvas element and adds it to the game board element. The dimensions of the board div element are determined by the .game-board CSS class and depend on the screen resolution of the device. The newly created canvas element has the default dimensions 300x150, so you need to set the correct width and height on the canvas element. Use getBoundingClientRect() to retrieve the CSS dimensions of the board div element. This function returns an object describing the position and dimensions of the element. This information also lets you calculate `jewelSize` by dividing the width by the number of columns specified in the `jewel.settings` object. The jewel size and the number of columns and rows are saved for later as they will be used repeatedly throughout the module.

Add the file to the loading sequence in `index.html`, as shown in Listing 7-10.

Listing 7-10 **Loading the canvas display module**

```
window.addEventListener("load", function() {
    jewel.load("scripts/dom.js");
    if (jewel.isStandalone()) {
        jewel.load("scripts/screen.splash.js", jewel.setup);
        jewel.load("scripts/screen.main-menu.js");
        if (jewel.hasWebWorkers()) {
            jewel.preload("scripts/board.worker.js");
            jewel.load("scripts/board.worker-interface.js");
        } else {
            jewel.load("scripts/board.js");
        }
        jewel.load("scripts/screen.game.js");
        jewel.load("scripts/display.canvas.js");
    } else {
        jewel.load("scripts/screen.install.js", jewel.setup);
    }
});
```

Jewel Warrior has seven different types of jewels. Each type has a different shape and color. I created a set of images for these jewel types; you can find them in the project archive for this chapter. The size of a jewel sprite depends on the resolution and orientation of the device, and although you can let the browser dynamically resize the images, you often get the best visual quality by providing images with matching resolution. I included four sets of images in the archive for this chapter. You can find the files in the `images` folders. Each file is named `jewelsNN.png`, where NN is 32, 40, 64, or 80, which refers to the width and height of each jewel. Figure 7-1 shows the jewel sprites.

FIGURE 7-1: Jewel Warrior has several jewel sprites.

You need to load the jewel sprite when the display module is initialized and make sure that the `callback` function isn't called before the image has been loaded and is ready to be drawn on the canvas. If you call the `drawImage()` method on the canvas context with an image that hasn't loaded yet, you get an error. Listing 7-11 shows the changes to the `initialize()` function in `display.canvas.js`.

Listing 7-11   Loading the jewel sprite

```
jewel.display = (function() {
    var jewelSprite,
    ...
    function initialize(callback) {
        if (firstRun) {
            setup();
            jewelSprite = new Image();
            jewelSprite.addEventListener(
                "load", callback, false);
            jewelSprite.src =
                "images/jewels" + jewelSize + ".png";
            firstRun = false;
        } else {
            callback();
        }
    }
    ...
})();
```

As you can see, the jewel sprite is loaded only the first time the `initialize()` function is called. If the user plays another round of the game, the image can simply be reused.

Creating the board background

Before drawing the jewels, add a semitransparent, checkered pattern in the background of the board. As long as the foreground content—in this case, the jewels—doesn't need to interact with the background, you can use separate canvas elements for the two layers. When modifying foreground content, always having to make sure the background remains nice can affect the performance and the complexity of the code. In Listing 7-12, you see how to create a second canvas element and add it to the document before the foreground content. Add the new `createBackground()` function to `display.canvas.js`.

Listing 7-12 **Adding a background pattern**

```
jewel.display = (function() {
    ...

    function createBackground() {
        var background = document.createElement("canvas"),
            bgctx = background.getContext("2d");

        jewel.dom.addClass(background, "background");
        background.width = cols * jewelSize;
        background.height = rows * jewelSize;

        bgctx.fillStyle = "rgba(225,235,255,0.15)";
        for (var x=0;x<cols;x++) {
            for (var y=0;y<cols;y++) {
                if ((x+y) % 2) {
                    bgctx.fillRect(
                        x * jewelSize, y * jewelSize,
                        jewelSize, jewelSize
                    );
                }
            }
        }
        return background;
    }

    function setup() {
        ...
        boardElement.appendChild(createBackground());
        boardElement.appendChild(canvas);
    }

    ...
})();
```

The pattern itself is not that interesting. The nested loops iterate over the entire board and fill semitransparent squares in every other cell. Now add the CSS rules shown in Listing 7-13 to main.css.

Listing 7-13 **Adding game board CSS rules**

```
#game-screen .game-board .board-bg,
#game-screen .game-board .board {
    position : absolute;
```

continued

Listing 7-13   continued
```
    left: 0;
    top: 0;
    width : 100%;
    height : 100%;
}

#game-screen .game-board .board {
    z-index : 10;
}

#game-screen .game-board .board-bg {
    z-index : 0;
}
```

Both the background canvas and board canvas are positioned using `absolute`, which places them on top of each other. Figure 7-2 shows the game screen with the checkered board background.

FIGURE 7-2: The game board background is checkered.

Filling the board with jewels

Time to draw some jewels! The display module needs a function that simply draws the entire board based on the board data. Listing 7-14 shows the new functions added to the `display.canvas.js` module.

Listing 7-14 **The display redraw function**

```
jewel.display = (function() {
    var jewels,
        ...

    function drawJewel(type, x, y) {
        ctx.drawImage(jewelSprite,
            type * jewelSize, 0, jewelSize, jewelSize,
            x * jewelSize, y * jewelSize,
            jewelSize, jewelSize
        );
    }

    function redraw(newJewels, callback) {
        var x, y;
        jewels = newJewels;
        ctx.clearRect(0,0,canvas.width,canvas.height);
        for (x = 0; x < cols; x++) {
            for (y = 0; y < rows; y++) {
                drawJewel(jewels[x][y], x, y);
            }
        }
        callback();
    }

    return {
        initialize : initialize,
        redraw : redraw
    };
})();
```

The `redraw()` function first clears the entire canvas before iterating over all board positions to paint a jewel image in each cell. A `drawJewel()` helper function takes care of the actual drawing. Note that the `redraw()` function gets the jewel data from the caller. The display module has no connection to the board module and has no concept of the game state other than what it's told to draw.

Triggering the initial redraw

Now you just need to call the `initialize()` function, and when it finishes, call the first `redraw()`. Listing 7-15 shows the additions to the `screen.game.js` module.

Listing 7-15   Triggering the initial redraw

```
jewel.screens["game-screen"] = (function() {
    ...
    function startGame() {
        var board = jewel.board,
            display = jewel.display;
        board.initialize(function() {
            display.initialize(function() {
                display.redraw(board.getBoard(), function() {
                    // do nothing for now
                });
            });
        });
    }
    ...
})();
```

Now you can start the game, and you should see something similar to Figure 7-3. Load the game and click the Play button on the main menu.

Exiting the game

Your work on the display module is done for now, but the player should have options to exit the current game and return to the main menu or temporarily pause the game. Listing 7-16 shows a footer element with exit and pause buttons added to the game screen in `index.html`.

Listing 7-16   Adding a footer to the game screen

```
...
<div id="game">
    ...
    <div class="screen" id="game-screen">
        ...
        <footer>
            <button class="exit">Exit</button>
```

```
            <button class="pause">Pause</button>
        </footer>
    </div>
</div>
...
```

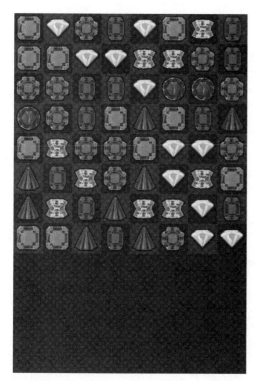

FIGURE 7-3: The game screen is loaded with jewels.

The CSS rules from `main.css` shown in Listing 7-17 position the footer at the bottom of the screen and style the button so it matches the rest of the game.

Listing 7-17   Styling the footer

```
.screen footer {
    display : block;
    position : absolute;
    bottom : 0;
    height : 1.0em;
```

continued

Listing 7-17   **continued**

```css
    width : 100%;
}

.screen footer button {
    margin-left : 0.25em;
    margin-right : 0.25em;
    padding : 0 0.75em;
    font-family : Geo, sans-serif;
    font-size : 0.5em;
    color : rgba(200,200,100,0.5);
    background : rgb(10,20,0);
    border : 1px solid rgba(200,200,100,0.5);
    border-radius : 0.2em;
}
```

Listing 7-18 shows the event handler attached in the setup() function in screen.game.js. If the player confirms that he wants to return to the menu, the game simply switches to the main menu screen.

Listing 7-18   **Responding to the Exit button**

```javascript
jewel.screens["game-screen"] = (function() {
    var firstRun = true;

    function exitGame() {
        pauseGame();
        var confirmed = window.confirm(
            "Do you want to return to the main menu?"
        );
        if (confirmed) {
            jewel.showScreen("main-menu");
        } else {
            resumeGame();
        }
    }

    function setup() {
        var dom = jewel.dom;
        dom.bind("footer button.exit", "click", exitGame);
    }

    ...
})();
```

The code in Listing 7-18 introduces two new functions: pauseGame() and resumeGame(). You now add these functions along with a pause button in the footer.

Pausing the game

The pauseGame() and resumeGame() functions simply change the value of a paused variable, as shown in Listing 7-19. Remember to reset the paused value when starting a new game.

Listing 7-19 Adding pause and resume functionality

```
jewel.screens["game-screen"] = (function() {
    var paused,
    ...
    function startGame() {
        ...
        paused = false;
    }

    function pauseGame() {
        if (paused) {
            return; // do nothing if already paused
        }
        paused = true;
    }

    function resumeGame() {
        paused = false;
    }
    ...
})();
```

You can add a dimming effect by placing a dark gray, semitransparent div element on top of the game screen. Listing 7-20 shows the new div element added to index.html.

Listing 7-20 Adding the dimming overlay

```
<div id="game">
    ...
    <div class="screen" id="game-screen">
        <div class="game-board"></div>
        <footer>
            <button class="exit">Exit</button>
```

continued

Listing 7-20   continued

```
            <button class="pause">Pause</button>
        </footer>
        <div class="pause-overlay">
            <div class="pause-text">Pause</div>
        </div>
    </div>
</div>
```

The CSS rules in Listing 7-21 place the overlay in front of the other content, make it take up the entire game screen and color the background. The "Pause" text is centered on the screen and given the same style as the logo.

Listing 7-21   Styling the overlay

```
/* Game screen pause overlay */
#game-screen .pause-overlay {
    display : none;
    position : absolute;
    left : 0;
    top : 0;
    width : 100%;
    height : 100%;
    z-index : 100;
    background : rgba(20,20,20,0.5);
}
#game-screen .pause-overlay .pause-text {
    width: 100%;
    text-align : center;
    margin-top : 50%;
    font-family : Slackey;
    font-size : 1.0em;
    text-shadow : 0.03em  0.03em  0.03em rgb(255,255,0),
                 -0.03em -0.03em  0.03em rgb(255,255,0),
                  0.10em  0.15em  0.15em rgb(0,0,0);
    color : rgb(70,120,20);
}
```

Now bind the click event on the pause button to the pauseGame() function and the click event on the pause overlay to the resumeGame() function so the user can resume the game. You should also modify the startGame(), pauseGame() and resumeGame() functions so they show and hide the pause overlay. Listing 7-22 shows how.

Listing 7-22 **Binding the pause event handlers**

```
jewel.screens["game-screen"] = (function() {
    ...
    function startGame() {
        ...
        paused = false;
        var dom = jewel.dom,
            overlay = dom.$("#game-screen .pause-overlay")[0];
        overlay.style.display = "none";
    }

    function pauseGame() {
        if (paused) {
            return; // do nothing if already paused
        }
        var dom = jewel.dom,
            overlay = dom.$("#game-screen .pause-overlay")[0];
        overlay.style.display = "block";
        paused = true;
    }

    function resumeGame() {
        var dom = jewel.dom,
            overlay = dom.$("#game-screen .pause-overlay")[0];
        overlay.style.display = "none";
        paused = false;
    }

    function setup() {
        var dom = jewel.dom;
        dom.bind("footer button.exit", "click", exitGame);
        dom.bind("footer button.pause", "click", pauseGame);
        dom.bind(".pause-overlay", "click", resumeGame);
    }
    ...
})();
```

In later chapters, you expand the pause and exit functionality so the game actually pauses and the game state is automatically saved when the user exits the game. Figure 7-4 shows the pause overlay in action.

FIGURE 7-4: The screen dims when the user pauses the game.

Summary

This chapter started with the game display, and the basic display routines for rendering the game board are now in place. You used the `canvas` element to put some jewels on the screen. In the beginning of the chapter, you also enhanced the splash screen with a progress bar that tracks the loading progress.

In the next chapter, you make more couplings between the display and board logic by adding user interactions. You then use those interactions to expand the capabilities of the display modules.

Chapter 8
Interacting with the Game

In This Chapter

- Capturing user input
- Working with touch events
- Binding inputs to actions
- Adding visual feedback to actions

IN THE PREVIOUS chapter, you implemented the first parts of the game display. So far, the display is just a static rendering of the jewel board, and the game doesn't react to any user input at all. In this chapter, you discover how to implement a new module that captures user input and enables the display and the rest of the game react to the input.

First, however, you walk through the different types of inputs available in the browser, paying special attention to touch-based input found in mobile devices such as smartphones and tablets. Using this knowledge, you return to the game and build a system that encapsulates the native input events and that enables you to translate these events into game actions.

After you implement the user input, you find out how to attach game actions to the display module to allow the player to select and swap jewels.

Capturing User Input

I'm sure you're more than familiar with basic keyboard and mouse events in desktop browsers, so here I focus on the more interesting topic of how these events behave on mobile devices with touch screens.

Mouse events on touch devices

Touch-enabled devices such as smartphones and tablets rarely come equipped with a mouse. Instead, they depend solely on interaction with the touch screen to navigate through applications and websites. The web, of course, was built without such devices in mind; however, most devices resolve this problem transparently by automatically firing mousedown, click, and mouseup events when the user taps the screen. If the site works with a mouse, there's a good chance it also works just fine on a touch-based device.

One thing doesn't translate easily to a touch screen, though, and that's the hover state. With a mouse, hovering the pointer over a UI element is commonplace and often provides, for example, additional information in the form of tooltips or just a bit of eye candy. Some designs even rely on mouseover events to trigger actions such as unfolding menus, displaying extra buttons, and so on.

This state of "almost but not quite" just doesn't exist on a touch device. Either you're touching the screen or you aren't. There's no way to mimic the mouseover event because there's no way to tell where the finger is until it actually touches the screen. This also has consequences for CSS because the :hover pseudo-class no longer makes sense.

> **TIP** Some modern touch-screen devices, such as the Sony Xperia sola, can actually detect when the finger is close to the screen but not actually touching. However, these features are far from ubiquitous, so don't assume support for anything beyond regular touch events yet.

The virtual keyboard

Both Android and iOS feature a virtual keyboard that automatically appears whenever the user needs to input text. For example, tapping an input field or a text area automatically brings up the keyboard.

Keyboard events such as keypress, keydown, and keyup do go through to JavaScript, so it is possible to map certain functions to keys on the virtual keyboard. However, the events aren't fired until you release the key, so you can't actually tell when the key is pressed, only when it's released. The events also fire only once, unlike on desktop browsers where they fire continuously when the key is held down.

You don't have much control over this keyboard. There's no nice and easy way to disable it, and you can't force it to pop up either. If you really need to be able to toggle the keyboard manually, you can place an input field out of view and toggle the keyboard by using the `blur()` and `focus()` methods. See Listing 8-1 for an example. You can find the code in the file `01-virtualkeyboard.html`.

Listing 8-1 Toggling the virtual keyboard

```
<button id="toggleButton">Toggle Keyboard</button><br/>
<span id="output"></span>
<script>

function toggleKeyboard() {
    var kbToggle = document.getElementById("kbToggle");
    // create element if it doesn't exist
    if (!kbToggle) {
        kbToggle = document.createElement("input");
        kbToggle.id = "kbToggle";
        kbToggle.style.position = "absolute";
        kbToggle.style.left = "-1000px";
        document.body.appendChild(kbToggle);
        // keep the focus
        kbToggle.addEventListener("blur", function() {
            kbToggle.focus();
        }, false);
    }
    // switch classes and focus
    if (kbToggle.className == "on") {
        kbToggle.className = "off";
        kbToggle.blur();
    } else {
        kbToggle.className = "on";
        kbToggle.focus();
    }
}

// output pressed key
document.addEventListener("keypress", function(e) {
    document.getElementById("output").innerHTML
        = "You pressed: " + String.fromCharCode(e.charCode);
}, false);
```

continued

Listing 8-1   continued
```
// toggle keyboard on click
document.getElementById("toggleButton").addEventListener(
    "click", toggleKeyboard, false);
</script>
```

In general, I advise against using the keyboard for anything other than text input. Not only is its functionality limited, but also it eats up a significant portion of the screen real estate.

Touch events

In addition to the regular mouse events, you can use touch events on platforms that support them. Touch events are standardized in the W3C Touch Events specification (www.w3.org/TR/touch-events), which reached recommendation status in October 2013. Both iOS and Android devices have had exposed touch events in the browser since early versions, so, it's safe to assume support for these events. Of course, if you're also targeting desktop browsers, you must check for support. You can detect whether the browser supports touch events by checking whether, for example, the ontouchstart property exists on the window object:

```
if ("ontouchstart" in window) {
    // touch events are supported
}
```

The touchstart event is fired whenever the user places her finger on the screen. The other two touch events that you need to know about are touchmove and touchend. The touch-move event fires when the user's finger moves across the screen, and the touchend event fires when the user removes her finger. These three touch events behave much like the mousedown, mousemove, and mouseup events.

In general, touch event objects are like any other event object, except they have a few extra properties. Event objects coming from mouse events carry information about the mouse position, for example, via the clientX and clientY properties:

```
document.addEventListener("click", function(e) {
    alert(e.clientX + ", " + e.clientY);
}, false);
```

Touch events have similar data about the touch position, but instead of providing it directly on the event object, they have a property called touches. The touches property is a list of all the currently active touches on the screen. To get information about the touch event, you must grab the first touch object from the touches list. A touch object has the same coordinate properties used in regular mouse event objects—that is, `clientX/Y`, `screenX/Y`, and so on. The example in Listing 8-2 shows how to retrieve the coordinates of the touch event. You can find the example in the file `02-touch.html`.

Listing 8-2 **Using touch events**

```
Touch X: <input id="touchx"><br/>
Touch Y: <input id="touchy">
<script>
    var touchx = document.getElementById("touchx"),
        touchy = document.getElementById("touchy");

    document.addEventListener("touchmove", function(e) {
        touchx.value = e.touches[0].clientX;
        touchy.value = e.touches[0].clientY;
        e.preventDefault();
    }, false);
</script>
```

This short example simply prints the x and y coordinates in the corresponding `input` elements when you move your finger across the screen. Note that because it accesses only the first element of the touches list, this event works only with the first finger that touches the screen. As you see in the next section, however, working with multiple touch objects is also easy.

Multitouch

The `touches` array lists `all` active touches, and if more than one finger is touching the screen, you don't know which one is the relevant touch object. The event object provides two additional lists that you can use to get around this problem: `targetTouches` and `changed-Touches`. The `targetTouches` list contains only the touch objects that are active on the target element. So, if a `touchstart` event fires on, say, a `div` element, the `targetTouches` list lists only the touch objects on that specific `div`, whereas the `touches` list might contain other, unrelated touch objects. The `changedTouches` list adds a further restriction and lists only the touch objects involved in that specific event. So, if you have two fingers on the `div` and move only one, the `targetTouches` list in the `touchmove` event contains both touch objects, but the `changedTouches` gives you only the one that moved.

The first example is a multitouch-enabled feature that lets you drag multiple elements around at the same time. Listing 8-3 shows the code, which you also can find in the file `03-multidrag.html`. This file also includes a bit of CSS to style the two draggable elements.

Listing 8-3 **Multitouch drag**

```
<div id="dragme1"></div>
<div id="dragme2"></div>
<script>
    var el1 = document.getElementById("dragme1"),
        el2 = document.getElementById("dragme2");

    el1.addEventListener("touchstart", startDrag, false);
    el2.addEventListener("touchstart", startDrag, false);

    function startDrag(e) {
        var touch = e.targetTouches[0],
            x = touch.clientX,
            y = touch.clientY,
            rect = this.getBoundingClientRect();

        function drag(e) {
            var touch = e.targetTouches[0],
                newX = touch.clientX,
                newY = touch.clientY;
            this.style.left = (rect.left + newX - x) + "px";
            this.style.top = (rect.top + newY - y) + "px";
            e.preventDefault();
        }

        function endDrag() {
            this.removeEventListener("touchmove", drag);
            this.removeEventListener("touchend", endDrag);
        }

        this.addEventListener("touchmove", drag, false);
        this.addEventListener("touchend", endDrag, false);
    };
</script>
```

The startDrag() function starts by grabbing a touch object from the targetTouches list and saving the original position. Ignore any extra fingers on the same elements, so picking the first element of targetTouches is fine. The startDrag() function then attaches a handler to the touchmove event that uses the difference between the new and old coordinates to move the div element. Had the startDrag() function used touches rather than targetTouches, you couldn't be sure that the touch object was actually the one that was on that element.

Another common feature in mobile applications is the two-finger, pinch-zoom gesture. When two fingers touch the screen and move either toward or away from each other, you can use the relative change in distance as a scaling factor. You can apply this factor to anything you want, be it the whole page or just a single element. Listing 8-4 shows an example of how you can create such a pinch-zoom feature. You can find the full code in the file 04-pinchzoom.html.

Listing 8-4   **Multitouch pinch-zoom effect**

```
<div id="zoomer"></div>
<script>
    var zoomer = document.getElementById("zoomer");
        zoomer.addEventListener("touchstart", startZoom, false);

    function startZoom(e) {
        if (e.targetTouches.length != 2) {
            return;
        }

        var touch1 = e.targetTouches[0],
            touch2 = e.targetTouches[1],
            dX = touch1.clientX - touch2.clientX,
            dY = touch1.clientY - touch2.clientY,
            startDist = Math.sqrt(dX * dX + dY * dY),
            scale = +this.getAttribute("data-scale") || 1;

        function zoom(e) {
            if (e.targetTouches.length != 2) {
                return;
            }
            var touch1 = e.targetTouches[0],
                touch2 = e.targetTouches[1],
                dX = touch1.clientX - touch2.clientX,
                dY = touch1.clientY - touch2.clientY,
                newDist = Math.sqrt(dX * dX + dY * dY),
                newScale = scale * newDist / startDist;
            this.style.webkitTransform = "scale("+newScale+")";
            this.setAttribute("data-scale", newScale);
            e.preventDefault();
        }
```

continued

Listing 8-4 **continued**

```
    function endZoom() {
        this.removeEventListener("touchmove", zoom);
        this.removeEventListener("touchend", endZoom);
    }

    this.addEventListener("touchmove", zoom, false);
    this.addEventListener("touchend", endZoom, false);
    }
</script>
```

When the user touches the element, the startZoom() function acts if exactly two fingers are touching that element—that is, if the length of targetTouches equals 2. The initial distance between the two touch events is stored, so you can compare it to calculate a new scale factor in the subsequent touchmove events. The scale factor is also stored as an attribute on the element. The startZoom() function then adds the touchmove event handler that does the actual zooming. When zoom() is triggered, the coordinates of at least one of the touch objects are changed. The ratio of new distance to the old distance is used as the scaling factor when setting the CSS scaling transformation. Finally, the touchend event handler cleans up by removing the touchmove and touchend handler functions.

Gestures

In addition to the touch* family of events, iOS devices also support a set of gesture events. These events can be useful for creating features such as the pinch-zoom effect shown in Listing 8-4. The three gesture events are

- gesturestart

- gesturechange

- gestureend

Gesture events are built on top of touch events and don't expose as much low-level information. Instead, they carry information that might be useful when acting on multitouch events. None of the gesture events react to single-touch input; the gesturestart event fires only when the second finger touches the screen. The gesturechange event fires whenever one of the touch points moves. The event object that this event sends has a few cool properties. Most interesting, perhaps, are the scaling and rotation values exposed through the scale and rotation properties. The scale value indicates the relative change in distance between the touch points since the gesturestart event. So, if scale is equal to 2.0, the distance has doubled since the beginning. Similarly, the rotation value indicates the number of degrees the touch points have rotated around their common center. Listing 8-5 shows how you can use those properties to create, for example, a touch-enabled zoom and rotate feature. You can find the example in the file 05-gesture.html.

Listing 8-5 **Gesture-based zoom and rotate**

```
<div id="mydiv"></div>
<script>
    var el = document.getElementById("mydiv");
    el.addEventListener("gesturestart", gestureStart, false);

    function gestureStart(e) {
        var rot = +this.getAttribute("data-rot") || 0,
            scale = +this.getAttribute("data-scale") || 1;

        function change(e) {
            this.style.webkitTransform =
                "rotate(" + (rot + e.rotation) + "deg) " +
                "scale(" + (scale * e.scale) + ")";
            e.preventDefault();
        }
        function end(e) {
            this.setAttribute("data-rot", rot + e.rotation);
            this.setAttribute("data-scale", scale * e.scale);
            this.removeEventListener("gesturechange", change);
            this.removeEventListener("gestureend", end);
        }
        this.addEventListener("gesturechange", change, false);
        this.addEventListener("gestureend", end, false);
    }
</script>
```

These events definitely simplify the code for these types of features, but remember that they are iOS-specific. Only devices such as iPhones and iPads support the gesture events, and there's no sign that other browser vendors are planning to adopt them.

Simulating touch events

Sometimes being able to use and test touch events is useful even, for example, if you're on a desktop PC with no touch support. Phantom Limb by Vodori is a nice tool that intercepts mouse events and translates them to touch events. It's a small JavaScript library that you have to include in your page. You can find the script at www.vodori.com/blog/phantom-limb.html.

Phantom Limb even supports multitouch when the user holds down the Alt/Option key. I included this small library in the sample code for this chapter; you can find it in the 02-touch.html, 03-multidrag.html, and 04-pinchzoom.html examples.

If you use Chrome, it's even easier to simulate touch events. Open the DevTools settings by clicking the "gear" icon in the lower right corner. In the "Overrides" section you can enable emulation of touch events, among other things. The mouse pointer now acts like a touch point and fires the relevant touch events.

Input events and canvas

Working with user input and canvas can be a bit tricky. Because a canvas element behaves like a bitmap image and the structure of the painted content isn't retained, you really can't attach event handlers to anything other than the canvas element. You may know perfectly well what the pixels mean, but the browser doesn't, so you have no way to attach event handlers directly to game sprites or any other art you've drawn on the canvas.

Using paths for hit detection

If you want to add mouse or touch interactions to the canvas, you'll have to keep track of object positions. That way, you can attach a single event handler on the canvas element and then search the list of objects to see whether any of them should react. If the elements that have been drawn on the canvas are all described by paths, you can save the path data and use the ctx.isPointInPath() method to test whether a touch or mouse event is in one of the paths. Listing 8-6 shows an example of this approach. You can find the code for this example in the file 06-canvaspath.html.

Listing 8-6　Detecting mouse events on canvas

```
<canvas id="canvas" width="400" height="300"></canvas>
<script>
    var canvas = document.getElementById("canvas"),
        ctx = canvas.getContext("2d");

    ctx.beginPath();
    ctx.moveTo(100, 50);
    ctx.lineTo(250, 200);
    ctx.lineTo(150, 250);
    ctx.lineTo(200, 300);
    ctx.lineTo(50, 250);
    ctx.lineTo(150, 150);

    ctx.fillStyle = "teal";
    ctx.fill();

    canvas.addEventListener("touchmove", function(e) {
        hitTest(e.targetTouches[0]);
```

```
        e.preventDefault();
    }, false);
    canvas.addEventListener("mousemove", hitTest, false);

    function hitTest(e) {
        var rect = canvas.getBoundingClientRect(),
            x = e.clientX - rect.left,
            y = e.clientY - rect.top,
            inPath = ctx.isPointInPath(x, y);
        ctx.fillStyle = inPath ? "orange" : "teal";
        ctx.fill();
    }
```

```
</script>
```

The example in Listing 8-6 declares a path on the canvas and then uses the `ctx.isPointIn-Path()` method in the `mousemove` and `touchmove` event handlers to decide which color to fill the path. This example shows how you can use that method to attach behavior to specific areas on the canvas. Of course, you do need to keep track of the points that make up the path and, if necessary, set up the path again in each test. This approach isn't always ideal, and it doesn't solve all problems, but depending on the task at hand, it might do the trick. Problems that are more complex can sometimes be solved by testing, for example, for nontransparent pixel values using the canvas image data methods.

You can use the `ctx.isPointInPath()` method for more than user input. Consider, for example, a game in which a projectile is fired at a target. If the outline of the target can be described by a path, the `ctx.isPointInPath()` method makes it easy to determine whether the projectile has hit the target.

Using hit regions

The canvas specification has recently been expanded with hit regions, a feature meant to make it easier to add user input and interaction to the canvas element. No browsers currently implement hit regions, but most browsers should catch up before long.

To specify a hit region, you use the `addHitRegion()` method on the canvas context object. This function takes a single argument, an options object describing the region:

```
ctx.addHitRegion({
    path: aPathObject,
    id: "myregion",
    cursor: "pointer"
});
```

The `path` property is a path object and is optional. If no path object is given, the current path is used. When the hit region is added, you can simply attach a listener to, for example, the `click` event, and if the user clicks inside a hit region, the relevant region ID will be available in the `region` property on the event object:

```
canvas.addEventListener("click", function(e) {
    if (e.region) {
        alert("You clicked the region: " + e.region);
    }
}, false);
```

Using gamepads and controllers

One of the most recent additions to HTML5 is the capability to use gamepads. The API for this feature is still in development (see `www.w3.org/TR/gamepad`), but Firefox and Chrome both already support at least some of the specification. To enable gamepad support in Firefox, go to `about:config` and enable the `dom.gamepad.enabled` flag.

Accessing gamepad data

According to the W3C specification, gamepads connected to the computer are accessible through a `gamepads` object on the `navigator` object. However, neither Chrome nor Firefox currently implement this object. Instead, you can use the `navigator.getGamepads()` function in Firefox and the `navigator.webkitGetGamepads()` function in Chrome to access the gamepads:

```
function getGamepads() {
    if (navigator.gamepads) {
        return navigator.gamepads;
    } else if (navigator.getGamepads) {
        return navigator.getGamepads();
    } else if (navigator.webkitGetGamepads) {
        return navigator.webkitGetGamepads();
    }
}
```

You'll find a couple of small differences in the way these functions work. In Firefox, `navigator.getGamepads()` returns a regular array containing gamepad objects for any connected gamepads. In Chrome, `navigator.webkitGetGamepads()` returns a `GamepadList` object that is array-like but always has a length of 4, even if no gamepads are connected. That means you need to check all four elements to see whether there's an actual object or whether the element is undefined. The gamepad objects in both types of lists are relatively simple and have the following properties:

- id
- index
- timestamp
- connected
- mapping
- axes
- buttons

The id property is a string identifying the gamepad, for example "45e-2a1-Controller (XBOX 360 For Windows)". The index property is the index of the gamepad—that is, the first connected gamepad has index 0, the second has index 1, and so forth. If the gamepad at index 0 is disconnected, the remaining gamepads keep their indices, and the next gamepad to connect reuses index 0. The timestamp property indicates when the state of the controller was last updated, but it isn't supported in Firefox yet. The connected property is a Boolean value indicating whether the gamepad is connected. Only Firefox currently uses this property.

The buttons property is an array of button states, each element in the array corresponding to a button on the gamepad. The button values are either 0 or 1 (or some value in between for analog buttons), where 1 is fully depressed. The number of available buttons depends on the controller, as does the mapping of button indices to actual buttons. To complicate matters further, Firefox and Chrome use different button and axis mappings. The mapping property is a string indicating the layout of the gamepad. This property is currently implemented only in Firefox and only partly. However, eventually this property will make it easier to support different types of controllers. Table 8-1 shows the button layout for the Xbox 360 controller.

Table 8-1 Xbox 360 gamepad buttons

Button Index	Button (Chrome)	Button (Firefox)
0	A button (green)	A button (green)
1	B button (red)	B button (red)
2	X button (blue)	X button (blue)
3	Y button (yellow)	Y button (yellow)
4	Left bumper	Left bumper
5	Right bumper	Right bumper
6	Left trigger	Back

continued

Table 8-1   **continued**

Button Index	Button (Chrome)	Button (Firefox)
7	Right trigger	Start
8	Back	Left stick
9	Start	Right stick
10	Left stick	
11	Right stick	
12	D-pad up	
13	D-pad down	
14	D-pad left	
15	D-pad right	

As you can see, Firefox doesn't map buttons for the triggers and the D-pad. These are treated as axes instead. The `axes` property is an array containing values for the sticks on the gamepad. Each stick has a value in the range [-1.0 .. 1.0] for each of its axes. For horizontal axes, a value of -1.0 is left and a value of 1.0 is right. For vertical axes, a value of -1.0 is up and a value of 1.0 is down. Table 8-2 shows the axes indices for the Xbox 360 controller.

Table 8-2   **Gamepad axes**

Axis index	Axis (Chrome)	Axis (Firefox)
0	Left stick horizontal	Left stick horizontal
1	Left stick vertical	Left stick vertical
2	Right stick horizontal	Left and right trigger
3	Right stick vertical	Right stick horizontal
4		Right stick vertical
5		D-pad left/right
6		D-pad up/down

Although the button and axis mappings have some differences, there's enough overlap that you can use the colored buttons and the left stick without having to code for each browser. The W3C specification also recommends that buttons and axes are indexed in order of decreasing importance, so using button 0 and axes 0 and 1 for your primary actions should be relatively safe.

Gamepad events
The official specification also specifies an event-based method of detecting connected gamepads through the `gamepadconnected` and `gamepaddisconnected` events. The relevant

gamepad object is passed to the event handler in the `gamepad` property on the event object. Unfortunately, only Firefox currently supports these events.

```
window.addEventListener("gamepadconnected", function(e) {
    alert("You connected a gamepad: " + e.gamepad.id);
}, false);
window.addEventListener("gamepaddisconnected", function(e) {
    alert("You disconnected a gamepad: " + e.gamepad.id);
}, false);
```

In addition, Firefox supports several other nonstandard events such as `gamepadbutton-down`, `gamepadbuttonup`, and `gamepadaxismove`. These events, or similar events, may or may not be included in the W3C standard at some point.

Firefox 25, which is the most recent version at the time of this writing, has a bug that prevents the browser from registering any gamepads at all unless you add an event listener to the `gamepadconnected` event. Fortunately, that's easy to fix by attaching an empty event handler:

```
window.addEventListener("gamepadconnected", function(){}, false);
```

Detecting changes to the gamepad state

Currently, the best way to register state changes such as button presses is to continuously poll the gamepad objects and check whether anything has changed. Before the gamepad is even available in the gamepad list, you often must press a button or wriggle a stick *while* reading the gamepad list, so don't be surprised if you don't see the gamepad in the list before you start polling. Listing 8-7 shows an example of a polling function.

Listing 8-7 Polling for connected gamepads

```
var gpStates = [];

function pollGamepads() {
    var gamepads = getGamepads(),
        i, gamepad, idx;
    for (i=0;i<gamepads.length;i++) {
        if (gamepads[i]) {
            gamepad = gamepads[i];
            idx = gamepad.index;
            if (gpStates[idx]) {
                if (gpStates[idx].gamepad != gamepad) {
                    gamepadDisconnected(gpStates[idx]);
```

continued

Listing 8-7   **continued**

```
                    gamepadConnected(gamepad);
                }
            } else {
                gamepadConnected(gamepad);
            }
            updateGamepadState(gamepad);
        }
    }
}
```

This function can be called repeatedly with, for example, `setInterval()`. The `gpStates` array stores the states of the currently known gamepads. The `pollGamepads()` function grabs the current gamepad list from the `getGamepads()` and checks whether a gamepad with that index already exists in the `gpStates` list. If there's no such gamepad, the `poll-Gamepads()` function calls the `gamepadConnected()` function, which adds the gamepad to the list. If there's already a gamepad with that index and it isn't the same gamepad, `poll-Gamepads()` removes the old one before adding the new gamepad. Listing 8-8 shows the `gamepadConnected()` and `gamepadDisconnected()` functions.

Listing 8-8   **Adding connected gamepads**
```
function gamepadConnected(gamepad) {
    gpStates[gamepad.index] = {
        gamepad: gamepad,
        buttons: gamepad.buttons,
        axes: gamepad.axes
    };
    console.log("Gamepad[" + gamepad.index + "] connected");
}

function gamepadDisconnected(gamepad) {
    console.log("Gamepad[" + gamepad.index + "] disconnected");
    delete gpStates[gamepad.index];
}
```

The `gamepadConnected()` function adds the gamepad state to the `gpStates` array, storing both the gamepad object and the current button and axis states. The `gamepadDisconnected()` function simply deletes the state object from the list.

The `pollGamepads()` function also calls `updateGamepadState()`, which compares the new state with the old state for each button and axis and logs changes. When the timestamp property on the gamepad objects is implemented in all browsers, you can use it to determine whether you need to update the state at all. Until then, you need to update it every time. Listing 8-9 shows this function.

Listing 8-9 **Updating the button and axis states**

```
function updateGamepadState(gamepad) {
    var state = gpStates[gamepad.index],
        i;
    for (i=0;i<gamepad.buttons.length;i++) {
        if (gamepad.buttons[i] != state.buttons[i]) {
            console.log("Gamepad[" + gamepad.index + "] button "
                    + i + " = " + gamepad.buttons[i]);
            state.buttons[i] = gamepad.buttons[i];
        }
    }
    for (i=0;i<gamepad.axes.length;i++) {
        if (gamepad.axes[i] != state.axes[i]) {
            console.log("Gamepad[" + gamepad.index + "] axis "
                    + i + " = " + gamepad.axes[i]);
            state.axes[i] = gamepad.axes[i];
        }
    }
}
```

You can find a complete example using these functions in the file 07-gamepad.html in the archive for this chapter.

Building the Input Module

The input module is responsible for capturing user input in the form of keyboard, mouse, and touch events and translating these events into a set of game events. For example, using the mouse to click on the game board triggers a "select jewel" event in the game. Tapping the touch screen on a mobile device triggers the same event. Other modules, such as the game screen module, can then bind handler functions to these events so that the appropriate actions are taken when the user interacts with the game.

To begin building the input module, start by creating a new module and placing it in the file input.js. Listing 8-10 shows the initial contents of this module.

Listing 8-10   **The input module**

```
jewel.input = (function() {
    var inputHandlers;

    function initialize() {
        inputHandlers = {};
    }

    function bind(action, handler) {
        // bind a handler function to a game action
    }

    function trigger(action) {
        // trigger a game action
    }

    return {
        initialize : initialize,
        bind: bind
    };
})();
```

Load the new file in index.html:

```
window.addEventListener("load", function() {
    jewel.load("scripts/dom.js");
    if (jewel.isStandalone()) {
        ...
        jewel.load("scripts/input.js");
    } else {
        ...
    }
});
```

Call the initialize() function from the game screen module in screen.game.js:

```
jewel.screens["game-screen"] = (function() {
    ...
    function setup() {
        ...
        jewel.input.initialize();
    }
    ...
})();
```

To create control bindings between input events and game actions, you give each input a keyword. For example, mouse clicks have the input keyword CLICK, a press of the Enter key has the keyword KEY_ENTER, and so on. The controls structure is stored in the game settings in index.html, as shown in Listing 8-11.

Listing 8-11   **Defining control bindings**

```
var jewel = (function() {
    var settings = {
        ...
        controls : {
            // keyboard
            KEY_UP : "moveUp",
            KEY_LEFT : "moveLeft",
            KEY_DOWN : "moveDown",
            KEY_RIGHT : "moveRight",
            KEY_ENTER : "selectJewel",
            KEY_SPACE : "selectJewel",
            // mouse and touch
            CLICK : "selectJewel",
            TOUCH : "selectJewel",
            // gamepad
            BUTTON_A: "selectJewel",
            LEFT_STICK_UP: "moveUp",
            LEFT_STICK_DOWN: "moveDown",
            LEFT_STICK_LEFT: "moveLeft",
            LEFT_STICK_RIGHT: "moveRight"
        }
    }
    ...
})();
```

Using keywords this way, you can change the game controls without having to modify the game code. You could even enable user-defined controls, optionally saving them in the local browser storage.

You use the bind() function, discussed in a bit, to attach handler functions to game actions. For example, a game action might employ the keyword selectJewel. Whenever the input module detects user input that should trigger that action, all the handler functions are called one by one.

The inputHandlers object keeps track of the bindings between input events and game actions. For each game action, a property on the inputHandlers object is an array of all the handler functions associated with that action. For example, inputHandlers·["selectJewel"] holds all the functions you need to call when the selectJewel action happens.

The other empty function, trigger(), does the function calling. You will implement this function later in this chapter. It simply takes an action name as its argument and calls any functions in the corresponding array in inputHandlers. If trigger() is called with any additional arguments, they are passed on to the handler functions. This way, handler functions can have access to information such as coordinates in the case of mouse events.

Handling input events

Jewel Warrior supports four types of input: mouse, keyboard, touch, and gamepad. The mouse and keyboard events make sense only on the desktop, and touch events, for the most part at least, are relevant only on mobile devices, which means there's some overlap of reactions to these input events. Because the input mechanics in this game are very simple, a user should be able to play the game using just one type of input.

Mouse input

The only type of mouse input you need to consider for Jewel Warrior is clicking, so the only mouse event that you need to worry about is the mousedown event. You could also listen for the click event, but because it fires only when the mouse button is released, using the mousedown event can make the game appear a bit more responsive. When the user clicks the jewel board and a game action is bound to the CLICK event, the handler functions for this action must be called. Listing 8-12 shows the DOM event handler added to the initialize() function in input.js.

Listing 8-12   **Capturing mouse clicks**

```
jewel.input = (function() {
    ...
    function initialize() {
        var dom = jewel.dom,
            $ = dom.$,
            controls = jewel.settings.controls,
            board = $("#game-screen .game-board")[0];

        inputHandlers = {};
        dom.bind(board, "mousedown", function(event) {
            handleClick(event, "CLICK", event);
        });
    }
    ...
})();
```

The DOM event object is passed on to a second function, handleClick(), along with the name of the game action. This behavior happens so that the same logic can be reused for touch events. The handleClick() function calculates the relative coordinates of the click and, from those, the jewel coordinates. Finally, the action is triggered, sending the jewel coordinates as parameters. Listing 8-13 shows the handleClick() function.

Listing 8-13 Handling click events

```
jewel.input = (function() {
    ...
    function handleClick(event, control, click) {
        // is any action bound to this input control?
        var settings = jewel.settings,
            action = settings.controls[control];
        if (!action) {
            return;
        }

        var board = jewel.dom.$("#game-screen .game-board")[0],
            rect = board.getBoundingClientRect(),
            relX, relY,
            jewelX, jewelY;

        // click position relative to board
        relX = click.clientX - rect.left;
        relY = click.clientY - rect.top;
        // jewel coordinates
        jewelX = Math.floor(relX / rect.width * settings.cols);
        jewelY = Math.floor(relY / rect.height * settings.rows);
        // trigger functions bound to action
        trigger(action, jewelX, jewelY);
        // prevent default click behavior
        event.preventDefault();
    }
    ...
})();
```

Touch input

The touch event functionality is almost identical to the mouse event handling. Instead of the mousedown event, you now listen for the touchstart event and use the input keyword TOUCH. Instead of passing the event object as the third argument to handleClick(), you must now pass the relevant touch object, event.targetTouches[0]. Listing 8-14 shows how.

Listing 8-14 Capturing touch input

```
jewel.input = (function() {
    ...
    function initialize() {
        var dom = jewel.dom,
            $ = dom.$,
            board = $("#game-screen .game-board")[0];

        inputHandlers = {};
        dom.bind(board, "mousedown", function(event) {
            handleClick(event, "CLICK", event);
        });
        dom.bind(board, "touchstart", function(event) {
            handleClick(event, "TOUCH", event.targetTouches[0]);
        });
    }
    ...
})();
```

Because event objects and touch objects both store their coordinates in clientX and clientY properties and those are the only properties used in handleClick(), passing both kinds of objects is safe.

Keyboard input

You can use a few different events to detect keystrokes. The keydown, keyup, and keypress events all fire, but the various browsers don't always agree on how to handle the keypress event. The keyup and keydown events are both reliable, but keydown usually responds better because it fires as soon as the key is pressed. The event object that this event creates has a keyCode property that holds the numeric code of the key that was pressed. For example, the following snippet alerts the key code when you press any key:

```
element.addEventListener("keydown", function(event) {
    alert("You pressed: " + event.keyCode);
}, false);
```

Working with numeric codes can get a bit confusing, and remembering which keys have which codes is hard. To make this code a bit easier to work with, you can use a structure that maps codes to key names. Listing 8-15 shows a keys object that does just that.

Listing 8-15 **Adding key codes**

```
jewel.input = (function() {
    var keys = {
        37 : "KEY_LEFT",
        38 : "KEY_UP",
        39 : "KEY_RIGHT",
        40 : "KEY_DOWN",
        13 : "KEY_ENTER",
        32 : "KEY_SPACE",
        65 : "KEY_A",
        66 : "KEY_B",
        67 : "KEY_C",
        /* ... alpha keys 68 - 87 ... */
        88 : "KEY_X",
        89 : "KEY_Y",
        90 : "KEY_Z"
    };
    ...
})();
```

The alphabetical A–Z keys have sequential codes, starting at 65 for the A key and going up to 90 for the Z key. I defined only these as well as a few special keys such as the arrow keys, Enter, and space.

You can now use these key names as input keywords together with the CLICK and TOUCH events you've already implemented. Now, you just listen for the keydown event and trigger the appropriate action, as shown in Listing 8-16.

Listing 8-16 **Capturing keyboard input**

```
jewel.input = (function() {
    ...
    function initialize() {
        var controls = jewel.settings.controls,
        ...
        dom.bind(document, "keydown", function(event) {
            var keyName = keys[event.keyCode];
            if (keyName && controls[keyName]) {
                event.preventDefault();
                trigger(controls[keyName]);
            }
        });
    }
    ...
})();
```

Gamepad input

You can use the polling technique discussed earlier in this chapter to add gamepad support to the input module. First, you need to detect whether gamepads are supported by the browser; if they are, you start polling for changes. Listing 8-17 shows the changes to input.js.

Listing 8-17   Detecting support for gamepads

```
jewel.input = (function() {
    var gpStates,
        gpPoller,
        ...

    function initialize() {
        ...
        if (getGamepads()) {
            gpStates = [];
            if (!gpPoller) {
                gpPoller = setInterval(pollGamepads, 1000/60);
                // workaround to make Firefox register gamepads
                window.addEventListener("gamepadconnected",
                                        function(){}, false);
            }
        }
    }

    function getGamepads() {
        if (navigator.gamepads) {
            return navigator.gamepads;
        } else if (navigator.getGamepads) {
            return navigator.getGamepads();
        } else if (navigator.webkitGetGamepads) {
            return navigator.webkitGetGamepads();
        }
    }

    function pollGamepads() {}

    function gamepadConnected() {}

    function gamepadDisconnected() {}

    ...
})();
```

The initialize() function simply uses the getGamepads() function for feature detection. If getGamepads() returns anything, you can assume gamepad support and use setInterval() to start continuously calling pollGamepads(). You can simply copy pollGamepads() along with gamepadConnected() and gamepadDisconnected() from the example earlier in this chapter. The updateGamepadState() function is a bit different and is shown in Listing 8-18.

Listing 8-18 Detecting button and axis changes

```
jewel.input = (function() {
    ...
    function updateGamepadState(gamepad) {
        var state = gpStates[gamepad.index];
        for (var i=0;i<gamepad.buttons.length;i++) {
            if (gamepad.buttons[i] != state.buttons[i]) {
                state.buttons[i] = gamepad.buttons[i];
                if (state.buttons[i]) {
                    gamepadButtonDown(gamepad, i);
                }
            }
        }
        for (var i=0;i<gamepad.axes.length;i++) {
            if (gamepad.axes[i] != state.axes[i]) {
                state.axes[i] = gamepad.axes[i];
                gamepadAxisChange(gamepad, i, state.axes[i]);
            }
        }
    }
    ...
})();
```

The gamepadButtonDown() function is called for buttons that have changed their value from 0 to 1, meaning that they were pressed. The gamepadAxisChange() is called for all axes that have changed in any way. Listing 8-19 shows these two functions.

Listing 8-19 Triggering gamepad actions

```
jewel.input = (function() {
    ...
    function gamepadButtonDown(gamepad, buttonIndex) {
        var gpButtons = {
                0:  "BUTTON_A"
            },
```

continued

Listing 8-19   **continued**

```
            controls = jewel.settings.controls,
            button = gpButtons[buttonIndex];
        if (button && controls[button]) {
            trigger(controls[button]);
        }
    }

    function gamepadAxisChange(gamepad, axisIndex, axisValue) {
        var controls = jewel.settings.controls,
            controlName;
        if (axisIndex === 0 && axisValue === -1) {
            controlName = "LEFT_STICK_LEFT";
        } else if (axisIndex === 0 && axisValue === 1) {
            controlName = "LEFT_STICK_RIGHT";
        } else if (axisIndex === 1 && axisValue === -1) {
            controlName = "LEFT_STICK_UP";
        } else if (axisIndex === 1 && axisValue === 1) {
            controlName = "LEFT_STICK_DOWN";
        }
        if (controlName && controls[controlName]) {
            trigger(controls[controlName]);
        }
    }
    ...
})();
```

The gamepadButtonDown() function searches the button index to see whether any game actions were bound to the corresponding button name. Similarly, the gamepadAxis-Change() identifies the control name from the axis index and the axis value and uses that information to trigger all actions bound to the stick direction.

Implementing game actions

Now it's time to revisit the game screen module in screen.game.js and start implementing action handlers for the input events.

You need to add a new piece of information to the game screen module. When the user clicks on the jewel board, the jewel at that location is activated. You can use a simple object to hold the information about where the cursor is and whether the jewel at that position is active. Listing 8-20 shows the cursor object and its initialization.

Listing 8-20   **Initializing the cursor**

```
jewel.screens["game-screen"] = (function() {
    var firstRun = true,
        paused,
        cursor;

    function startGame() {
        var board = jewel.board,
            display = jewel.display;
        board.initialize(function() {
            display.initialize(function() {
                cursor = {
                    x : 0,
                    y : 0,
                    selected : false
                };
                display.redraw(board.getBoard(), function() {
                    // do nothing for now
                });
            });
        });
    }
    ...
})();
```

The cursor object has three properties. The x and y properties are the jewel coordinates, and the selected property is a Boolean value indicating whether the jewel is selected or whether the cursor is just sitting passively at that position. If the jewel is selected, the game tries to swap with the next activated jewel.

You also need an easy way to update these cursor values. Listing 8-21 shows a setCursor() function that sets the cursor values and tells the game display to update the rendering of the cursor.

Listing 8-21   **Setting the cursor properties**

```
jewel.screens["game-screen"] = (function() {
    ...
    function setCursor(x, y, select) {
        cursor.x = x;
        cursor.y = y;
        cursor.selected = select;
    }
    ...
})();
```

Selecting jewels

The input module can trigger the following actions:

- `selectJewel`

- `moveLeft`

- `moveRight`

- `moveUp`

- `moveDown`

The `selectJewel` action selects a jewel on the board or, if possible, swaps two jewels in case another jewel is already selected. The `move*` actions move the cursor around the board.

A player can select a jewel on the board in various ways. For example, tapping the jewel on the touch screen and clicking it with the mouse both trigger the `selectJewel` game action. This action should call a `selectJewel()` function that determines the appropriate action. Listing 8-22 shows the code for the function.

Listing 8-22   Selecting jewels

```
jewel.screens["game-screen"] = (function() {
    ...
    function selectJewel(x, y) {
        if (arguments.length === 0) {
            selectJewel(cursor.x, cursor.y);
            return;
        }
        if (cursor.selected) {
            var dx = Math.abs(x - cursor.x),
                dy = Math.abs(y - cursor.y),
                dist = dx + dy;

            if (dist === 0) {
                // deselected the selected jewel
                setCursor(x, y, false);
            } else if (dist == 1) {
                // selected an adjacent jewel
                jewel.board.swap(cursor.x, cursor.y,
                    x, y, playBoardEvents);
                setCursor(x, y, false);
            } else {
                // selected a different jewel
```

```
                setCursor(x, y, true);
            }
        } else {
            setCursor(x, y, true);
        }
    }
    ...
})();
```

If another jewel was already selected, you can use the distance between the two jewels to determine the appropriate action. As noted earlier in the board module, a distance of 1 means that the two positions are adjacent, a distance of 0 means that the same jewel is selected again, and any other distance means that some other jewel is selected. If the player selects the same jewel twice, the jewel is deselected by calling the setCursor() function with false as the value of the selected parameter. If the selected jewel is a neighbor of the position already selected, you try to swap the two jewels by calling the board.swap() function. The fifth argument to the swap() method is the callback function. Here, a function called playBoardEvents() is passed. (I get to that function in a bit.) The final case, in which a very different jewel is selected, you simply move the cursor to that position and enable the selected parameter.

The playBoardEvents() function passed to board.swap() is called whenever the board module finishes moving jewels and updating the board data. The swap() function calls its callback function with a single argument, which is an array of all the events that take place between the board's old and new state. You can now use those events to, for example, animate the display. Later, you also see how to add sound effects to these board events, but right now, look at the function in Listing 8-23.

Listing 8-23   **Sending board changes to the display**

```
jewel.screens["game-screen"] = (function() {

    ...
    function playBoardEvents(events) {
        var display = jewel.display;
        if (events.length > 0) {
            var boardEvent = events.shift(),
                next = function() {
                    playBoardEvents(events);
                };
            switch (boardEvent.type) {
                case "move" :
                    display.moveJewels(boardEvent.data, next);
```
continued

Listing 8-23   continued

```
                    break;
                case "remove" :
                    display.removeJewels(boardEvent.data, next);
                    break;
                case "refill" :
                    display.refill(boardEvent.data, next);
                    break;
                default :
                    next();
                    break;
            }
        } else {
            display.redraw(jewel.board.getBoard(), function() {
                // good to go again
            });
        }
    }
    ...
})();
```

If the events array contains elements, the first event is removed from the array and stored in the boardEvent variable. The next() function is a small helper that calls playBoard-Events() recursively on the rest of the events. The event objects in the events array all have a type property that indicates the type of the event and a data property that holds data relevant to that specific event. Each type of event triggers a different function on the display module. These functions don't exist yet but are all asynchronous functions that you use to animate the display. The next() function is passed as a callback function to make sure the rest of the events are processed after the animation finishes.

Moving the cursor

Now, turn your attention to the functions moveLeft, moveRight, moveUp, and move-Down. As their names imply, they move the cursor a single step in one of the four directions.

To do so, use a generic moveCursor() function that takes two parameters, an x and a y value, and that moves the cursor the specified number of steps along either axis. As was the case with selectJewel(), this function has two different behaviors depending on whether a jewel is currently selected. If the player has already selected a jewel, moveCursor() instead selects the new jewel rather than move the cursor. Because you already have the select Jewel() function, you can just pass the new coordinates on to that function. If no jewel is selected, the position of the cursor is changed by calling setCursor(). The moveCursor() code is shown in Listing 8-24.

Listing 8-24 **Moving the cursor**

```
jewel.screens["game-screen"] = (function() {
    ...
    function moveCursor(x, y) {
        var settings = jewel.settings;
        if (cursor.selected) {
            x += cursor.x;
            y += cursor.y;
            if (x >= 0 && x < settings.cols &&
                y >= 0 && y < settings.rows) {
                selectJewel(x, y);
            }
        } else {
            x = (cursor.x + x + settings.cols) % settings.cols;
            y = (cursor.y + y + settings.rows) % settings.rows;
            setCursor(x, y, false);
        }
    }
    ...
})();
```

Now that the generic `moveCursor()` function is implemented, you can easily add directional move functions that move the cursor in one of the four directions. Depending on the direction, these functions simply add or subtract 1 from one of the cursor coordinates, as shown in Listing 8-25.

Listing 8-25 **Directional move functions**

```
jewel.screens["game-screen"] = (function() {
    ...
    function moveUp() {
        moveCursor(0, -1);
    }

    function moveDown() {
        moveCursor(0, 1);
    }

    function moveLeft() {
        moveCursor(-1, 0);
    }
```

continued

Listing 8-25 **continued**
```
    function moveRight() {
        moveCursor(1, 0);
    }
    ...
})();
```

Binding inputs to game functions

With both the game functions and input events defined, you can return to the input module
in input.js and bind the two sets together in the inputHandlers object. First, implement the bind() function introduced earlier in this chapter. This function takes two parameters: the name of a game action and a function that should be attached to that action. You
can see the function in Listing 8-26.

Listing 8-26 **The bind function**
```
jewel.input = (function() {
    ...
    function bind(action, handler) {
        if (!inputHandlers[action]) {
            inputHandlers[action] = [];
        }
        inputHandlers[action].push(handler);
    }
    ...
})();
```

Responding to inputs

Next up is the trigger() function, which is also mentioned earlier in this chapter. This is
the function you used in the DOM event handlers to trigger game actions. The trigger()
function shown in Listing 8-27 takes a single argument, the name of a game action, and calls
all handler functions that were bound to that action.

Listing 8-27 **Triggering game functions**
```
jewel.input = (function() {
    ...
    function trigger(action) {
        var handlers = inputHandlers[action],
            args = Array.prototype.slice.call(arguments, 1);
        console.log("Game action: " + action);
        if (handlers) {
```

```
            for (var i=0;i<handlers.length;i++) {
                handlers[i].apply(null, args);
            }
        }
    }
    ...
})();
```

If handlers are bound to the specified action—that is, if a property with that name is on the `inputHandlers` object—all the handler functions are called. Arguments passed to `trigger()` beyond the named `action` argument are extracted by borrowing the `slice()` method from `Array`. The resulting array of argument values is then used when calling the handler functions via `apply()`.

> **NOTE** You need to be careful with error handling in this implementation of `trigger()`, especially if you're making a game or framework where you have no control over the handler functions. If one of the bound handlers fails and throws an error, the loop is interrupted and no other handlers are called. Whether this is a problem will depend on the specific project, but it's something to keep in mind. To ensure that a single, failing handler doesn't keep the other handlers from executing, you can wrap the `apply()` call in a `try-catch` statement. That does, however, add extra overhead to the process.

Initializing the input module

Now, you just need to attach the functions in the game screen module to the action names from the input module, which is where the `input.bind()` method comes in. After initializing the input module in `screen.game.js`, bind the functions to the relevant actions using `bind()`, as shown in Listing 8-28.

Listing 8-28   Binding inputs to game actions

```
jewel.screens["game-screen"] = (function() {
    ...
    function setup() {
        ...
        var input = jewel.input;
        input.initialize();
        input.bind("selectJewel", selectJewel);
        input.bind("moveUp", moveUp);
        input.bind("moveDown", moveDown);
        input.bind("moveLeft", moveLeft);
        input.bind("moveRight", moveRight);
    }
    ...
})();
```

You can now interact with the game, but clicking the jewels gives no visual feedback and try-ing to swap jewels will likely produce errors. It's time to make the board display react to your input.

Rendering the cursor

The input module is now properly linked to the game mechanics, but the display module should also indicate which jewel is currently selected. The display module needs to keep track of the cursor position in much the same way as the game screen module. You mimic that by adding a cursor object to the display module in display.canvas.js.

You access the cursor via the setCursor() function shown in Listing 8-29. If this function is called without parameters, it clears the cursor by setting it to null; otherwise, it updates the coordinates.

Listing 8-29   Adding the cursor to the display module

```
jewel.display = (function() {
    var cursor,
        ...

    function clearCursor() {
        if (cursor) {
            var x = cursor.x,
                y = cursor.y;
            clearJewel(x, y);
            drawJewel(jewels[x][y], x, y);
        }
    }

    function setCursor(x, y, selected) {
        clearCursor();
        if (arguments.length > 0) {
            cursor = {
                x : x,
                y : y,
                selected : selected
            };
        } else {
            cursor = null;
        }
```

```
        renderCursor();
    }

    return {
        initialize : initialize,
        redraw : redraw,
        setCursor : setCursor
    };
})();
```

The clearCursor() function clears the jewel at the cursor position and redraws the jewel.
Listing 8-30 shows the simple clearJewel() helper function. This function simply clears a
square on the canvas at the specified coordinates.

Listing 8-30   Clearing a jewel position

```
jewel.display = (function() {
    ...
    function clearJewel(x, y) {
        ctx.clearRect(
            x * jewelSize, y * jewelSize, jewelSize, jewelSize
        );
    }
    ...
})();
```

Now you're ready to render the cursor. You can indicate where the cursor is in many ways. I
chose simply to add a highlight effect by drawing the jewel an extra time using the lighter
composite operation. Listing 8-31 shows the cursor rendering.

Listing 8-31   The cursor rendering function

```
jewel.display = (function() {
    ...

    function redraw(newJewels, callback) {
        ...
        renderCursor();
    }
```

continued

Listing 8-31   **continued**

```
    function renderCursor() {
        if (!cursor) {
            return;
        }
        var x = cursor.x,
            y = cursor.y;

        clearCursor();

        if (cursor.selected) {
            ctx.save();
            ctx.globalCompositeOperation = "lighter";
            ctx.globalAlpha = 0.8;
            drawJewel(jewels[x][y], x, y);
            ctx.restore();
        }
        ctx.save();
        ctx.lineWidth = 0.05 * jewelSize;
        ctx.strokeStyle = "rgba(250,250,150,0.8)";
        ctx.strokeRect(
            (x + 0.05) * jewelSize, (y + 0.05) * jewelSize,
            0.9 * jewelSize, 0.9 * jewelSize
        );
        ctx.restore();
    }

    ...
})();
```

Now you just need to link the setCursor() function in the game screen module to the one in the display module. Listing 8-32 shows the necessary addition to screen.game.js.

Listing 8-32   **Updating the displayed cursor**

```
jewel.screens["game-screen"] = (function() {
    ...
    function setCursor(x, y, select) {
        cursor.x = x;
        cursor.y = y;
        cursor.selected = select;
        jewel.display.setCursor(x, y, select);
    }
    ...
})();
```

The cursor is now automatically updated and rendered when the user moves it or selects a jewel. Figure 8-1 shows what the cursor looks like.

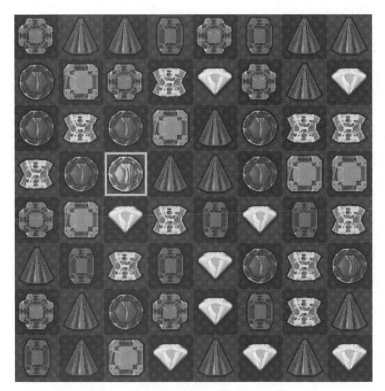

FIGURE 8-1: The currently selected jewel is now highlighted.

Reacting to game actions

The player can now select jewels on the jewel board, but the game fails when the player tries to swap two jewels because the `playBoardEvents()` function calls some display functions that aren't yet implemented. In the next chapter, you find out how to create animated responses to the board events, but for now, you can add simpler versions that just update the board instantly.

The missing functions in `display.canvas.js` are `moveJewels()`, `removeJewels()`, and `refill()`. Listing 8-33 shows the temporary functions.

Listing 8-33　Temporary display functions

```
jewel.display = (function() {
    ...
    function moveJewels(movedJewels, callback) {
        var n = movedJewels.length,
            mover, i;
        for (i=0;i<n;i++) {
            mover = movedJewels[i];
            clearJewel(mover.fromX, mover.fromY);
        }
        for (i=0;i<n;i++) {
            mover = movedJewels[i];
            drawJewel(mover.type, mover.toX, mover.toY);
        }
        callback();
    }

    function removeJewels(removedJewels, callback) {
        var n = removedJewels.length;
        for (var i=0;i<n;i++) {
            clearJewel(removedJewels[i].x, removedJewels[i].y);
        }
        callback();
    }

    return {
        ...
        moveJewels : moveJewels,
        removeJewels : removeJewels,
        refill : redraw
    };

})();
```

The moveJewels() function iterates through all the specified jewels in two separate loops, first clearing the old positions and then drawing the jewels at their new positions. It's important to iterate through two steps; otherwise, you'll accidentally clear a freshly drawn jewel. The removeJewels() function is even simpler because it just clears all the specified positions. The refill() function is an alias of redraw() for now. You will implement an animated refill() function in Chapter 9.

Try loading the game. You can now select jewels and swap them to form chains using mouse, touch, and keyboard input. You may find it difficult to follow the board reactions because the changes happen instantly, but you'll deal with that problem in the next chapter when you implement game animations.

The input module you created in this chapter only manages input on the actual game board. If you want to enable, for example, keyboard navigation on the main menu, you will have to expand the input module to cover more than just the game screen. I will leave that as an extra challenge for you.

Summary

Over the course of this chapter, you learned how to intercept the native input events coming from the browser and turn them into game actions. You read about user input in desktop browsers as well as on touch-enabled mobile devices. With a few simple examples, you saw how to easily create touch-based gestures such as zooming and rotating using the multitouch capabilities in devices like the iPhone. You then found out about the new gamepad API and saw how you can easily add basic gamepad support to your games, even though these features aren't yet fully developed.

You also implemented a cursor object in the Jewel Warriors game and enabled jewel selection and swapping via keyboard, mouse, touch, and gamepad. The game is finally taking shape and now has actual gameplay. In the next chapter, you find out how to make the game more interesting by tying animation and effects to the game actions that you just implemented.

Chapter 9
Animating Game Graphics

In This Chapter

- Creating animation cycles
- Making animations for game actions
- Adding score and level UI elements
- Animating the game timer

YOUR GAME IS now developed to the point that a player can select and swap jewels. It still needs a lot of polish, though, and in this chapter, I show you how to spruce up the game display with some animated effects. First, you find out how to create a basic animation cycle using the animation timing API and its `requestAnimationFrame()` function.

With the basics in place, you see how to implement animations in the canvas display module, including animations for moving and removing jewels and refilling the jewel board.

In the latter part of the chapter, you implement some of the game's missing parts—namely, the points and the game timer. These additions allow you to create the level up and game over events and their animations.

Making the Game React

So far, you've dealt with only the player's actions. In addition, the game must react to what the player does. Most importantly, the display needs to be updated so the player can make her next move. Although you're able to make all the changes instantly, the game is more visually pleasing if the changes are animated so that jewels move smoothly around the board.

Animation timing

The general idea when creating JavaScript-based animations is to set up a function so that it's called repeatedly and quickly enough for the movement to appear smooth. In JavaScript, the easiest way to do so is to use the setInterval() function:

```
function updateAnimation() {
    // update graphic elements
    ...
}
setInterval(updateAnimation, 1000 / 30);
```

This function calls the updateAnimation() function roughly 30 times per second. Alternatively, you can use the setTimeout() function to achieve the same result:

```
function updateAnimation() {
    // update graphic elements
    ...
    setTimeout(updateAnimation, 1000 / 30);
}
setTimeout(updateAnimation, 1000 / 30);
```

The setTimeout() function calls the specified function only once, so the updateAnimation() function needs to set up a new timer for the next animation frame.

A third option is currently being developed by the W3C. Because these timers are used for many purposes other than animations, you'll soon have access to timing functions designed specifically with animation in mind. The specification for the new animation timing API is available at www.w3.org/TR/animation-timing.

This new API is supported in all current versions of the common desktop browsers as well as mobile Safari (beginning with iOS 6) and Android (beginning with Android 4.4). The most important function is the `requestAnimationFrame()` function, which has the following syntax:

```
function updateAnimation(time) {
    // update graphic elements
    ...
    requestAnimationFrame(updateAnimation);
}
requestAnimationFrame(updateAnimation);
```

This function looks a lot like the `setTimeout()` example, but notice that it doesn't have a time argument for specifying when the update function needs to be called. Instead, the update function is called with a `time` argument containing the time (in milliseconds) that the next repaint is scheduled. This time is relative to the time the page loaded.

The `requestAnimationFrame()` function tells the browser to call the specified function when the browser deems best. Therefore, the browser can use its own internal animation cycle and even ensure that CSS and JavaScript animations are synchronized. Because the browser is now free to hold off rendering if the page isn't visible, use of this function also affects use of resources. If the user is looking at another tab, there's no need to spend precious processing time on updating animations. Not updating animations can be significant on mobile devices where both processing power and battery time are limited.

Of course, doing so also means that you can't be sure the update function is actually called, so don't let `requestAnimationFrame()` calls handle critical logic. The traditional `setTimeout()` and `setInterval()` timers are still the best fit for tasks that have side effects that *need* to happen at a specific time.

As mentioned previously, `requestAnimationFrame()` is fully supported in most modern browsers, but some older versions use vendor-prefixed functions, so for the time being, you can't assume that Android supports the new timing API. Fortunately, it's relatively easy to simulate the behavior with a regular `setTimeout()` function for browsers that lack support.

Listing 9-1 shows a polyfill that creates a `requestAnimationFrame()` method on the `window` object if one doesn't already exist. If no implementation is available, the functionality is simulated using a regular `setTimeout()` call.

Listing 9-1 Polyfill for requestAnimationFrame()

```
window.requestAnimationFrame = (function() {
    var startTime = Date.now();
    return window.requestAnimationFrame ||
            window.webkitRequestAnimationFrame ||
            window.mozRequestAnimationFrame ||
            function(callback) {
                return window.setTimeout(
                    function() {
                        callback(Date.now() - startTime);
                    }, 1000 / 60
                );
            };
})();
```

The setTimeout() and setInterval() functions return integer handles that can be used to remove the timers with clearTimeout() and clearInterval(). The new animation timing API borrows this behavior and provides a function for canceling a request, aptly named cancelRequestAnimationFrame(). The polyfill for this function, shown in Listing 9-2, is again straightforward and ultimately falls back to clearTimeout().

Listing 9-2 Polyfill for cancelRequestAnimationFrame()

```
window.cancelRequestAnimationFrame = (function() {
    return window.cancelRequestAnimationFrame ||
            window.webkitCancelRequestAnimationFrame ||
            window.mozCancelRequestAnimationFrame ||
            window.clearTimeout;
})();
```

You can also find the polyfills in the file requestAnimationFrame.js in the code archive for this chapter. To use it, just load it with the other scripts in index.html.

Using requestAnimationFrame()

This section shows a few examples that demonstrate how to use requestAnimation-Frame() to create animations. The first example, shown in Listing 9-3, uses a regular set-Timeout() function to call the animate() function repeatedly.

Listing 9-3   A simple animation with setTimeout()

```
function animate() {
    var element = document.getElementById("anim"),
        time = Date.now();

    // element is assumed to have position:absolute
    element.style.left = (50 + Math.cos(time / 500) * 25) + "%";
    element.style.top = (50 + Math.sin(time / 500) * 25) + "%";

    setTimeout(animate, 1000 / 30);
}
animate();
```

You can find the resulting animation in the file `01-settimeout.html`, which shows a simple `div` moving around in circles. Now look at the example in Listing 9-4. Here, the timer is replaced with `requestAnimationFrame()`.

Listing 9-4   A simple animation with requestAnimationFrame()

```
function animate(time) {
    var element = document.getElementById("anim");

    // element is assumed to have position:absolute
    element.style.left = (50 + Math.cos(time / 500) * 25) + "%";
    element.style.top = (50 + Math.sin(time / 500) * 25) + "%";

    requestAnimationFrame(animate);
}
requestAnimationFrame(animate);
```

This example shows how easily you can replace the old `setTimeout()` calls. The modified example is located in the `02-requestanimationframe.html` file.

The Mozilla implementation of the `requestAnimationFrame()` function offers another way to use it. Instead of supplying a callback function, you call `requestAnimation-Frame()` without parameters. Firefox then fires a special `MozBeforePaint` event on the `window` object when the callback function would have been called, had one been supplied. Instead of passing the current time to the handler function as a parameter, `requestAni-mationFrame()` now makes it available via the `timeStamp` property on the event object. Listing 9-5 shows the example redone to use the Mozilla event.

Listing 9-5   **A simple animation with Mozilla events**

```
function animate(event) {
    var element = document.getElementById("anim"),
        time = event.timeStamp;

    element.style.left = (50 + Math.cos(time / 500) * 25) + "%";
    element.style.top = (50 + Math.sin(time / 500) * 25) + "%";

    requestAnimationFrame();
}

window.addEventListener("MozBeforePaint", animate);

requestAnimationFrame();
```

This method might be useful in some situations, but because it's restricted to Firefox and isn't part of the draft specification, sticking to callback functions is safer.

Creating the animation cycle

Now that you know how to use the timing API, you can use it to create a simple cycle in the display module. Listing 9-6 shows the new cycle() function and the necessary changes to setup().

Listing 9-6   **The animation cycle**

```
jewel.display = (function() {
    var previousCycle,
        ...

    function setup() {
        ...
        previousCycle = Date.now();
        requestAnimationFrame(cycle);
    }

    function cycle() {
        var time = Date.now();
        previousCycle = time;
        requestAnimationFrame(cycle);
    }

    ...
})();
```

Creating an animation cycle is as simple as that. The `cycle()` function doesn't do anything interesting yet; it simply schedules another cycle. The initial call in `setup()` starts the cycle. Note that it also keeps track of the time of the previous cycle. Tracking time is important because you need to know how much time has passed since the last time the animations were updated.

Animating the cursor

The cursor that you implement in Chapter 8 is just a static border around the selected position. A small animation can make it more visually appealing. It doesn't have to be anything advanced; something simple will do just fine. Here, I show you how to enhance the glowing appearance with a pulsating effect. Listing 9-7 shows the new `renderCursor()` function.

Listing 9-7 The modified cursor rendering function

```
jewel.display = (function() {
    ...
    function renderCursor(time) {
        if (!cursor) {
            return;
        }
        var x = cursor.x,
            y = cursor.y,
            t1 = (Math.sin(time / 200) + 1) / 2,
            t2 = (Math.sin(time / 400) + 1) / 2;

        clearCursor();

        if (cursor.selected) {
            ctx.save();
            ctx.globalCompositeOperation = "lighter";
            ctx.globalAlpha = 0.8 * t1;
            drawJewel(jewels[x][y], x, y);
            ctx.restore();
        }
        ctx.save();
        ctx.lineWidth = 0.05 * jewelSize;
        ctx.strokeStyle =
            "rgba(250,250,150," + (0.5 + 0.5 * t2) + ")";
        ctx.strokeRect(
            (x + 0.05) * jewelSize, (y + 0.05) * jewelSize,
            0.9 * jewelSize, 0.9 * jewelSize
        );
        ctx.restore();
    }
    ...
})();
```

Note that `Math.sin()` creates the `t1` and `t2` factors. You can use sines and cosines for many things with animations. Here, the `Math.sin()` function provides an easy way to create values that vary over time, going smoothly from -1 to +1 and back, as shown in Figure 9-1. If you add 1 to the value and divide by 2, as `renderCursor()` does, the range is modified to [0, 1]. You apply these factors to the alpha values when compositing the jewel and when drawing the border rectangle. You can alter the period of the pulse by changing the argument passed to the `Math.sin()` calls.

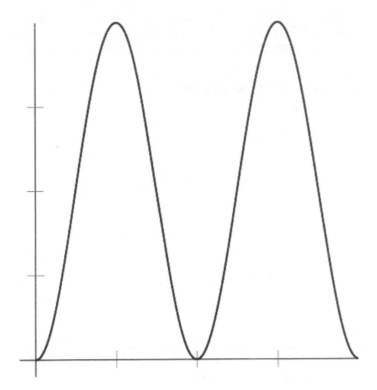

FIGURE 9-1: This visual display represents the cursor pulse.

Now you need to add only the `renderCursor()` function to the animation cycle:

```
function cycle() {
    var time = Date.now();
    renderCursor(time);
    previousCycle = time;
    requestAnimationFrame(cycle);
}
```

The cursor now automatically updates in each cycle. Also, remember to remove the old `renderCursor()` call from the `setCursor()` and `redraw()` functions.

Animating game actions

Next, you must handle five different game animations:

- Moving jewels
- Removing jewels
- Refilling the board
- Advancing to the next level
- Ending the game

Because you haven't implemented the game timer, the game doesn't have a *game over* state. In addition, you don't keep track of the score, so there's no way to advance to the next level. However, you can implement the other three animations right away.

The display module needs to keep track of all currently running animations so they can be rendered during each animation cycle. For that, you use an array called `animations`. The animation cycle doesn't need to know the specifics of each animation; it just needs a reference to a function that it can call in each frame. It also needs to know the amount of time the animation takes. That way, finished animations can automatically be removed from the list. You add animations using the `addAnimation()` function shown in Listing 9-8.

Listing 9-8 Adding animations

```
jewel.display = (function() {
    var animations = [],
        ...

    function addAnimation(runTime, fncs) {
        var anim = {
            runTime : runTime,
            startTime : Date.now(),
            pos : 0,
            fncs : fncs
        };
        animations.push(anim);
    }

    ...
})();
```

Each animation is added to the list as a simple object structure describing the start time, the time it takes to finish, and the fncs property, which holds references to three functions: fncs. before(), fncs.render(), and fncs.done(). These functions are called at various times when the animation is rendering. The pos property is a value in the range [0, 1], indicating the current position of the animation, where 0 is at the beginning and 1 is when the animation is done. The rendering function in Listing 9-9 handles the calls to the fncs functions.

Listing 9-9   Rendering animations

```
jewel.display = (function() {
    ...
    function renderAnimations(time, lastTime) {
        var anims = animations.slice(0), // copy list
            n = anims.length,
            animTime,
            anim,
            i;

        // call before() function
        for (i=0;i<n;i++) {
            anim = anims[i];
            if (anim.fncs.before) {
                anim.fncs.before(anim.pos);
            }
            anim.lastPos = anim.pos;
            animTime = (lastTime - anim.startTime);
            anim.pos = animTime / anim.runTime;
            anim.pos = Math.max(0, Math.min(1, anim.pos));
        }

        animations = []; // reset animation list

        for (i=0;i<n;i++) {
            anim = anims[i];
            anim.fncs.render(anim.pos, anim.pos - anim.lastPos);
            if (anim.pos == 1) {
                if (anim.fncs.done) {
                    anim.fncs.done();
                }
            } else {
                animations.push(anim);
            }
        }
    }
}
```

```
    function cycle() {
        var time = Date.now();
        // hide cursor while animating
        if (animations.length === 0) {
            renderCursor(time);
        }
        renderAnimations(time, previousCycle);
        previousCycle = time;
        requestAnimationFrame(cycle);
    }
    ...
}) ();
```

Each animation object has at least a `render()` function and optionally a `before()` function. The `before()` function is called in each cycle before the `render()` function. The idea is that the `before()` function prepares for the next frame and, if necessary, cleans up after the previous frame. It's important that all animations have their `before()` functions called before any `render()` calls. Otherwise, one animation's `before()` function could interfere with the `render()` function of another.

Every time the animation timer calls `renderAnimations()`, the `animations` array is cleared and rebuilt in the rendering loop. This makes it easy to add only those animations that haven't finished yet. If an animation is done—that is, if its position is at least equal to 1—it's `done()` function is called; otherwise, it's added back into the list.

Moving jewels

When the user swaps jewels and the board is updated, the board module generates game events for each event, such as moving jewels, disappearing jewels, and so on. These events are handled by the `playBoardEvents()` function that you added to the game screen module earlier in this chapter. The code in `screen.game.js` for the move event looked something like this:

```
function playBoardEvents(events) {
    ...
        switch (boardEvent.type) {
            case "move" :
                display.moveJewels(boardEvent.data, next);
                break;
    ...
}
```

However, the board doesn't generate move events if the attempted swap isn't valid. When the swap is invalid, the visual feedback would be improved if the jewels swapped places and then moved back to their original positions.

Now expand the `swap()` function in `board.js` so it generates these extra events. Listing 9-10 shows the new `swap()` function in `board.js`.

Listing 9-10　**Generating move events for invalid swaps**

```
jewel.board = (function() {
    ...
    function swap(x1, y1, x2, y2, callback) {
        var tmp, swap1, swap2,
            events = [];
        swap1 = {
            type : "move",
            data : [{
                type : getJewel(x1, y1),
                fromX : x1, fromY : y1, toX : x2, toY : y2
            }, {
                type : getJewel(x2, y2),
                fromX : x2, fromY : y2, toX : x1, toY : y1
            }]
        };
        swap2 = {
            type : "move",
            data : [{
                type : getJewel(x2, y2),
                fromX : x1, fromY : y1, toX : x2, toY : y2
            }, {
                type : getJewel(x1, y1),
                fromX : x2, fromY : y2, toX : x1, toY : y1
            }]
        };
        if (isAdjacent(x1, y1, x2, y2)) {
            events.push(swap1);
            if (canSwap(x1, y1, x2, y2)) {
                tmp = getJewel(x1, y1);
                jewels[x1][y1] = getJewel(x2, y2);
                jewels[x2][y2] = tmp;
                events = events.concat(check());
            } else {
                events.push(swap2, {type : "badswap"});
            }
            callback(events);
        }
    }
    ...
})();
```

The swap() function now adds a move event to the initial events array so the jewels switch places. If the canSwap() test fails, a second event is added to move the jewels back.

The moveJewels() function is passed an array of jewel objects describing the jewels that it must move. Each jewel object has the following properties:

- type
- fromX
- fromY
- toX
- toY

These properties describe the jewel type and the start and end positions. Now add the moveJewels() function in Listing 9-11 to the display module in display.canvas.js.

Listing 9-11 Animating moving jewels

```
jewel.display = (function() {
    ...
    function moveJewels(movedJewels, callback) {
        var n = movedJewels.length,
            oldCursor = cursor;
        cursor = null;
        movedJewels.forEach(function(e) {
            var x = e.fromX, y = e.fromY,
                dx = e.toX - e.fromX,
                dy = e.toY - e.fromY,
                dist = Math.abs(dx) + Math.abs(dy);
            addAnimation(200 * dist, {
                before : function(pos) {
                    pos = Math.sin(pos * Math.PI / 2);
                    clearJewel(x + dx * pos, y + dy * pos);
                },
                render : function(pos) {
                    pos = Math.sin(pos * Math.PI / 2);
                    drawJewel(
                        e.type,
                        x + dx * pos, y + dy * pos
                    );
                },
                done : function() {
```

continued

Listing 9-11   **continued**

```
                    if (-n == 0) {
                        cursor = oldCursor;
                        callback();
                    }
                }
            });
        });
    }
    ...
})();
```

The main portion of the moveJewels() code iterates through all the specified jewels and sets up an animation for each one. The before method clears the area where the jewel was located in the last frame. The movement factor is calculated using the same Math.sin() trick that you also saw in the cursor rendering. The pos value that is passed to the before and render methods is in the range [0, 1], so the resulting motion eases out nicely at the end. The plot in Figure 9-2 shows a visual representation of the motion factor.

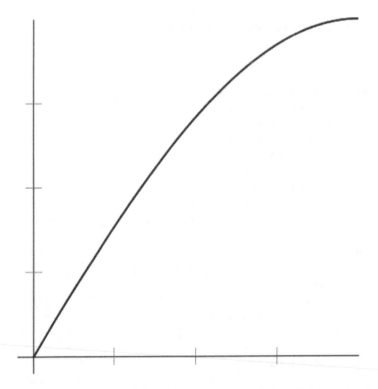

FIGURE 9-2: The motion of the jewels eases out toward the end of the animation.

Removing jewels

The procedure for removing jewels is similar to the one in moveJewels(). The removeJewels() function is passed a list of objects that describe the jewels that need to disappear. Each object has these properties:

- type
- x
- y

The animations are set up so the jewel is cleared before each frame and then redrawn in a scaled-down and rotated version using the canvas transformation methods. See Listing 9-12 for the complete removeJewels() function.

Listing 9-12   Removing jewels

```
jewel.display = (function() {
    ...
    function removeJewels(removedJewels, callback) {
        var n = removedJewels.length;
        removedJewels.forEach(function(e) {
            addAnimation(400, {
                before : function() {
                    clearJewel(e.x, e.y);
                },
                render : function(pos) {
                    ctx.save();
                    ctx.globalAlpha = 1 - pos;
                    drawJewel(
                        e.type, e.x, e.y,
                        1 - pos, pos * Math.PI * 2
                    );
                    ctx.restore();
                },
                done : function() {
                    if (-n == 0) {
                        callback();
                    }
                }
            });
        });
    }
    ...
})();
```

As you can see, the drawJewel() call in render() now has new fourth and fifth arguments. These arguments are the scale and rotation that you want to apply to the jewel before drawing it. Listing 9-13 shows the changes to the drawJewel() function in display.canvas.js.

Listing 9-13   **Adding scaling and rotation to drawJewel()**

```
jewel.display = (function() {
    ...
    function drawJewel(type, x, y, scale, rot) {
        ctx.save();
        if (typeof scale !== "undefined" && scale > 0) {
            ctx.beginPath();
            ctx.translate(
                (x + 0.5) * jewelSize,
                (y + 0.5) * jewelSize
            );
            ctx.scale(scale, scale);
            if (rot) {
                ctx.rotate(rot);
            }
            ctx.translate(
                -(x + 0.5) * jewelSize,
                -(y + 0.5) * jewelSize
            );
        }
        ctx.drawImage(jewelSprite,
            type * jewelSize, 0, jewelSize, jewelSize,
            x * jewelSize, y * jewelSize,
            jewelSize, jewelSize
        );
        ctx.restore();
    }
    ...
})();
```

In Chapter 6, you learned how to use the canvas and its various transformation methods. So, if you've worked through that chapter, you shouldn't have a problem with the added transformations. In removeJewels(), the scale argument is passed as (1 - pos), which makes the value go from 1 to 0 as the animation progresses. The pos value is also used in the rot argument, only it's multiplied by 2 pi to get a full 360 degrees of rotation.

Now that you can add a scaling factor when drawing jewels, try adding a scale value of 1.1 or
so in the `renderCursor()` function. The result is a more glowing appearance. **TIP**

Refilling the board

When the board module detects that no valid moves are left, it sends a `refill` event. The argument sent along with the event contains the jewels that make up the new board. For the refill animation, I used a mix of canvas animation and CSS 3D transforms. Look at the `refill()` function in Listing 9-14. As in the `moveJewels()` and `removeJewels()` functions, this example sets up an animation using `addAnimation()`. The `render()` function does two things: It replaces all the old jewels with the new ones and rotates the board around the x-axis.

Listing 9-14 Refilling the board with fresh jewels

```
jewel.display = (function() {
    ...
    function refill(newJewels, callback) {
        var lastJewel = 0;
        addAnimation(1000, {
            render : function(pos) {
                var thisJewel = Math.floor(pos * cols * rows),
                    i, x, y;
                for (i = lastJewel; i < thisJewel; i++) {
                    x = i % cols;
                    y = Math.floor(i / cols);
                    clearJewel(x, y);
                    drawJewel(newJewels[x][y], x, y);
                }
                lastJewel = thisJewel;
                jewel.dom.transform(canvas,
                    "rotateX(" + (360 * pos) + "deg)");
            },
            done : function() {
                canvas.style.webkitTransform = "";
                callback();
            }
        });
    }
    ...
    return {
        ...
        refill : refill
    }
})();
```

The rotation is done with a 3D CSS transformation. The CSS `rotateX()`, `rotateY()`, and `rotateZ()` transformations all rotate the element a number of degrees around their axes. The `jewel.dom.transform()` function is just a shortcut for the vendor-specific versions. Add the function to `dom.js`:

```
jewel.dom = (function() {
    ...
    function transform(element, value) {
        if ("transform" in element.style) {
            element.style.transform = value;
        } else if ("webkitTransform" in element.style) {
            element.style.webkitTransform = value;
        } else if ("mozTransform" in element.style) {
            element.style.mozTransform = value;
        } else if ("msTransform" in element.style) {
            element.style.msTransform = value;
        }
    }
    return {
        ...
        transform : transform
    };
})();
```

To get the right 3D effect, however, you must add some depth to the rotation, which you do by setting the `perspective` property on a parent element. Simply add the following to the `.game-board` rule in `main.css`:

```
/* Game screen */
#game-screen .game-board {
    ...
    perspective : 16em;
    -webkit-perspective : 16em;
    -moz-perspective : 16em;
    -ms-perspective : 16em;
}
```

You can play around with the value to alter the appearance of the 3D effect. Smaller values make it appear more flat, whereas a high value increases the effect. The refill animation finishes in the `done()` method by resetting the CSS transformation and calling the callback function to let the caller know that it's done. Figure 9-3 shows a frame from the refill animation.

FIGURE 9-3: This animation flips the board.

To test the refill animation without having to play until a refill is automatically triggered, you trigger the animation manually by entering the following into the JavaScript console:

```
jewel.display.refill(jewel.board.getBoard(), function(){})
```

It doesn't replace the jewels with new ones, but you can see the CSS rotation.

Adding Points and Time

The player can now swap jewels, and the board display reacts nicely. The game has no real goal, however. You still need to implement a timer that counts down and threatens to end the game early, and you need to award the player points so that he gets the feeling of progressing as he advances to higher levels. All this game data should be visible to the player and be constantly updated. The actual values are maintained in the game screen module in a simple object that contains the current level and score as well as a few properties for keeping track of the game timer. The values need to be reset every time a new game starts, which you do in the startGame() function shown in Listing 9-15.

Listing 9-15   **Initializing the game info and starting the game**

```
jewel.screens["game-screen"] = (function() {
    var gameState,
        ...
    function startGame() {
        var board = jewel.board,
            display = jewel.display;
        gameState = {
            level : 0,
            score : 0,
            timer : 0, // setTimeout reference
            startTime : 0, // time at start of level
            endTime : 0 // time to game over
        };
        board.initialize(function() {
            display.initialize(function() {
                cursor = {
                    x : 0,
                    y : 0,
                    selected : false
                };
                display.redraw(board.getBoard(), function() {});
            });
        });
    }
    ...
})();
```

Creating the UI elements

Before you can start using the game state object, you need a few more DOM elements on the game screen. Listing 9-16 shows the modified HTML code for the game screen in index. html. The new elements include labels for the current level and score as well as a progress bar you use for the game timer.

Listing 9-16   **Adding new interface elements on the game screen**

```
<div id="game">
    ...
    <div class="screen" id="game-screen">
        <div class="game-board"></div>
        <div class="game-info">
            <label class="level">Level: <span></span></label>
```

```
            <label class="score">Score: <span></span></label>
        </div>
        <div class="time"><div class="indicator"></div></div>
        ...
    </div>
</div>
```

In the future, when the new HTML5 elements are more universally supported, you'll be able to use the more semantic output element instead of span in the label elements. You'll also get the progress element, which simplifies implementing various kinds of progress bars. The CSS to go along with the new markup goes in main.css and is shown in Listing 9-17.

Listing 9-17 **Styling the game info elements**
```
/* Game screen - Game state */
#game-screen .game-info {
    width : 100%;
    float : left;
}

#game-screen .game-info label {
    display : inline-block;
    height : 1.5em;
    float : left;
    font-size : 0.6em;
    padding : 0.25em;
}

#game-screen .game-info .score {
    float : right;
}

#game-screen .time {
    height : 0.25em;
    border-radius : 0.5em;
}

#game-screen .time .indicator {
    width : 100%;
}
```

The new CSS rules aren't particularly interesting. They simply arrange the elements below the game board and style the time bar to look a bit like the progress bar on the splash screen. Figure 9-4 shows the new elements.

FIGURE 9-4: The new UI elements. The jewels appear above the time bar.

This setup works well in a desktop browser or when you're viewing the game in portrait mode on a mobile device. However, if you rotate the device to landscape mode, the layout isn't ideal. You can use CSS media queries to target only landscape mode. Add the rules in Listing 9-18 to mobile.css to improve the looks of the landscape mode.

Listing 9-18　**Adjusting the UI for large screens**

```
@media (orientation: landscape) {
    #game-screen .game-board {
        float : left;
    }
}
```

```css
#game-screen .game-info {
    width : auto;
    height : 2em;
    white-space : nowrap;
}

#game-screen .game-info label {
    font-size : 0.5em;
}

#game-screen .game-info .score {
    float : left;
    clear : both;
}
 #game-screen .time {
    margin : 0;
    position: absolute;
    top : 2.0em;
    left: 8.7em;
    width : 5em;
    /* vendor specific transforms */
    -webkit-transform : rotate(-90deg)
        translate(-2.5em, -2.5em);
    -moz-transform : rotate(-90deg)
        translate(-2.5em, -2.5em);
    -ms-transform : rotate(-90deg)
        translate(-2.5em, -2.5em);
    /* standard transform */
    transform : rotate(-90deg) translate(-2.5em, -2.5em);
}

#game-screen footer button.exit {
    float: right;
}
}
```

The level and score labels now automatically move to the upper-right corner to take advantage of the extra horizontal space in landscape mode. The timer bar gets a special treatment because it's rotated 90 degrees, which allows it to maintain its full size even as it's moved to the narrow space next to the board. Figure 9-5 shows the result in landscape mode on a smartphone.

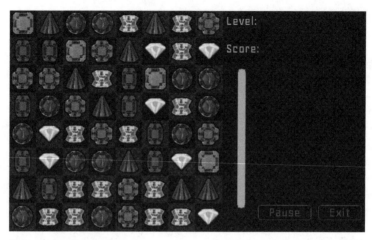

FIGURE 9-5: The game UI elements automatically adjust to landscape mode.

You can now update these elements with the current values. First, they should be updated at the beginning of the game, so create an `updateGameInfo()` function that updates the score and level elements as shown in Listing 9-19.

Listing 9-19   Updating the game info

```
jewel.screens["game-screen"] = (function() {
    ...
    function startGame() {
        ...
        updateGameInfo();
        board.initialize(function() {
            ...
        });
    }

    function updateGameInfo() {
        var $ = jewel.dom.$;
        $("#game-screen .score span")[0].innerHTML =
            gameState.score;
        $("#game-screen .level span")[0].innerHTML =
            gameState.level;
    }
    ...
})();
```

The updateGameInfo() call in startGame() resets the display to the initial values when a new game starts.

Creating the game timer

Now you can move on to the game timer. When the game starts, the timer must slowly count down, and when it reaches the end, the game is over. Visually, this animation is represented by the timer progress bar going from full to empty. The only way for the player to stay alive is to score enough points to advance to the next level and make the timer reset. To make the game more and more difficult, you need to speed up the timer as the game progresses. First, add a base time to the game settings in jewel.js:

```
var jewel = (function() {
    var settings = {
        ...,
        baseLevelTimer : 60000
    }
    ...
})();
```

This value is the time in milliseconds for the first level. As the level number increases, the amount of time decreases, but it's still based on this one base number.

When you need to update the timer progress bar, the timer value must be converted to a relative value. You can then use this relative value to adjust the width of the inner element using percentages. Listing 9-20 shows the timer update function in screen.game.js.

Listing 9-20   Checking and updating the game timer
```
jewel.screens["game-screen"] = (function() {
    ...
    function setLevelTimer(reset) {
        var $ = jewel.dom.$;
        if (gameState.timer) {
            clearTimeout(gameState.timer);
            gameState.timer = 0;
        }
        if (reset) {
            gameState.startTime = Date.now();
            gameState.endTime =
                settings.baseLevelTimer *
                Math.pow(gameState.level,
                    -0.05 * gameState.level);
        }
```

continued

Listing 9-20   **continued**

```
        var delta = gameState.startTime +
                    gameState.endTime - Date.now(),
            percent = (delta / gameState.endTime) * 100,
            progress = $("#game-screen .time .indicator")[0];
        if (delta < 0) {
            gameOver();
        } else {
            progress.style.width = percent + "%";
            gameState.timer = setTimeout(setLevelTimer, 30);
        }
    }

    function startGame() {
        ...
        updateGameInfo();
        setLevelTimer(true);
        ...
    }
    ...
})();
```

If `setLevelTimer()` is called with the reset flag, it resets the timer based on the current level. The `startTime` value is simply the current time, which is saved so that later calls can calculate how much time has passed. The `endTime` value represents how much time the player is given at this particular level. Because of the negative exponent, the value of the `Math.pow()` expression decreases as the level number increases.

Regardless of the reset flag, the function then calculates how much time has passed since the timer was set. Dividing this number with the total time given for this level gives you a number from 0 to 1, which you can then use to set the CSS width of the inner element of the timer progress bar. If more time has passed than was allowed, the timer function then calls a `gameOver()` function to end the game. I show you the implementation of the game over function later in this chapter. If the player is still alive, a new `setTimeout()` call sets up the next timer check.

The reason you're not using `requestAnimationFrame()` here instead of `setTimeout()` is that the timer functionality is a bit more critical than animations. Remember that the browser may not update any of the animations if its resources are needed elsewhere.

Pausing the game

The pause button doesn't actually temporarily stop the game yet. It needs to halt both the game timer and any animations that may be playing. If you simply choose not to update the animations and the timer while the game is paused, you also need to take the lost time into consideration when resuming the game. Because both the game timer and the animations depend on their start times, you need to offset this time when the game resumes so that animations don't finish instantly and the game isn't suddenly over just because the player paused it for a bit.

One way to do this is by calculating the time the game has been paused and then adding that to the start time when resuming. You will also want to disallow any game actions such as moving the cursor or selecting jewels while the game is paused. Listing 9-21 shows the changes to screen.game.js.

Listing 9-21   Pausing the game timer

```javascript
jewel.screens["game-screen"] = (function() {
    var paused,
        pauseStart,
        . . .

    function pauseGame() {
        . . .
        paused = true;
        pauseStart = Date.now();
        clearTimeout(gameState.timer);
        jewel.display.pause();
    }

    function resumeGame() {
        . . .
        var pauseTime = Date.now() - pauseStart;
        gameState.startTime += pauseTime;
        setLevelTimer();
        jewel.display.resume(pauseTime);
    }

    function selectJewel(x, y) {
        if (paused) {
            return;
        }
        . . .
    }
```

continued

Listing 9-21   **continued**

```
    function moveCursor(x, y) {
        if (paused) {
            return;
        }
        ...
    }
    ...
})();
```

To pause the animations, you add pause and resume functions to the display module. These functions don't need to track the time because they can simply use the `pauseTime` value calculated by the game screen module. When the game display is resumed, it will run through all the active animations and add the pause time to the `startTime` value on the animation objects. Listing 9-22 shows the changes to `display.canvas.js`.

Listing 9-22   **Pausing animations in the display module**

```
jewel.display = (function() {
    var paused,
        ...

    function initialize(callback) {
        paused = false;
        ...
    }

    function cycle() {
        var now = Date.now();
        if (!paused) {
            // hide cursor while animating
            if (animations.length === 0) {
                renderCursor(now);
            }
            renderAnimations(now, previousCycle);
        }

        previousCycle = now;
        requestAnimationFrame(cycle);
    }

    function pause() {
        paused = true;
    }
```

```
function resume(pauseTime) {
    paused = false;
    for (var i=0;i<animations.length;i++) {
        animations[i].startTime += pauseTime;
    }
}

return {
    ...
    pause : pause,
    resume : resume
}
})();
```

The `cycle()` function has also been modified so it doesn't call the `renderCursor()` and `renderAnimations()` functions when the game is paused. If you pause the game in the middle of an animation, the animation stops and resumes where it left off when you resume the game.

Awarding points

In Chapter 4, when you implemented the jewel-swapping logic, you made it register both jewel-related events and the points that are awarded. The `playBoardEvents()` function handles the score event, so add a case for that event as well, as shown in Listing 9-23.

Listing 9-23   **Awarding points**
```
jewel.screens["game-screen"] = (function() {
    ...
    function playBoardEvents(events) {
        var display = jewel.display;
        if (events.length > 0) {
            var boardEvent = events.shift(),
                next = function() {
                    playBoardEvents(events);
                };
            switch (boardEvent.type) {
                case "move" :
                    display.moveJewels(boardEvent.data, next);
                    break;
                case "remove" :
                    display.removeJewels(boardEvent.data, next);
                    break;
```

continued

Listing 9-23 **continued**

```
                case "refill" :
                    display.refill(boardEvent.data, next);
                    break;
                case "score" : // new score event
                    addScore(boardEvent.data);
                    next();
                    break;
                default :
                    next();
                    break;
            }
        } else {
            display.redraw(jewel.board.getBoard(), function() {
                // good to go again
            });
        }
    }
    ...
})();
```

Updating the UI score element is straightforward, as shown in Listing 9-24.

Listing 9-24 **Updating the score**

```
jewel.screens["game-screen"] = (function() {
    ...
    function addScore(points) {
        gameState.score += points;
        updateGameInfo();
    }
    ...
})();
```

Leveling up

The player should advance to the next level when she reaches certain numbers of points. For this, you need some more functionality in the addScore() function. Modify the function as shown in Listing 9-25.

Listing 9-25   Checking the number of points

```
jewel.screens["game-screen"] = (function() {
    ...
    function addScore(points) {
        var settings = jewel.settings,
            nextLevelAt = Math.pow(
                settings.baseLevelScore,
                Math.pow(settings.baseLevelExp,
                    gameState.level-1)
            );
        gameState.score += points;
        if (gameState.score >= nextLevelAt) {
            advanceLevel();
        }
        updateGameInfo();
    }
    ...
})();
```

The modified `addScore()` function uses two new values that you must add to the settings in `jewel.js`:

```
var jewel = (function() {
    var settings = {
        baseLevelScore : 1500,
        baseLevelExp : 1.05,
        ...
    }
    ...
})();
```

You use these values to calculate the number of points needed to advance to the next level. When you raise the base `baseLevelScore` to an exponent that increases with each level, the gap between levels becomes greater and greater, further adding to the difficulty of the game. The values I chose give limits of 1500, 2162, 3174, 4750, and 7254 points for the first five levels. Play around with the settings if you'd rather have another distribution.

The `addScore()` function calls an `advanceLevel()` function that increments the level value and sets up a new game timer. Add the `advanceLevel()` function shown in Listing 9-26 to `screen.game.js`, remove the `setLevelTimer()` call from `startGame()`, and call `advanceLevel()` when the display is initialized.

Listing 9-26 **Advancing to the next level**

```
jewel.screens["game-screen"] = (function() {
    ...

    function startGame() {
        ...
        updateGameInfo();
        board.initialize(function() {
            display.initialize(function() {
                display.redraw(board.getBoard(), function() {
                    cursor = {
                        x : 0,
                        y : 0,
                        selected : false
                    };
                    advanceLevel();
                });
            });
        });
    }
    function advanceLevel() {
        gameState.level++;
        updateGameInfo();
        gameState.startTime = Date.now();
        gameState.endTime = jewel.settings.baseLevelTimer *
            Math.pow(gameState.level, -0.05 * gameState.level);
        setLevelTimer(true);
    }
}
```

The `level` value on the `gameInfo` object is 0 at the beginning of the game. The player should advance to level 1 right away, so you also add an initial `advanceLevel()` call to the `startGame()` function, as shown in Listing 9-26. You can then remove the initial call to `setLevelTime()` because `advanceLevel()` has already taken care of that.

The `advanceLevel()` function increments the `level` value and updates the UI elements. Of course, advancing to the next level should trigger some visual feedback. Listing 9-27 shows a new animation added to the display module in `display.canvas.js`.

Listing 9-27 **Adding a visual effect when the level changes**

```
jewel.display = (function() {
    ...
    function levelUp(callback) {
        addAnimation(1000, {
            before : function(pos) {
                var j = Math.floor(pos * rows * 2),
                    x, y;
                for (y=0,x=j;y<rows;y++,x-) {
                    if (x >= 0 && x < cols) { // boundary check
                        clearJewel(x, y);
                        drawJewel(jewels[x][y], x, y);
                    }
                }
            },
            render : function(pos) {
                var j = Math.floor(pos * rows * 2),
                    x, y;
                ctx.save(); // remember to save state
                ctx.globalCompositeOperation = "lighter";
                for (y=0,x=j;y<rows;y++,x-) {
                    if (x >= 0 && x < cols) { // boundary check
                        drawJewel(jewels[x][y], x, y, 1.1);
                    }
                }
                ctx.restore();
            },
            done : callback
        });
    }

    return {
        ...,
        levelUp : levelUp
    };
})();
```

Take a closer look at the loop that appears in both the before and the render functions:

```
var j = Math.floor(pos * rows * 2),
    x, y;
for (y=0,x=j;y<rows;y++,x--) {
    ...
}
```

Because pos goes from 0 to 1, j is an integer value that starts at 0 and ends at (2 * rows). The loop starts at y=0 and x=j. It then moves down the board, and at every row, it moves the x position one step to the left. The result is that the matching jewels form a diagonal row that moves down or across the board during the animation. The before function just clears and redraws the previous jewel, and the render function highlights the currently active jewels by drawing copies on top with the lighter composite operation.

Add the call to the jewel.display.levelUp() function in advanceLevel() in screen.game.js:

```
function advanceLevel() {
    ...
    display.levelUp();
}
```

Announcing game events

Letting the player know that he's moved on to a new level is probably a good idea. The game info labels aren't big enough to ensure that the player notices the change. Add a new div element to the game screen for announcements and give it the class announcement. Listing 9-28 shows the modifications to index.html.

Listing 9-28　**Adding the announcement container**
```
<div id="game">
    ...
    <div class="screen" id="game-screen">
        <div class="game-board">
            <div class="announcement"></div>
        </div>
        ...
    </div>
</div>
```

Now you can add text in that div and make it appear in the middle of the game board so the player doesn't miss it. Add the CSS in Listing 9-29 to main.css to style the announcements.

Listing 9-29　**Styling the announcements**
```
/* Game screen - Announcement */
#game-screen .announcement {
    position : absolute;
    left: 0;
```

```
    top : 50%;
    margin-top : -0.5em;
    width : 100%;

    font-family : Slackey, sans-serif;
    color : rgb(150,150,75);
    text-shadow : 0.03em 0.03em 0.03em rgb(255,255,0),
                  -0.03em -0.03em 0.03em rgb(255,255,0),
                  0.1em 0.15em 0.15em rgb(0,0,0);
    text-align : center;
    white-space : nowrap;

    z-index : 20; /* in front of everything else */
    opacity : 0; /* start out transparent */
    cursor : default;
}
```

This code makes the announcements look nice, but you can do even better and add a zoom and fade animation using a bit of CSS. Listing 9-30 shows how.

Listing 9-30   **Creating a zoom and fade CSS animation**
```
/* Announcement animation */
/* Keyframes for webkit */
@-webkit-keyframes zoomfade {
    0%   { opacity : 1; -webkit-transform : scale(0.5); }
    25%  { opacity : 1; }
    100% { opacity : 0; -webkit-transform : scale(1.5); }
}
/* Keyframes for Firefox */
@-moz-keyframes zoomfade {
    0%   { opacity : 1; -moz-transform : scale(0.5); }
    25%  { opacity : 1; }
    100% { opacity : 0; -moz-transform : scale(1.5); }
}
/* Keyframes for W3C compliant browsers */
@keyframes zoomfade {
    0%   { opacity : 1; transform : scale(0.5); }
    25%  { opacity : 1; }
    100% { opacity : 0; transform : scale(1.5); }
}
```

continued

Listing 9-30   **continued**

```
/* zoom-fade animation class */
.zoomfade {
    animation-name : zoomfade;
    animation-duration : 2s;
    -webkit-animation-name : zoomfade;
    -webkit-animation-duration : 2s;
    -moz-animation-name : zoomfade;
    -moz-animation-duration : 2s;
}
```

These rules declare a CSS animation called zoomfade with three keyframes at 0%, 25%, and 100%. Over the course of the entire animation, the element scales from 0.5 to 1.5. The opacity is also changed but only after the 25% keyframe, which gives the user a better chance of actually reading the text before it fades away. Finally, the CSS assigns the animation to a class called zoomfade and gives it a duration of two seconds. Now you need to attach the zoomfade class to the announcement element in screen.game.js as shown in Listing 9-31. To get the animation to play again the next time you need it, just remove the class and add it again. Be sure you use setTimeout() to add the class so the browser has time to register that it was removed.

Listing 9-31   **Announcing significant events**

```
jewel.screens["game-screen"] = (function() {
    ...
    function announce(str) {
        var dom = jewel.dom,
            $ = dom.$,
            element = $("#game-screen .announcement")[0];
        element.innerHTML = str;
        dom.removeClass(element, "zoomfade");
        setTimeout(function() {
            dom.addClass(element, "zoomfade");
        }, 1);
    }
    ...
})();
```

Now add an announcement to the advanceLevel() function in screen.game.js to let the player know that he's advanced. Listing 9-32 shows where to add the call.

Listing 9-32 **Announcing the next level**

```
jewel.screens["game-screen"] = (function() {
    ...
    function advanceLevel() {
        gameInfo.level++;
        announce("Level " + gameState.level);
        ...
    }
    ...
}
```

Figure 9-6 shows the level announcement.

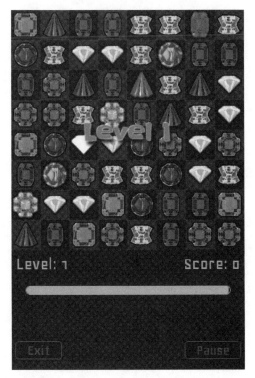

FIGURE 9-6: This announcement lets the player know the game level.

While you're at it, add an announcement when the game board is refilled. You can add the announce() call in playBoardEvents(), as shown in Listing 9-33.

Listing 9-33   Announcing the refill event

```
jewel.screens["game-screen"] = (function() {
    ...
    function playBoardEvents(events) {
        ...
        switch (boardEvent.type) {
            ...
            case "refill" :
                announce("No moves!");
                display.refill(boardEvent.data, next);
                break;
            ...
        }
    }
    ...
})();
```

Game over

When the game ends, there should also be a nice animation. To that end, make the jewel board start shaking and make the jewels seem to explode apart. First, add the missing gameOver() function to screen.game.js:

```
jewel.screens["game-screen"] = (function() {
    ...
    function gameOver() {
        jewel.display.gameOver(function() {
            announce("Game over");
        });
    }
    ...
})();
```

This function tells the display module to play the game animation and then displays an announcement when the animation is done. Listing 9-34 shows the gameOver() function in display.canvas.js.

Listing 9-34 **The game over animation**

```
jewel.display = (function() {
    ...
    function gameOver(callback) {
        addAnimation(1000, {
            render : function(pos) {
                canvas.style.left =
                    0.2 * pos * (Math.random() - 0.5) + "em";
                canvas.style.top =
                    0.2 * pos * (Math.random() - 0.5) + "em";
            },
            done : function() {
                canvas.style.left = "0";
                canvas.style.top = "0";
                explode(callback);
            }
        });
    }
    ...
    return {
        ...
        gameOver : gameOver
    }
})();
```

The render() function in this animation adjusts the position of the jewel board canvas by a small random amount. When you use the animation position as a multiplier, the intensity of the effect increases as the animation progresses. When the animation ends, it passes the callback function on to an explode() function, which sets up the explosion-like behavior.

Create the explosion effect by making all the jewels blow apart in random directions. To do so, you need a list of objects representing the pieces. Each piece should contain information about its current position, its rotation speed, and its current velocity. The position is represented by simple x and y coordinates and starts at the jewel's original position on the board. The rotation speed is a randomly picked number that represents the number of radians the jewel should rotate during the animation. The velocity is the direction in which the piece is moving and the speed at which it moves. This is also represented by a pair of x and y values. The explode() function is shown in Listing 9-35.

Listing 9-35   Setting up the explosion

```
jewel.display = (function() {
    ...
    function explode(callback) {
        var pieces = [],
            piece,
            x, y;
        for (x=0;x<cols;x++) {
            for (y=0;y<rows;y++) {
                piece = {
                    type : jewels[x][y],
                    pos : {
                        x : x + 0.5,
                        y : y + 0.5
                    },
                    vel : {
                        x : (Math.random() - 0.5) * 20,
                        y : -Math.random() * 10
                    },
                    rot : (Math.random() - 0.5) * 3
                }
                pieces.push(piece);
            }
        }

        addAnimation(2000, {
            before : function(pos) {
                ctx.clearRect(0,0,canvas.width,canvas.height);
            },
            render : function(pos, delta) {
                explodePieces(pieces, pos, delta);
            },
            done : callback
        });
    }
    ...
})();
```

The explode() function iterates over the entire board and creates a list of pieces from all the jewels. It saves the jewel type and then sets up the initial position, rotation, and velocity values. Notice that the vel.y value is forced to be negative, whereas vel.x can be either positive or negative. This is so all the pieces are initially moving upward. The render function calls the `explodePieces()` function, which moves all the pieces and also applies a gravity effect to the pieces, forcing them to come down. The `explodePieces()` function needs both the `pos` and `delta` values to be able to move the pieces just the right amount. The `before()` function of the animation clears the entire canvas so it's ready for the next frame. Listing 9-36 shows the `explodePieces()` function.

Listing 9-36   Animating the falling jewels

```
jewel.display = (function() {
    ...
    function explodePieces(pieces, pos, delta) {
        var piece, i;
        for (i=0;i<pieces.length;i++) {
            piece = pieces[i];

            piece.vel.y += 50 * delta;
            piece.pos.y += piece.vel.y * delta;
            piece.pos.x += piece.vel.x * delta;

            if (piece.pos.x < 0 || piece.pos.x > cols) {
                piece.pos.x = Math.max(0, piece.pos.x);
                piece.pos.x = Math.min(cols, piece.pos.x);
                piece.vel.x *= -1;
            }

            ctx.save();
            ctx.globalCompositeOperation = "lighter";
            ctx.translate(piece.pos.x * jewelSize,
                        piece.pos.y * jewelSize);
            ctx.rotate(piece.rot * pos * Math.PI * 4);
            ctx.translate(-piece.pos.x * jewelSize,
                        -piece.pos.y * jewelSize);
            drawJewel(piece.type,
                piece.pos.x - 0.5,
                piece.pos.y - 0.5
            );
            ctx.restore();
        }
    }
    ...
})();
```

The `explodePieces()` function does two things. First, it alters the position and velocity of all the jewel pieces. It then renders each of them on the now-blank canvas.

The velocity is changed by adding a constant multiplied by the delta. This change in velocity simulates the effect of gravity. On Earth, for example, a falling object increases its velocity with roughly 9.8 meters per second toward the surface every second (if you ignore air resistance, at least). Play around with the constant to increase or decrease the gravity. The position is then altered by adding the velocity multiplied by delta. If the x value of the position is negative or if it exceeds the value of `cols`, the piece has reached the left or right edge of the board. You can choose to let it continue moving out of view, or you can flip the x component of the velocity to make it bounce back, which is the option I chose.

It's now easy to render the jewel piece in the right spot. The rotation is done in the usual way by translating to the position of the jewel, rotating, and then translating back. Note that 0.5 is subtracted from the coordinates used in the `drawJewel()` call. The reason is that the `pos.x` and `pos.y` values represent the center of the jewel, but `drawJewel()` wants the upper-left corner. The `lighter` compositing operation gives the jewels a translucent appearance when they move over each other. Figure 9-7 shows a still image from the final animation.

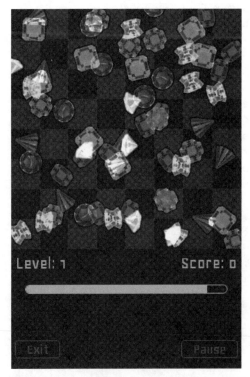

FIGURE 9-7: In the game over animation, the jewels tumble.

Summary

The game experience of Jewel Warrior is enhanced immensely with the help of a few animated effects in the right places. In this chapter, you learned how to set up an animation cycle using the new animation timing API, and you used it to create a simple animation framework for the canvas display.

You found out how to make a variety of animations for game actions, such as swapping jewels and adding the game over animation. In addition, you added some key elements to the game, namely the game timer, as well as the ability to score points and advance in levels.

Part III

Adding 3D and Sound

Chapter 10
Creating Audio for Games

In This Chapter

- Introducing HTML5 audio
- Dealing with audio formats
- Using the Web Audio API
- Implementing an audio module
- Adding sound effects to the game

NOW THAT THE visual aspect of the game is taken care of, you can turn to adding audio. This chapter introduces you to the new HTML5 audio element that aims to solve the age-old problem of adding sound to web applications.

First, you explore the basics of the audio element, covering most of the details and API functions described in the HTML5 specification. You also see an example of how the new Web Audio API enables even cooler things such as positional audio and advanced audio processing.

Finally, you use the HTML5 audio element to implement an audio module for Jewel Warrior. You also see how to bind sound effects to game events, thereby adding an extra dimension to the game experience.

HTML5 Audio

In the early days of the web, there was no way to put sound on web pages, nor was there a need for it because the web was largely just a way to display documents. However, with the games and applications being produced today, it's suddenly a feature that makes sense.

Microsoft introduced a bgsound element to Internet Explorer that allowed authors to attach a single audio file to a page, which then played in the background. Its use was frowned upon, however, because users couldn't turn the sound off, so instead of enhancing the page, it was distracting and annoying.

Over time, various alternatives have been used for audio. Embedding sound files in web pages is relatively straightforward using embed tags; however, doing so depends on plug-ins, and control of the audio leaves much to be desired. Eventually, Flash took over and has dominated both audio and video on the web. Until now, at least.

The HTML5 specification introduces new media elements that let you work with both audio and video without using plug-ins. The two new HTML elements, audio and video, are very easy to use and, in their basic form, require just a single line of HTML. For example, embedding an autoplaying sound can be as simple as this:

```
<audio src="mysound.mp3" autoplay></audio>
```

Similarly, a video player with UI controls can be embedded with the following:

```
<video src="myvideo.avi" controls></video>
```

Both the audio and video elements implement the HTML5 MediaElement interface and therefore share a good portion of their APIs. Therefore, although I don't discuss the video element directly, you still can take some of what you learn in this chapter and apply it to the video element. You can read more about the MediaElement interface at https://devel oper.mozilla.org/en-US/docs/Web/API/HTMLMediaElement.

Detecting audio support

One way to determine whether a browser supports the audio element is to create one using document.createElement() and test whether one of the audio-specific methods exists on the created element. One such method is the canPlayType() method, which you see again in a bit:

```
var audio = document.createElement("audio");
if (typeof audio.canPlayType == "function") {
```

```
    // HTML5 audio is supported
} else {
    // Load fallback code
}
```

If you need a good fallback solution, I recommend Scott Schiller's excellent Sound Manager 2, available at `www.schillmania.com/projects/soundmanager2`. This library makes it easy to use audio with HTML5 and JavaScript. If the browser doesn't support HTML5 audio, it falls back seamlessly to a Flash-based audio player.

Understanding the audio format wars

Just knowing that the `audio` element is available isn't enough, however. You also need to make sure the browser can play the type of audio you're using, be it MP3, Ogg Vorbis, or some other audio format.

The HTML5 specification describes the functionality of the `audio` element in plenty of detail, but it doesn't specify a standard audio format or even hint as to what formats a browser should support. It's entirely up to the browser vendors to include the formats that they deem suitable. Now, you might think that innovative companies and organizations such as Mozilla, Google, and Microsoft would quickly come to some sort of agreement and settle on a common format. Unfortunately, that has yet to happen.

Apparently, every browser vendor has its own idea of what makes a good audio format and which formats simply don't align with its own strategies and agendas. Formats such as MP3, Ogg Vorbis, AAC, and Google's WebM all have advantages and drawbacks, and issues such as software ideals and patent concerns have slowed down the standardization process. What you, as a web developer, are left with is a fragmented landscape of audio support where it's actually impossible to find a single audio format that's supported across the board. Table 10-1 shows the formats supported by the major browsers.

Table 10-1 Audio format support

	WAV	MP3	Ogg Vorbis	AAC (MP4)	WebM
Internet Explorer 11		x		x	(x)
Chrome 31	x	x	x	x	x
Firefox 25	x	(x)	x	(x)	x
Safari 7	x	x		x	
Opera 18	x		x		x
iOS 7	x	x		x	
Android 4.4		x			

As Table 10-1 shows, no format is universally supported. Firefox can play MP3 and AAC audio but relies on the operating system to support it, which means only on Windows Vista/7+ and Android for now. Internet Explorer supports WebM only with a plug-in. To get audio working reliably in as many browsers as possible, you need at least two versions of all your audio files, for example, Ogg Vorbis and MP3.

Detecting supported formats

Because HTML5 audio isn't meant for one specific audio format, the API provides a method for detecting whether the browser can play a given type of audio. This function is, of course, `audio.canPlayType()`, which was used earlier to detect audio support.

The `audio.canPlayType()` method takes a single argument, a string containing the MIME type of the format you want to test. For example, the following tests whether Ogg Vorbis audio is supported:

```
var canPlayOGG = audio.canPlayType(
                    "audio/ogg; codecs='vorbis'");
```

Notice the `codecs` parameter in the MIME type. Some MIME types allow this optional parameter to specify not only the format, which in this case is an Ogg container, but also the codec, here Vorbis.

The equivalent test for MP3 audio is

```
var canPlayMP3 = audio.canPlayType("audio/mpeg");
```

Now, you might think that the `audio.canPlayType()` method returns either `true` or `false`, but it's slightly more complicated than that. The return value is a string that has one of three values:

- `probably`
- `maybe`
- an empty string

The value `probably` means that the browser is reasonably sure that it can play audio files of this type. If the browser isn't confident that it can play the specified type but doesn't know that it can't either, you get the value `maybe`. The empty string is returned when the browser knows there's no way it can play that type of audio. Depending on how optimistic you want your application to be, you can choose to accept either just the `probably` value or both `probably` and `maybe`:

```
if (canPlayMP3 == "probably") {
    ... // browser is confident that it can play MP3
}
if (canPlayMP3 == "probably" || canPlayMP3 == "maybe") {
    ... // there's a chance that it can play MP3
}
```

Note that, because the empty string evaluates to `false` when coerced to a Boolean value, you can simplify the last test to

```
if (canPlayMP3) {
    ... // there's a chance that it can play MP3
}
```

Finding sound effects

Not everyone has the talents necessary to create great sounding sound effects and background music, and for hobby developers, budget concerns often get in the way of licensing readymade audio or hiring outside talent. Fortunately, plenty of sites offer both sound effects and music with few or no restrictions on how you use them.

The Freesound Project (`www.freesound.org`) is a great site for finding samples and sound effects of all kinds. The sound files are all licensed under the Creative Commons (CC) Sampling Plus license, which means you are free to use them in your projects as long as you properly attribute the authors of the sound clips.

If you need full music tracks to add a little ambience to your game, SoundClick (`www.soundclick.com`) features thousands of music tracks, many of them licensed under various CC licenses.

You can find many more sites that provide CC licensed content at the Creative Commons website at http://`wiki.creativecommons.org/Content_Directories`.

Often, the sounds you find need a few adjustments before they're perfect for your game. For that purpose, I recommend the free, open-source audio editor, Audacity (`http://audacity.sourceforge.net`). It has more features than you'll probably ever need and lets you easily modify the audio, add effects, and convert between various formats.

Using the audio Element

You can create `audio` elements either by adding them to the HTML markup or by creating them with JavaScript. Adding an `audio` element to the HTML is as simple as using

```
<audio src="mysound.mp3" />
```

Just like the `canvas` element, the `audio` element lets you put arbitrary content inside the tag that's rendered only if HTML5 audio isn't supported. You can use that feature to, for example, include a Flash-based fallback solution or simply to display a helpful message:

```
<audio src="mysound.mp3">
    Sorry, your browser doesn't support HTML5 Audio!
</audio>
```

In the preceding snippet, any browser that supports the audio element will ignore the message.

You can also create audio elements with JavaScript:

```
var myaudio = new Audio("mysound.mp3");
```

If you don't specify the source file in the `Audio()` constructor, you can specify it later by setting the `src` property on the `audio` element.

Adding user controls

The `audio` element comes with built-in UI controls. You can enable these controls by adding the `controls` attribute to the element:

```
<audio src="mysound.mp3" controls />
```

This line tells the browser to render the element with the browser's own controls. The specification doesn't dictate what controls must be available or what they should look like; it recommends only that the browser provide controls for standard behavior such as playing, pausing, seeking, changing volume, and so on. Figure 10-1 shows audio elements with controls as rendered in Firefox, Chrome, and Internet Explorer.

FIGURE 10-1: These audio elements can be rendered with native controls in Firefox (top), Chrome (middle), and Internet Explorer (bottom).

As you can see, the overall appearance is the same, although the default dimensions vary a bit. If necessary, you can use CSS to change, for example, the width of the element.

> The `controls` attribute is a *Boolean attribute*, which means that its mere presence enables the feature. The only allowed value for a Boolean attribute is the name of the attribute itself, that is, `controls="controls"`. The value is optional; however; most often, you just want to use the shortened version.

NOTE

If the `controls` attribute is absent, the `audio` element is simply not rendered and doesn't affect the rest of the page content. You can still play the sound using the JavaScript API, though.

Preloading audio

In some cases, loading the audio before you're going to use it makes sense. You can tell the browser to preload the audio file by setting the `preload` attribute on the `audio` element to one of three values:

- `none`

- `metadata`

- `auto`

Note that the `preload` attribute is just a hint to the browser. The browser is allowed to ignore the attribute altogether for any reason, such as available resources or user preferences.

The value `none` hints that the browser should not preload any data at all and start loading data only after the playback begins. For example, the following code hints that no data should be preloaded at all:

```
<audio src="mysound.mp3" preload="none" />
```

The `metadata` value makes the browser load only enough data that it knows the duration of the audio file. If the `preload` attribute is set to `auto` or if the attribute is absent, the browser decides for itself what gives the best user experience. This includes potentially loading the entire file.

You also can control the preloading in JavaScript through a property on the element:

```
audio.preload = "metadata"; // load only metadata
```

Although having the file ready for immediate playback is nice, you should always weigh this advantage against the added network traffic it requires. Preload only the files you are reasonably sure will be used.

Specifying multiple source files

I already mentioned that no single format is supported in all browsers, forcing you either to provide source files in multiple formats or to leave out support for one or more browsers.

Fortunately, you can easily specify a list of audio files that the browser should try to play. The `audio` element can have one or more `source` child elements. These `source` elements must each point to an audio file. When the `audio` tag is parsed, the browser goes over the list of `source` elements and stops at the first one that it can play. The `source` element is relevant only as a child of an `audio` (or `video`) element; you can't use it for anything on its own.

```
<audio controls>
    <source src="mysound.mp3" type="audio/mpeg">
    <source src="mysound.ogg" type='audio/ogg; codecs="vorbis"'>
</audio>
```

The preceding example makes the browser test for MP3 support first and then Ogg Vorbis, picking the first format that works. The `type` attribute specifies the MIME type of the audio file, optionally with a codec value. You can also use this attribute when specifying the audio source directly on the `audio` element with the `src` attribute. The `type` attribute is not required, but you should include it whenever you can. Without the MIME type, the browser is forced to download the audio file to determine whether it can play the file. If you let the browser know the type of audio, it can skip the resource fetching and just use the same mechanism as the `canPlayType()` method.

TIP   Firefox is a bit picky with respect to the format of the MIME type string and requires you to use double quotation marks around the `codecs` value, so be sure to use single quotation marks around the `type` value.

If you specify both an src attribute on the audio element and add source child elements, the src attribute takes precedence. Only the audio source specified by the src attribute is considered; the source elements are disregarded, even if the file from the src attribute is unplayable.

If you need to know which file ended up being selected, you can read the value from the currentSrc property on the audio element:

```
alert("Picked the file: " + audio.currentSrc);
```

If none of the specified audio sources are playable, the currentSrc property is set to the empty string.

Controlling playback

The audio element API exposes a few methods on the element, most importantly the play() method, which is used to start the playback:

```
audio.play();
```

This method begins playing the sound. If the audio was already at the end, the playback is restarted from the beginning. If you want to make the sound start playing automatically as soon as possible, you can use the autoplay attribute:

```
<audio src="mysound.mp3" autoplay />
```

The other method on the audio element is the pause() method:

```
audio.pause();
```

This method pauses the playback and sets the paused property on the audio element to true. Calling pause() more than once has no effect; to resume playing, you must call play() again. Using these two methods and the paused property, you can easily create a function that toggles the pause state:

```
function togglePause(audio) {
    if (audio.paused) {
        audio.play();
    } else {
        audio.pause();
    }
}
```

A common usage pattern is to make a sound loop back to the beginning and continue playing when it reaches the end. To make an audio clip loop, simply add the Boolean `loop` attribute to the audio element:

```
<audio src="mysound.mp3" loop />
```

You can also set the `loop` property with JavaScript after the element is created:

```
audio.loop = true; // audio is now looping
```

Depending on the browser and platform, you may experience a small pause before the audio begins playing when moving back to the beginning. Unfortunately, there's no easy fix for this problem. It's hoped the implementations of HTML5 audio will improve with time so that this problem is eliminated.

If you need to control the playback position in a more detailed manner, you can do so via the `audio.currentTime` property:

```
audio.currentTime = 60 * 1000; // skip to 1 minute into the clip
```

The audio specification describes no `stop()` method, but constructing one yourself is easy. Just reset `currentTime` to 0 and pause the playback:

```
function stopAudio(audio) {
    audio.pause(); // pause playback
    audio.currentTime = 0; // move to beginning
}
```

Controlling the volume

You can adjust the volume of the audio clip by setting the `volume` property on the audio element. The value of the `volume` property is a number between 0 and 1, where 0 is completely silent and 1 is maximum output:

```
audio.volume = 0.75; // set the volume to 75%
```

You can also mute the audio by setting the `mute` property to `true`. This property sets the effective volume to 0 but doesn't touch the `volume` value, so when you unmute the audio by setting `mute` to `false`, the original volume is restored:

```
audio.volume = 0.75; // effective volume = 0.75;
audio.muted = true;  // effective volume = 0.0;
...
audio.muted = false; // effective volume = 0.75;
```

Because mute is a Boolean, toggling between the two states is as easy as setting mute to its negated value:

```
function toggleMute(audio) {
    audio.muted = !audio.muted;
}
```

Using audio events

You can use a number of events to detect when various events take place on the audio event. Table 10-2 shows a subset of the events.

Table 10-2 Audio events

Event name	Description
loadstart	Fires when the browser starts loading the audio resource.
abort	Fires if the loading is aborted for reasons other than an error.
error	Fires if there was an error while trying to load the audio.
loadedmetadata	Fires when the browser has loaded enough to know the duration of the sound.
canplay	Fires when the browser can start playing from the current position.
canplaythrough	Fires when the browser estimates that it can start playing from the current position and keep playing without running out of data.
ended	Fires when the audio reaches the end.
durationchange	Fires if the duration of the audio clip changes.
timeupdate	Fires every time the position changes during playback.
play	Fires when the audio starts playing.
pause	Fires when the audio is paused.
volumechange	Fires when the volume of the audio is changed.

This list of events in Table 10-2 is not exhaustive but shows the most important events you need for most use cases. You can find the full list of events in the W3C specification (http://www.w3.org/TR/html5/embedded-content-0.html#mediaevents).

Creating custom UI controls

Sometimes, you may want to provide your own custom UI elements for controlling the audio playback. Perhaps the style of the native controls doesn't fit with your application; perhaps you just want more control over their behavior. As you've probably already figured out, you can easily use the aforementioned methods and events to create your controls, which is what the following example shows. Listing 10-1 shows the HTML elements.

Listing 10-1   **Custom elements for audio control**

```
<audio id="myaudio" loop>
    <source src="beat.mp3" type="audio/mpeg" />
    <source src="beat.ogg" type='audio/ogg; codecs="vorbis"' />
</audio>
<section id="controls">
    <header><h3>Player Controls</h3></header>
    <div class="progress"><div class="value"></div></div>
    <button class="play">Play</button>
    <button class="pause">Pause</button>
    <button class="stop">Stop</button>
    <button class="mute">Mute</button>
</section>
```

You can find this example in the file `01-customcontrols.html`. I also added a few CSS rules to style the progress bar. The play, pause, stop, and mute buttons are easy to implement. Listing 10-2 shows the `click` event handlers attached to the buttons.

Listing 10-2   **Binding click events to audio actions**

```
function $(str) {
    return document.querySelectorAll(str);
};
var audio = $("#myaudio")[0];

$("button.play")[0].addEventListener("click", function() {
    audio.play();
}, false);

$("button.pause")[0].addEventListener("click", function() {
    audio.pause();
}, false);
```

```
$("button.stop")[0].addEventListener("click", function() {
    audio.pause();
    audio.currentTime = 0;
}, false);

$("button.mute")[0].addEventListener("click", function() {
    audio.muted = !audio.muted;
}, false);
```

The audio element should also automatically update the progress bar when it's playing. You can use the timeupdate event to read the currentTime value and update the progress bar element accordingly. Listing 10-3 shows how.

Listing 10-3 **Updating the custom progress bar**
```
function updateProgress() {
    var prog = $(".progress .value")[0],
        pos = audio.currentTime / audio.duration * 100;
    prog.style.width = pos + "%";
}
audio.addEventListener("timeupdate", updateProgress, false);
```

Finally, the progress bar should respond to mouse clicks by changing the audio playback position. This problem is also easy to solve because you just need to update the currentTime value according to the relative click position. Listing 10-4 shows the click event handler for the progress bar.

Listing 10-4 **Updating playback position**
```
$(".progress")[0].addEventListener("click", function(e) {
    var rect = this.getBoundingClientRect(),
        pos = (e.clientX - rect.left) / rect.width;
    audio.currentTime = audio.duration * pos;
}, false);
```

That's all it takes to use your DOM elements to control the audio playback.

Using audio on mobile devices

But what about mobile devices? Things are progressing, but there are still some issues to work out. Current versions of iOS (from 3.0) and Android (from 2.3) both have support for HTML5 audio. Some earlier versions of Android had partial and broken audio support, but not until 2.3 was it possible to actually play sounds with HTML5 audio.

One of the issues concerns volume control. As you've now learned, the audio element has its own volume value that you can use to control the volume of that specific audio clip. On iOS devices, audio elements always play at full volume, and you can't change the volume value. The sound volume is completely in the hands of the user, and any attempt to modify it via JavaScript is ignored. In addition to the limitations on volume control, iOS is further crippled because only one audio stream is allowed to play at any time. Starting a new sound pauses any sound that's already playing. That means you can't have overlapping sound effects or, for example, play background music while also playing smaller clips tied to game events.

Android does allow multiple audio clips playing simultaneously but comes with the same volume restrictions as iOS. It also has some serious latency issues when starting playback, making it hard to get responsive sound effects.

Working with Audio Data

The specification for HTML5 audio is far from finished, and even today work is being put into expanding the audio element with capabilities such as direct, sample-level access to audio data to allow both advanced audio analysis and audio generation and filters. Because these features are far from mature, you don't get to use them in the Jewel Warrior game, but I discuss the APIs a bit and show you a few examples.

Until recently, there were two different APIs for manipulating audio data. People at Mozilla were working on the Audio Data API (https://wiki.mozilla.org/Audio_Data_API) while the Chromium project spawned the Web Audio API, which the W3C audio working group eventually settled on (www.w3.org/TR/webaudio). Mozilla has since deprecated its own API and added support for the Web Audio API. All major desktop browsers except Internet Explorer support the API, although Safari 7 and Opera 18 use a prefixed implementation. See the CanIUse site (http://caniuse.com/#feat=audio-api) for the most up-to-date information on browser support. For the most recent developments in the W3C specification, refer to the latest "Editor's Draft" at http://webaudio.github.io/web-audio-api.

NOTE   Like the image data methods on the canvas element, the audio data API is also subject to same-origin restrictions. That means you can access audio data only from files hosted on the same domain as your application. You also need to run the code from a web server because access to local files (that is, file://) is similarly restricted.

Using the Web Audio API

The basic concept of the Web Audio API revolves around audio contexts and audio nodes. You can use many different types of audio nodes. Some have both inputs and outputs and transform the data in a specific way—for example by modifying the volume or passing it through filters—whereas others serve as source nodes and have only an output.

The Web Audio API is fairly complex, and to cover it completely is beyond the scope of this book. In this chapter, I show enough basics that you can get started with this exciting new technology.

The audio context

The first thing you need is an audio context object, which you create using the `AudioContext()` constructor. Only Firefox currently implements the API without vendor prefixes; Chrome, Safari, and Opera all use the `webkit` prefix. To cover both cases, you can use a function like this:

```
function createAudioContext() {
    if (window.AudioContext) {
        return new window.AudioContext()
    } else if (window.webkitAudioContext) {
        return new window.webkitAudioContext()
    }
}
```

The audio context is basically a collection of audio nodes that route audio through each other and ultimately into a destination node, which is what the user will hear. You can think of it as a directed graph where each audio connects its output to the input of another node, ending at the destination node.

Audio nodes

Audio nodes are the objects that actually produce and transform the audio. They can be audio sources, processing nodes, or destination nodes. Source nodes have only an output and generate audio either programmatically or from an audio source. Only the destination node has an input. Processing nodes go in between and have both inputs and outputs. You can use these nodes to alter the audio in some way before it reaches the user. Both source nodes and processing nodes are created with methods on the audio context object—for example:

```
// create an OscillatorNode node that creates a 440hz tone
var source = context.createOscillator();
source.frequency.value = 440;
```

```
// create a GainNode that lowers the gain/volume to 0.8
var gain = context.createGain();
gain.gain.value = 0.8;
```

Audio nodes connect to each other using the connect() function:

```
source.connect(gain);
```

When the audio has been routed through all the nodes you want, connect the output of the final node to the destination node on the audio context and start source node:

```
gain.connect(context.destination);
```

```
source.start(0.5); // play in 0.5 seconds
```

Positional audio

Now for a small example of how you can use the Web Audio API to create positional audio, among many other things. A common problem with audio in games involves how to dynamically alter the volume and direction of sounds in the environment depending on where the sound originated. The Web Audio API provides an audio node that lets you do this rather easily. The PannerNode transforms audio given a position, direction, and even velocity if you also want Doppler effects. Simply connect the source node to the panner node and the panner node to the destination on the audio context.

This example connects two audio sources to an audio context and draws their positions on a canvas surface. You then add mouse events so the two sounds can be repositioned. You can find the finished example in the file 02-webaudio.html in the archive for this chapter. Note that a bug is currently in Firefox 25 that prevents this example from working. I recommend using Chrome or Opera for this example as they appear to have the least buggy implementations. First, a bit of HTML to get started. Listing 10-5 shows the canvas element and the two audio elements.

Listing 10-5   **Setting up the HTML elements**
```
<canvas id="canvas" width="512" height="512"></canvas>
<br/>
<audio id="beat" autoplay loop>
    <source src="beat.mp3" type="audio/mpeg" />
    <source src="beat.ogg" type="audio/ogg; codecs='vorbis'" />
</audio>
<audio id="footsteps" autoplay loop>
```

```
    <source src="steps.mp3" type="audio/mpeg" />
    <source src="steps.ogg" type="audio/ogg; codecs='vorbis'" />
</audio>
```

The canvas is used to draw the sound positions relative to the listener. For the JavaScript, start by creating the audio context and the necessary audio nodes as shown in Listing 10-6.

Listing 10-6   **Creating and connecting audio nodes**
```
var context = createAudioContext(),
    audio1 = document.getElementById("beat"),
    audio2 = document.getElementById("footsteps"),
    mediaNode1 = context.createMediaElementSource(audio1),
    mediaNode2 = context.createMediaElementSource(audio2),
    pannerNode1 = context.createPanner(),
    pannerNode2 = context.createPanner();

mediaNode1.connect(pannerNode1);
pannerNode1.connect(context.destination);
pannerNode1.refDistance = 50;

mediaNode2.connect(pannerNode2);
pannerNode2.connect(context.destination);
pannerNode2.refDistance = 50;
```

Listing 10-6 creates source nodes for each of the two sounds with the `context.creat-eMediaElementSource()` method. This method takes an `audio` (or `video`) element and returns an audio node representing that audio source. The `context.createPanner()` method returns a `PannerNode` audio node that is used to position an audio source in a 3D space. These nodes have methods for setting the position, orientation, and velocity of the sound along with several properties for describing sound parameters such as the sound cone, maximum distance, and so on. The coordinate system used in these calculations is independent of any units such as meters or feet, so to control how loud a sound is at a given distance, you can use the `refDistance` property, which specifies a reference distance.

Next, initialize the positions of the sounds as well as the listener as shown in Listing 10-7. The "world" in this example is just the two-dimensional 512x512 surface of the canvas, so only the x and y coordinates are needed.

```
var soundPos1 = [Math.random() * 512, Math.random() * 512],
    soundPos2 = [Math.random() * 512, Math.random() * 512],
    listenPos = [256, 256];

function updatePositions() {
    context.listener.setPosition(listenPos[0], listenPos[1], 0);
    pannerNode1.setPosition(soundPos1[0], soundPos1[1], 0);
    pannerNode2.setPosition(soundPos2[0], soundPos2[1], 0);
    updateCanvas();
}

function updateCanvas() {
}

updatePositions();
```

The `listener` property on the audio context is an `AudioListener` object that represents the listener. As with the panner nodes, you can set the position, orientation, and velocity of the listener. In this simple example, I use only the position and place the listener at the center of the canvas, but in a more complex game scenario, you can use the direction and velocity to add realism to the sounds. The `updateCanvas()` function is empty for now.

Now for some interactivity. Add mouse events to the canvas so you can position the two audio sources with the mouse. Listing 10-8 shows you how.

```
var canvas = document.getElementById("canvas"),
    ctx = canvas.getContext("2d"),
    mouseIsDown = false;

function update(e) {
    var rect = canvas.getBoundingClientRect(),
        x = e.clientX - rect.left,
        y = e.clientY - rect.top;

    if (e.shiftKey) {
        soundPos2 = [x, y];
    } else {
        soundPos1 = [x, y];
    }
    updatePositions();
}
```

```
canvas.addEventListener("mousedown", function(e) {
    mouseIsDown = true;
    update(e);
    e.preventDefault();
}, false);

canvas.addEventListener("mouseup", function(e) {
    mouseIsDown = false;
}, false);

canvas.addEventListener("mousemove", function(e) {
    if (mouseIsDown) {
        update(e);
    }
}, false);
```

The mousedown and mouseup event handlers toggle the mouseIsDown flag, which is then checked in the mousemove handler before calling the update() function. This way, update() is called only when the mouse is down.

The update() function first calculates the position of the mouse event on the canvas and then changes the position of either the first or the second sound, depending on whether the shift key is pressed. That way, you can move both sounds with the mouse. Finally, the updateCanvas() method that is called from updatePositions() is shown in Listing 10-9.

Listing 10-9 **Redrawing the positions on the canvas**
```
function updateCanvas() {
    ctx.clearRect(0, 0, canvas.width, canvas.height);

    ctx.beginPath();
    ctx.arc(listenPos[0], listenPos[1], 10, 0, 2 * Math.PI);
    ctx.stroke();

    ctx.beginPath();
    ctx.fillStyle = "red";
    ctx.arc(soundPos1[0], soundPos1[1], 5, 0, 2 * Math.PI);
    ctx.fill();

    ctx.beginPath();
    ctx.fillStyle = "blue";
    ctx.arc(soundPos2[0], soundPos2[1], 5, 0, 2 * Math.PI);
    ctx.fill();
}
```

This function simply clears the canvas and draws the listener as a circle and each of the sounds as smaller, filled circles. Find the full example in the file 02-webaudio.html in the archive for this chapter.

Building the Audio Module

Now that you've seen how easy it is to use audio with HTML5, you can put that knowledge to use by adding an audio module to Jewel Warrior. Create a new audio module in a fresh audio.js file and start out with the basic module structure as shown in Listing 10-10.

Listing 10-10   **The audio module**

```
jewel.audio = (function() {

    function initialize() {
    }

    return {
        initialize : initialize
    };

})();
```

Preparing for audio playback

The first task is to determine which audio format the audio module is going to use. In the code archive for this chapter, I included MP3 and Ogg Vorbis versions of all the sound effects to implement. The sound effects have been released into the public domain so feel free to use them for your own projects. Listing 10-11 shows a formatTest() function that returns the file extension of the most suitable audio format.

Listing 10-11   **Determining a suitable format and file extension**

```
jewel.audio = (function() {
    var extension;

    function initialize() {
        extension = formatTest();
        if (!extension) {
            return;
        }
    }
```

```
function formatTest() {
    var audio = new Audio(),
        types = [
            ["ogg", "audio/ogg; codecs='vorbis'"],
            ["mp3", "audio/mpeg"]
        ];
    for (var i=0;i<types.length;i++) {
        if (audio.canPlayType(types[i][1]) == "probably") {
            return types[i][0];
        }
    }
    for (i=0;i<types.length;i++) {
        if (audio.canPlayType(types[i][1]) == "maybe") {
            return types[i][0];
        }
    }
}
...
})();
```

The test is done by iterating over a list of audio formats and returning the first format for which the `canPlayType()` function returns `probably`. If no such format is found, a second loop looks for the less-confident `maybe` value. This test ensures that, for example, a `probably` value for WAV files can be chosen over a `maybe` value for Ogg Vorbis, even if the former is usually a less desirable format for web applications.

Playing sound effects

The most important function of the audio module is to play sounds. Each sound effect that's played needs its own `audio` element. Listing 10-12 shows the `createAudio()` function responsible for creating these elements.

Listing 10-12   Creating audio elements

```
jewel.audio = (function() {
    var extension,
        sounds;

    function initialize() {
        extension = formatTest();
        if (!extension) {
            return;
        }
```

continued

Listing 10-12 **continued**

```
        sounds = {};
    }

    function createAudio(name) {
        var el = new Audio("sounds/" + name + "." + extension);

        sounds[name] = sounds[name] || [];

        sounds[name].push(el);
        return el;
    }
    ...
})();
```

The `createAudio()` function has a single parameter, the name of the sound file minus the extension, which was determined previously in the initialization of the audio module. It doesn't just return the element, however; it also keeps a reference to that element in the `sounds` object. This object contains an array for each sound effect with all the `audio` elements created so far for that specific sound. As a result, it's possible to reuse elements that have finished playing. You can see this being used in the `getAudioElement()` function in Listing 10-13.

Listing 10-13   Getting an audio element

```
jewel.audio = (function() {
    ...
    function getAudioElement(name) {
        if (sounds[name]) {
            for (var i=0,n=sounds[name].length;i<n;i++) {
                if (sounds[name][i].ended) {
                    return sounds[name][i];
                }
            }
        }
        return createAudio(name);
    }
    ...
})();
```

The `getAudioElement()` function checks whether there's already an `audio` element that it can use. A new element is created only if no element is available, either because no elements have been created yet or because they're all playing. Now you can easily create a `play()` function that plays a given sound effect. Listing 10-14 shows the new function.

Listing 10-14 The play function

```
jewel.audio = (function() {
    var extension,
        sounds,
        activeSounds;

    function initialize() {
        extension = formatTest();
        if (!extension) {
            return;
        }
        sounds = {};
        activeSounds = [];
    }

    function play(name) {
        var audio = getAudioElement(name);
        audio.play();
        activeSounds.push(audio);
    }

    return {
        initialize : initialize,
        play : play
    };
})();
```

When the play() function plays a sound, it also stores a reference to that sound in an activeSounds array. You use this array to solve the next problem: stopping sounds.

Stopping sounds

Stopping currently playing sounds is easy. Simply iterate through the activeSounds array, call the audio.stop() method on all the audio elements, and empty the array. Listing 10-15 shows the stop() function added to audio.js.

Listing 10-15 The stop function

```
jewel.audio = (function() {

    ...

    function stop() {
        for (var i=activeSounds.length-1;i>=0;i-) {
```

continued

Listing 10-15 **continued**

```
                activeSounds[i].stop();
        }

        activeSounds.length = 0;
    }
    return {
        initialize : initialize,
        play : play,
        stop : stop
    };

})();
```

Cleaning up

You have one more thing left to do. When a sound starts, it's added to the activeSounds array. You need to make sure the sound is removed again after the playback finishes. To solve this problem, you can take advantage of the ended event that's fired when the end of the sound is reached. Whenever a new audio element is created, attach an event handler to the ended event that removes the audio element from the activeSounds array. Listing 10-16 shows the new event handler.

Listing 10-16   **Maintaining the active sounds list**

```
jewel.audio = (function() {

    function createAudio(name) {
        var el = new Audio("sounds/" + name + "." + extension);
        jewel.dom.bind(el, "ended", cleanActive);


        ...
    }
    function cleanActive() {
        for (var i=0;i<activeSounds.length;i++) {
            if (activeSounds[i].ended) {
                activeSounds.splice(i,1);
            }
        }
    }


    ...
})();
```

Because you don't keep track of where in the `activeSounds` array the `audio` element exists, the easiest approach is to do a blanket removal of any `audio` element that has ended. The elements are removed by using the `splice()` method, which modifies an array by removing a specified number of elements starting at a given index. Doing so, of course, changes the length of the array, which is why it's important that the loop condition keeps comparing i to the current length and not, as is usually the best practice, a previously cached value.

Finally, remember to load the `audio.js` file in `index.html` along with the other script modules.

Adding Sound Effects to the Game

Now that the audio module is complete, you can start adding sound effects to the game. I included a set of sound effects in the `sounds` folder in the code archive for this chapter. The included sound effects are to be used for the following game events:

- Successfully matching jewels
- Performing an invalid jewel swap
- Advancing to the next level
- Indicating the game is over

Playing audio from the game screen

Time to return to the game screen module, `screen.game.js`. The first thing to do is make sure the audio module is initialized when the game starts—that is, when the `startGame()` function in the game screen module is called. Listing 10-17 shows the modifications.

Listing 10-17 **Initializing the audio module**

```
jewel.screens["game-screen"] = (function() {
    ...
    function startGame() {
        ...
        jewel.audio.initialize();
        board.initialize(function() {
            ...
        });
    }
    ...
})();
```

Playing sound effects is now as simple as adding `audio.play()` calls wherever you need them, as shown in Listing 10-18.

Listing 10-18 Adding sound effects

```
jewel.screens["game-screen"] = (function() {
    ...
    function advanceLevel() {
        jewel.audio.play("levelup");
        ...
    }

    function gameOver() {
        jewel.audio.play("gameover");
        ...
    }

    function playBoardEvents(events) {
        if (events.length > 0) {
            ...
            switch (boardEvent.type) {
                ...
                case "remove" :
                    jewel.audio.play("match");
                    ...
                case "badswap" :
                    jewel.audio.play("badswap");
                    next();
                    break;
                ...
            }
        }
    }
    ...
})();
```

And there you have it. The game now plays sound effects for the most significant events.

Summary

In this chapter, you learned how to use the new `audio` element to add sound to your games and applications without Flash or other plug-in-based technologies. It's not all roses, though, because of audio format conflicts and issues on mobile devices.

Nevertheless, the level of support in modern desktop browsers has reached a level where you can confidently use HTML5 audio. The last part of this chapter showed you how to make an audio module and use it to add sound effects to Jewel Warrior.

You also got a peek at some of the more advanced features such as the Web Audio API that is available in some browsers. Although it's still a work in progress and lacks universal support, it's easy to see how such features will eventually greatly enhance the audio capabilities of the browser.

Chapter 11
Creating 3D Graphics with WebGL

In This Chapter

- Introducing WebGL
- Using the OpenGL Shading Language
- Using Collada models
- Texturing and lighting 3D objects
- Creating a WebGL display module

YOU ARE ALREADY familiar with drawing 2D graphics with the `canvas` element. In this chapter, you move forward and use 3D graphics and the WebGL context. You find out enough about the WebGL API to render simple 3D scenes with lighting and textured objects.

In the first part of the chapter, you focus on the OpenGL Shading Language (GLSL), a language made specifically to render graphics with OpenGL. You then go systematically through the process of rendering simple 3D objects. You also see how to import the commonly used Collada model format into your WebGL applications.

Before wrapping up, you learn how the techniques throughout the chapter come together to create a WebGL version of the Jewel Warrior game display.

3D for the Web

The `canvas` element is designed so that the actual functionality is separate from the element. A so-called *context* provides all graphics functionality. In Chapter 6, you drew graphics on the canvas using a path-based API provided by the 2D context. WebGL extends the `canvas` element with a 3D context.

WebGL is based on the OpenGL ES 2.0 graphics API, a variant of OpenGL aimed at embedded systems and mobile devices. This is also the version of OpenGL you use for developing native applications on, for example, iPhone and Android devices. The Khronos Group manages the WebGL specification and oversees the various OpenGL specifications. Much of the WebGL specification is a straight mapping of the functionality in OpenGL ES, which means that guides, books, and sample code already exist that you can use for inspiration. Even if the context isn't web-related, OpenGL ES code examples in other languages such as C can still be valuable. You can also find plenty of GLSL code to plug directly into WebGL applications.

WebGL is so popular that Khronos is already working on the specification for WebGL 2, an update that will bring it in line with the OpenGL ES 3.0 API and add a number of cool features such as 3D textures and new compression formats. WebGL 2 will be backward-compatible with WebGL, so the apps and games you make with WebGL today will also work in the future.

Where you can use WebGL

Firefox has had WebGL support since version 4.0, Chrome since version 9, and Safari (OS X) since version 5.1. Safari's WebGL is disabled by default but you can enable it in the Developer menu, which is enabled in the Advanced section of the preferences. WebGL is also coming to Opera, but at the moment, it's available only in special test builds. Initially, Microsoft expressed concern over WebGL, claiming that security problems inherent in the design keep WebGL from living up to its standards. Eventually, they reversed this stance, and Internet Explorer 11 was the first version of IE to include WebGL.

Support for WebGL on mobile devices is rather limited. The standard Android browser doesn't support WebGL in versions currently available. Firefox for Android does support WebGL as does Chrome for Android, although the latter requires it to be enabled on the `chrome://flags` page. Apple has included WebGL in iOS since iOS 5, but so far, it's been limited in the iAds framework. I hope that we'll soon find this feature making its way to the mobile Safari browser.

Getting started with WebGL

Most current 3D graphics, including those you see in this chapter, are based on objects made of small triangles, also called *faces*. Even very detailed 3D models with seemingly smooth surfaces reveal their polygonal nature when you zoom in close enough. Each triangle is described by three points, where each point, also called a *vertex*, is a three-dimensional vector. Put two triangles together to form a rectangle, put six squares together and you have a cube, and so on.

WebGL stores this 3D geometry in buffers that are uploaded to the graphics processing unit (GPU). The geometry is then rendered onto the screen, passing it through first a *vertex shader* and then a *fragment shader*. The vertex shader transforms the coordinates of the 3D points in accordance with the object's rotation and position as well as the desired 2D projection. Finally, the fragment shader calculates the color values used to fill the projected triangles on the screen. Shaders are the first topic I discuss after this introductory section because they're fundamental to creating WebGL applications.

WebGL and OpenGL ES are much too complex to cover in full detail in a single chapter. If you're serious about WebGL development and OpenGL, I recommend spending time on websites such as Learning WebGL (`http://learningwebgl.com`) where you can find many tutorials and WebGL-related articles. **NOTE**

Because WebGL is based on canvas, the first step to using WebGL is to create a `canvas` element and grab a WebGL context object:

```
var canvas = document.createElement("canvas"),
    gl = canvas.getContext("webgl");
```

Only Firefox and Chrome currently support the `webgl` context. Opera, Internet Explorer 11, and Safari all use the name `experimental-webgl`, but that will most likely change to `webgl` as these implementations mature. To cover both cases, you can either use `experimental-webgl` (because Firefox and Chrome also allow this name) or a function like this:

```
function createContext(canvas) {
    var gl = canvas.getContext("webgl") ||
             canvas.getContext("experimental-webgl");
    return gl;
}
```

The context object, `gl`, implements all the functionality of WebGL through various methods and constants.

Debugging WebGL

Debugging WebGL applications can be a bit tricky because most WebGL errors don't trigger JavaScript errors. Instead, you must use the `gl.getError()` function to check whether an error has occurred. This function returns the value 0 if there are no errors or a WebGL error code indicating the type of error:

```
var error = gl.getError();
if (error != 0) {
    alert("An error occurred: " + error);
}
```

Putting code like this after every WebGL function call causes bloated code and a lot of extra work. To make debugging a bit easier and less cumbersome, the Chromium team put together a small helper library that lets you enable a special debug mode on a WebGL context object:

```
var gl = canvas.getContext("webgl");
gl = WebGLDebugUtils.makeDebugContext(gl);
```

When you use this debug context, the `gl.getError()` function is automatically called every time you call one of the WebGL functions. If an error occurs, `gl.getError()` translates the error code into a more meaningful text and throws a real JavaScript error. That makes it much easier to catch errors that might otherwise go unnoticed.

The debug helper works in all WebGL-capable browsers and is also available at `https://www.khronos.org/registry/webgl/sdk/debug/webgl-debug.js`. I have also included the script in the code archive for this chapter.

WARNING   Enabling the debug mode adds extra function calls to all WebGL functions, which can have a negative effect on the performance of your application or game. Make sure you use the debug mode only during development and switch back to the plain WebGL context in production.

Creating a helper module

To simplify the implementation of Jewel Warrior's WebGL display, you can put some of the more general WebGL functionality into a separate module. Create a new module in `webgl.js` and start by adding the module definition, as shown in Listing 11-1.

Listing 11-1   **The empty WebGL helper module**
```
jewel.webgl = (function() {

    function createContext(canvas) {
        var gl = canvas.getContext("webgl") ||
                 canvas.getContext("experimental-webgl");
```

```
        return gl;
    }

    return {
        createContext : createContext
    };
})();
```

As you progress through this chapter, you add more and more functions to the module.

I don't list the complete code for the examples and the WebGL display module. Doing so **NOTE**
would involve a fair amount of repetition, and going over every detail would detract from the
focus. You can find the full examples and code in the archive for this chapter.

Using Shaders

You need to know about two kinds of shaders: *vertex shaders* and *fragment shaders*. You can
think of shaders as small programs used to instruct the GPU on how to turn the data in the
buffers into what you see rendered on the screen. For example, you use shaders to project
points from 3D space to the 2D screen, calculate lighting effects, and apply textures, among
other things.

Shaders use a special language called OpenGL Shading Language (GLSL). As its name implies,
this language is designed specifically for programming shaders for OpenGL. Other graphics
frameworks use similar languages, such as DirectX and its High-Level Shading Language
(HLSL). GLSL uses a C-like syntax, like JavaScript, so it shouldn't be too difficult to grasp
what's going on, even though you will come upon a few new concepts.

For the most part, you won't have trouble with the syntax, but there are a few traps if you're
mostly accustomed to JavaScript. One example is the lack of JavaScript's automatic semico-
lon insertion. Semicolons are not optional in GLSL, and failing to add them at the end of
lines of code causes errors.

Variables and data types

Variable declarations are similar to those in JavaScript but use the data type in place of the
var keyword:

```
data_type variable_name;
```

As in JavaScript, you can also assign an initial value:

```
data_type variable_name = init_value;
```

GLSL introduces several data types that aren't available in JavaScript. One data type that does behave the same in both JavaScript and GLSL is the Boolean type called bool:

```
bool mybool = true;
```

Besides bool, GLSL also has a few numeric types as well as several vector and matrix types.

Numeric types

Unlike JavaScript, GLSL has two numeric data types. Whereas all numbers in JavaScript use the number type, GLSL distinguishes between floating point and integer values using the data types float and int, respectively.

You can write literal integer values in decimal, octal, and hexadecimal form:

```
int mydec = 461; // decimal 461
int myoct = 0715; // octal 461
int myhex = 0x1CD; // hexadecimal 461
```

Literal floating point values must include either a decimal point or an exponent part:

```
float myfloat = 165.843;
float myfloatexp = 43e-6; // 0.000043
```

GLSL cannot cast integer values to floating point, so be careful to remember the decimal point in literal float values, even for values like 0.0 and 7.0.

Vectors

Vector types are used for many things in shaders. Everything from positions, normals, and colors are described using vectors. In GLSL, vector types come in three flavors: vec2, vec3, and vec4, where the number indicates the dimension of the vector. You create vectors as follows:

```
vec2 pos2d = vec3(3.42, 109.45);
vec3 pos3d = vec3(3.42, 109.45, 45.15);
```

You can also create vectors using other vectors in place of the components:

```
vec2 myXY = vec2(1.0, 2.0); // new two-dimensional vector
vec3 myXYZ = vec3(myXY, 3.0); // extend with a third dimension
```

This example combines the x and y components of the vec2 with a z value of 3.0 to create a new vec3 vector. You can use this capability for many things—for example, converting RGB color values to RGBA:

```
vec3 myColor = vec3(1.0, 0.0, 0.0); // red
float alpha = 0.5; // semi-transparent
vec4 myRGBA = vec4(myColor, alpha);
```

So far, all the vectors have been floating-point vectors. The vec2, vec3, and vec4 types allow only floating point values. If you need vectors with integer values, you can use the ivec2, ivec3, and ivec4 types. Similarly, bvec2, bvec3, and bvec4 allow vectors with Boolean values. In most cases, you use only floating point vectors.

If math is not your strong suit, wrapping your head around vectors, matrices, and linear algebra can be a bit daunting. I recommend visiting the Khan Academy (`https://www.khanacademy.org/math/linear-algebra`), where you'll find a series of excellent videos that explain this area much better than I can.

TIP

Vector math

You add and subtract vectors just as you do `float` and `int` values. The addition is performed component-wise:

```
vec2 v0 = vec2(0.5, 1.0);
vec2 v1 = vec2(1.5, 2.5);
vec2 v2 = v0 + v1; // = vec2(2.0, 3.5)
```

You can also add or subtract a single value to a vector:

```
float f = 7.0;
vec2 v0 = vec2(1.5, 2.5);
vec2 v1 = v0 + f; // = vec2(8.5, 9.5)
```

You add the `float` value to each component of the vector. The same applies to multiplication and division:

```
float f = 4.0;
vec2 v0 = vec2(3.0, 1.5);
vec2 v1 = v0 + f; // = vec2(12.0, 6.0)
```

If you use the multiplication operator on two vectors, the result is a component-wise multiplication of the vectors:

```
vec2 v0 = vec2(3.5, 4.0);
vec2 v1 = vec2(2.0, 0.5);
vec2 v2 = v0 * v1; // = vec2(3.5 * 2.0, 4.0 * 0.5)
                   // = vec2(7.0, 2.0)
```

The dot product can be calculated with the dot() function:

```
float d = dot(v0, v1); // = 3.5 * 2.0 + 4.0 + 0.5 = 9.0
```

The dot() function is just one of several functions that make life easier when you're working with vectors. Another example is the length() function, which calculates the length of a vector:

```
vec2 v0 = vec2(3.4, 5.2);
float len = length(v0); // = sqrt(3.4 * 3.4 + 5.2 * 5.2) = 6.21
```

Accessing vector components

The components of a vector are available via the properties x, y, z, and w on the vectors:

```
vec2 v = vec2(1.2, 7.3);
float x = v.x; // = 1.2
float y = v.y; // = 7.3
```

The properties r, g, b, and a are aliases of x, y, z, and w:

```
vec3 v = vec3(1.3, 2.4, 4.2);
float r = v.r; // = 1.3
float g = v.g; // = 2.4
float b = v.b; // = 4.2
```

A third option is to think of these components as a small array and access them with array subscripts:

```
vec2 v = vec2(1.2, 7.3);
float x = v[0]; // = 1.2
float y = v[1]; // = 7.3
```

Swizzling

A neat feature of GLSL vector types is *swizzling*. This feature enables you to extract multiple components of a vector and have them returned as a new vector. Suppose you have a three-dimensional vector and you want a two-dimensional vector with just the x and y values. Consider the following code:

```
vec3 myVec3 = vec3(1.0, 2.0, 3.0);
float x = myVec3.x; // = 1.0
float y = myVec3.y; // = 2.0
vec2 myVec2 = vec2(x, y);
```

This code snippet simply extracts the x and y components of vec3 to a couple of float variables that you can then use, for example, to create a new two-dimensional vector. This approach works just fine, but the following example achieves the same effect:

```
vec3 myVec3 = vec3(1.0, 2.0, 3.0);
vec2 myVec2 = myVec3.xy; // = vec2(1.0, 2.0)
```

Instead of accessing the x and y properties of the vector, you can combine any of the components to create new vectors.

```
vec3 myVec3 = vec3(1.0, 2.0, 3.0);
myVec3.xy = vec2(9.5, 4.7); // myVec3 = vec3(9.5, 4.7, 3.0);
vec2 myVec2 = myVec3.zx; // = vec2(3.0, 9.5)
```

You can even use the same component multiple times in the same swizzle expression:

```
vec3 myVec3 = vec3(1.0, 2.0, 3.0);
vec2 myVec2 = myVec3.xx; // = vec2(1.0, 1.0)
```

The dimensions of the vector limit which components you can use. Trying to access, for example, the z component of a vec2 causes an error.

You can use both xyzw and rgba to swizzle the vector components:

```
vec4 myRGBA = vec4(1.0, 0.0, 0.0, 1.0);
vec3 myRGB = myRGBA.rgb; // = vec3(1.0, 0.0, 0.0)
```

You cannot mix the two sets, however. For example, myRGBA.xyga isn't valid and produces an error.

Matrices

Matrices also have their own types, mat2, mat3, and mat4, which let you work with 2x2, 3x3, and 4x4 matrices. Only square matrices are supported. Matrices are initialized much like vectors by passing the initial values to the constructor:

```
mat2 myMat2 = mat2(
    1.0, 2.0,
    3.0, 4.0
);
mat3 myMat3 = mat3(
    1.0, 2.0, 3.0,
    4.0, 5.0, 6.0,
    7.0, 8.0, 9.0
);
```

The columns of a matrix are available as vectors using a syntax similar to array subscripts:

```
vec3 row0 = myMat3[0]; // = vec3(1.0, 4.0, 7.0)
```

This syntax, in turn, lets you access individual components with syntax such as

```
float m12 = myMat3[1][2]; // = 8.0
```

You can add and subtract matrices as you do vectors and numbers:

```
mat2 m0 = mat2(
    1.0, 5.7,
    3.6, 2.1
);
mat2 m1 = mat2(
    3.5, 2.0,
    2.3, 4.0
);
mat2 m2 = m0 + m1; // = mat2(4.5, 7.7, 5.9, 6.1)
mat2 m3 = m0 - m1; // = mat2(-2.5, 3.7, 1.3, -1.9)
```

You can also multiply two matrices. This operation doesn't operate component-wise but performs a real matrix multiplication. If you need component-wise matrix multiplication, you can use the matrixCompMult() function.

It's also possible to multiply a matrix and a vector with matching dimensions, producing a new vector:

```
vec2 v0 = vec2(2.5, 4.0);
mat2 m = mat2(
    3.5, 7.0,
    2.0, 5.0
);
vec v1 = v0 * m; // = vec2(
                 //        m[0].x * v0.x + m[1].x * v0.y,
                 //        m[0].y * v0.x + m[1].y * v0.y,
                 // . )
                 // = vec2(36.75, 25.0)
```

Using shaders with WebGL

As mentioned earlier, the two types of shaders are vertex shaders and fragment shaders. You need one of each to render a 3D object. Vertex shaders and fragment shaders have the same basic structure:

```
declarations

void main(void) {

    calculations

    output_variable = output_value;
}
```

The declarations section declares variables that the shader needs—both local variables and input variables coming from, for example, the vertex data. This section can also declare any helper functions utilized by the shader. Function declarations in GLSL look like this:

```
return_type function_name(parameters) {
    ...
}
```

This means that the function in the previous example is called `main`, has no return value, and takes no parameters. The `main()` function is required and is called automatically when the shader is executed. The shader ends by writing a value to an output variable. Vertex shaders write the transformed vertex position to a variable called `gl_Position`, and fragment shaders write the pixel color to `gl_FragColor`.

Vertex shaders

The vertex shader runs its code for each of the vertices in the buffer. Listing 11-2 shows a simple vertex shader.

Listing 11-2   A basic vertex shader

```
attribute vec3 aVertex;

void main(void) {
    gl_Position = vec4(aVertex, 1.0);
}
```

This simple shader declares an *attribute* variable called aVertex with the data type vec3, which is a vector type with three components. Attributes point to data passed from the WebGL application—in this case, the vertex buffer data. In this example, the vertex is converted to a four-dimensional vector and assigned, otherwise unaltered, to the output variable gl_Position. Later, you see how you can use view and projection matrices to transform the 3D geometry and add perspective.

Fragment shaders

Fragment shaders, also called *pixel shaders*, are similar to vertex shaders, but instead of vertices, fragment shaders operate on pixels on the screen. After the vertex shader processes the three points in a triangle and transforms them to screen coordinates, the fragment shader colorizes the pixels in that area. Listing 11-3 shows a simple fragment shader.

Listing 11-3   A basic fragment shader

```
#ifdef GL_ES
    precision mediump float;
#endif

void main(void) {
    gl_FragColor = vec4(1.0, 0.0, 0.0, 1.0);
}
```

The output variable in fragment shaders is a vec4 called gl_FragColor. This example sets the fragment color to a nontransparent red.

NOTE The term *fragment* refers to a piece of data that potentially ends up as a pixel if it passes depth testing and other requirements. A fragment doesn't need to be the size of a pixel. Fragments along edges, for example, could be smaller than a full pixel. Despite these differences, the terms *fragment* and *pixel*, as well as *fragment shader* and *pixel shader*, are often used interchangeably.

You're probably wondering about the first three lines in Listing 11-3. The OpenGL ES version of GLSL requires that fragment shaders specify the precision of `float` values. Three precisions are available: `lowp`, `mediump`, and `highp`. You can give each `float` variable a precision by putting one of the precision qualifiers in front of the declaration:

```
mediump float myfloatvariable;
```

You can also specify a default precision by adding a precision statement at the top of the shader code:

```
precision mediump float;
```

Earlier versions of desktop OpenGL don't support the `precision` keyword, though, and using it risks errors. However, GLSL supports a number of preprocessor statements such as `#if`, `#ifdef`, and `#endif`. You can use these statements to make sure a block of code is compiled only under certain conditions:

```
#ifdef GL_ES
    precision highp float;
#endif
```

This example causes the precision code to be ignored if `GL_ES` isn't defined—it's defined only in GLSL ES.

Including shader code in JavaScript

Getting the GLSL source code into your WebGL application can be a bit tricky. The browser doesn't understand GLSL, but you can still include the code in a `script` element directly in the HTML. Just give it a custom script type so the browser doesn't attempt to interpret the code as JavaScript:

```
<script id="fragment" type="x-shader/x-fragment">
    ... // GLSL source code
</script>
```

You can then extract the contents of the `script` element with standard DOM scripting. Note, however, that you can't reference an external GLSL file by adding an `src` attribute to the `script` element because the browser doesn't download scripts it can't execute.

Another option is to pack the GLSL in a string literal and embed it in the JavaScript code:

```
var fsource =
    "#ifdef GL_ES\r\n" +
```

```
"    precision highp float;\r\n" +
"#endif\r\n" +
"void main(void) {\r\n" +
"    gl_FragColor = vec4(0.7, 1.0, 0.8, 1.0); \r\n" +
"}\r\n";
```

You can add \r\n at the end of each line to include line breaks in the source. Otherwise, the source code is concatenated to a single line, making it harder to debug because shader error messages include line numbers. This is the method I chose to use in the examples included in the code archive for this chapter. It may not be the prettiest solution, but it gets the job done. For the sake of readability, the code listings in the rest of this chapter show the GLSL code without quotation marks and newline characters.

A third option is to load the shader code from separate files with Ajax. Although this approach adds extra HTTP requests, it has the advantage of storing the GLSL as is and encourages reuse of the shader files.

Creating shader objects

The shader source needs to be loaded into a shader object and compiled before you can use it. Use the gl.createShader() method to create shader objects:

```
var shader = gl.createShader(shaderType);
```

The shader type can be either gl.VERTEX_SHADER or gl.FRAGMENT_SHADER. The rest of the process for creating shader objects is the same regardless of the shader type.

You specify the GLSL source for the shader object with the gl.shaderSource() method. When the source is loaded, you can compile it with the gl.compileShader() method:

```
gl.shaderSource(shader, source);
gl.compileShader(shader);
```

You don't get JavaScript errors if the compiler fails because of bad GLSL code, but you can check for compiler errors by looking at the value of the gl.COMPILE_STATUS parameter:

```
if (!gl.getShaderParameter(shader, gl.COMPILE_STATUS)) {
    throw gl.getShaderInfoLog(shader);
}
```

The value of the gl.COMPILE_STATUS is true if no compiler errors occurred. If there are errors, you can use the gl.getShaderInfoLog() method to get the relevant error message. To test this error-catching check, just add invalid GLSL code to your shader source.

Listing 11-4 shows these calls combined to form the first function for the WebGL helper module.

Listing 11-4 Creating shader objects

```
jewel.webgl = (function() {
    ...
    function createShaderObject(gl, shaderType, source) {
        var shader = gl.createShader(shaderType);
        gl.shaderSource(shader, source);
        gl.compileShader(shader);
        if (!gl.getShaderParameter(shader, gl.COMPILE_STATUS)) {
            throw gl.getShaderInfoLog(shader);
        }
        return shader;
    }

    return {
        createShaderObject : createShaderObject,
        ...
    };
})();
```

Creating program objects

After both shaders are compiled, they must be attached to a program object. Program objects join a vertex shader and fragment shader to form an executable that can run on the GPU. Create a new program object with the `gl.createProgram()` method:

```
var program = gl.createProgram();
```

Now attach the two shader objects:

```
gl.attachShader(program, vshader);
gl.attachShader(program, fshader);
```

Finally, the program must be linked:

```
gl.linkProgram(program);
```

As with the shader compiler, you need to check for linker errors manually. Examine the `gl.LINK_STATUS` parameter on the program object and throw a JavaScript error if necessary:

```
if (!gl.getProgramParameter(program, gl.LINK_STATUS)) {
```

```
      throw gl.getProgramInfoLog(program);
}
```

Listing 11-5 shows these function calls combined to form the createProgramObject()
function for the WebGL helper module.

Listing 11-5   **Creating program objects**

```
jewel.webgl = (function() {
    ...
    function createProgramObject(gl, vs, fs) {
        var program = gl.createProgram();
        gl.attachShader(program, vs);
        gl.attachShader(program, fs);
        gl.linkProgram(program);
        if (!gl.getProgramParameter(program, gl.LINK_STATUS)) {
            throw gl.getProgramInfoLog(program);
        }
        return program;
    }

    return {
        createProgramObject : createProgramObject,
        ...
    }
})();
```

The shaders and program object are now ready for use:

```
gl.useProgram(program);
```

The program is now enabled and set as the active shader program. If you use more than one
program to render different objects, make sure you call gl.useProgram() to tell WebGL to
switch programs.

You must enable attribute variables in the vertex shader before they can be used. On the
JavaScript side of WebGL, you refer to an attribute variable by its location, which you can get
with the gl.getAttribLocation() function:

```
var aVertex = gl.getAttribLocation(program, "aVertex");
```

You can now enable the attribute:

```
gl.enableVertexAttribArray(aVertex);
```

Uniform variables

If you need to set values that are global to the entire group of vertices or pixels currently being rendered, you can use *uniform variables*. The value of a uniform variable is set with JavaScript and doesn't change until you assign a new value. Listing 11-6 shows a fragment shader with a uniform value.

Listing 11-6   **A fragment shader with a uniform variable**

```
#ifdef GL_ES
    precision highp float;
#endif

uniform vec4 uColor;

void main(void) {
    gl_FragColor = uColor;
}
```

Just add the `uniform` keyword to the variable declaration to make it a uniform variable. Because the value is set on the JavaScript side of WebGL, you cannot write to these variables from within the shader.

Uniform variables are referenced by their location in the same way as attribute variables. Use the `gl.getUniformLocation()` function to get the location:

```
var location = gl.getUniformLocation(program, "uColor");
```

The function you need to call to update a uniform variable depends on the data type of the variable. No fewer than 19 functions exist that update uniform variables, so picking the right one might seem a bit daunting at first.

To update a single float or vector variable, you can use functions of the form `uniform[1234] f()`. For example, if `loc` is the location of a uniform `vec2`, the following updates the value to `vec2(2.4, 3.2)`:

```
gl.uniform2f(location, 2.4, 3.2);
```

For arrays, you can use functions of the form `uniform[1234] fv()`. For example, the following updates an array of three `vec2` values:

```
gl.uniform2fv(location, [
    2.4, 3.6,
```

```
    1.6, 2.0,
    9.2, 3.4
]);
```

The `uniform[1234]i()` and `uniform[1234]fv()` forms allow you to update integer values.

Matrix values are set with the functions of the form `uniformMatrix[234]fv()`:

```
gl.uniformMatrix3fv(location, false, [
    4.3, 6.5, 1.2,
    2.3, 7.4, 0.9,
    5.5, 4.2, 3.0
]);
```

The second parameter specifies whether the matrix values should be transposed. This capability isn't supported, however, and the argument must always be set to `false`. You can pass the matrix values as a regular JavaScript array or as a `Float32Array` typed array object.

Returning to the fragment color, the `uColor` uniform value is `vec4`, so you can set this value with `gl.uniform4f()` or `gl.uniform4fv()`:

```
gl.uniform4f(location, 0.5, 0.5, 0.5, 1.0); // 50%  gray
gl.uniform4fv(location, [1.0, 0.0, 1.0, 1.0]); // magenta
```

Varying variables

In addition to uniforms and local variables, you can have varying variables that carry over from the vertex shader to the fragment shader. Consider a triangle in 3D space. The vertex shader does its work on all three vertices of the triangle before the fragment shader takes over and processes the pixels that make up the triangle. When the varying variable is read in the fragment shader, its value varies depending on where the pixel is located on the triangle. Listing 11-7 shows an example of a varying variable used in the vertex shader.

Listing 11-7   **Vertex shader with varying variable**
```
attribute vec3 aVertex;

varying vec4 vColor;

void main(void) {
    gl_Position = vec4(aVertex, 1.0);
    vColor = vec4(aVertex.xyz / 2.0 + 0.5, 1.0);
}
```

In the example in Listing 11-7, the position of the vertex determines the color value assigned to the vColor variable. The variable is declared as varying, making it accessible in the fragment shader as shown in Listing 11-8.

Listing 11-8 Fragment shader with varying variable

```
#ifdef GL_ES
    precision highp float;
#endif

varying vec4 vColor;

void main(void) {
    gl_FragColor = vColor;
}
```

Because different colors were assigned to the vertices, the result is a smooth gradient across the triangle.

Not all data types are equal when it comes to varying variables. Only float and the floating point vector and matrix types can be declared as varying. **NOTE**

Rendering 3D Objects

Now that you have some basic knowledge about how shaders work in WebGL, it's time to move forward to constructing and rendering some simple 3D objects. Most applications have some setup code and a render cycle that continuously updates the rendered image.

The amount of setup code depends entirely on the nature of the application and the amount of 3D geometry and shaders. A few things usually need to be taken care of, however. One example is the clear color, which is the color to which the canvas is reset whenever it's cleared. You can set this color with the gl.clearColor() method:

```
gl.clearColor(0.15, 0.15, 0.15, 1.0);
```

The gl.clearColor() method takes four parameters, one for each of the red, green, blue, and alpha channels. WebGL always works with color values from 0 to 1. Usually, you should also enable depth testing:

```
gl.enable(gl.DEPTH_TEST);
```

This method makes WebGL compare the distances between the objects and the point of view so that elements that are farther away don't appear in front of closer objects. The `gl.DEPTH_TEST` argument passed to `gl.enable()` is a constant numeric value. WebGL has many of these constants, but you see only a small subset of them throughout this chapter. Some of the constants are capabilities that you can toggle on and off with the `gl.enable()` and `gl.disable()` methods, whereas others are parameters that you can query with the function `gl.getParameter()`. You can, for example, query the clear color with the `COLOR_CLEAR_VALUE` parameter:

```
var color = gl.getParameter(gl.COLOR_CLEAR_VALUE);
```

The type of the return value depends on the parameter; in the case of `gl.COLOR_CLEAR_VALUE`, the return value is a `Float32Array` with four numerical elements, corresponding to the RGBA values of the clear color.

Using vertex buffers

WebGL uses buffer objects to store vertex data. You load the buffer with values, and when you tell WebGL to render the 3D content, the data is loaded to the GPU. Any time you want to change the vertex data, you must load new values into the buffer. You create buffer objects with the `gl.createBuffer()` function:

```
var buffer = gl.createBuffer();
gl.bindBuffer(gl.ARRAY_BUFFER, buffer);
```

The `gl.bindBuffer()` function binds the buffer object to the `gl.ARRAY_BUFFER` target, telling WebGL to use the buffer as a vertex buffer.

```
gl.bufferData(
    gl.ARRAY_BUFFER, data, gl.STATIC_DRAW
);
```

Notice that the buffer object isn't passed to the `gl.bufferData()` function. Instead, the function acts on the buffer currently bound to the target specified in the first argument.

The third parameter specifies how the buffer is used in terms of how often the data is updated and accessed. The three available values are `gl.STATIC_DRAW`, `gl.DYNAMIC_DRAW`, and `gl.STREAM_DRAW`. The `gl.STATIC_DRAW` value is appropriate for data loaded once and drawn many times, `gl.DYNAMIC_DRAW` is for repeated updates and access, and `gl.STREAM_DRAW` is used when the data is loaded once and drawn only a few times.

The data is passed to `gl.bufferData()` as a `Float32Array` typed array object. This process is generic enough that you can add it to the `webgl.js` helper module. Listing 11-9 shows the `gl.createFloatBuffer()` function.

Listing 11-9   **Creating floating-point buffers**

```
jewel.webgl = (function() {
    ...
    function createFloatBuffer(gl, data) {
        var buffer = gl.createBuffer();
        gl.bindBuffer(gl.ARRAY_BUFFER, buffer);
        gl.bufferData(gl.ARRAY_BUFFER,
            new Float32Array(data), gl.STATIC_DRAW
        );
        return buffer;
    }

    return {
        createFloatBuffer : createFloatBuffer,
        ...
    }
})();
```

You can then use the function to create a buffer object from an array of coordinates:

```
var vbo = webgl.createFloatBuffer(gl, [
    -0.5, -0.5, 0.0, // triangle 1, vertex 1
     0.5, -0.5, 0.0, // triangle 1, vertex 2
     0.5,  0.5, 0.0, // triangle 1, vertex 3
    -0.5, -0.5, 0.0, // triangle 2, vertex 1
     0.5,  0.5, 0.0, // triangle 2, vertex 2
    -0.5,  0.5, 0.0  // triangle 2, vertex 3
]);
```

This code snippet creates the vertex data necessary to render a two-dimensional square.

Using index buffers

If you look at the vertices in the preceding example, you can see that some of the vertices are duplicated. The vertex buffer is created with six vertices when only four are really needed to make a square.

```
var vbo = webgl.createFloatBuffer(gl, [
    -0.5, -0.5, 0.0,
     0.5, -0.5, 0.0,
     0.5,  0.5, 0.0,
    -0.5,  0.5, 0.0
]);
```

You then need to declare how these vertices are used to create the triangles. You do this with an *index* buffer, which is a list of indices into the vertex list that describes which vertices belong together. Each three entries in the index buffer make up a triangle. The index buffer is created in a way similar to the vertex buffer, as Listing 11-10 shows.

Listing 11-10   **Creating index buffers**

```
jewel.webgl = (function() {
    ...
    function createIndexBuffer(gl, data) {
        var buffer = gl.createBuffer();
        gl.bindBuffer(gl.ELEMENT_ARRAY_BUFFER, buffer);
        gl.bufferData(
            gl.ELEMENT_ARRAY_BUFFER,
            new Uint16Array(data), gl.STATIC_DRAW
        );
        return buffer;
    }

    return {
        createIndexBuffer : createIndexBuffer,
        ...
    }
})();
```

The important differences here are that the buffer is initialized with the type gl.ELEMENT_ ARRAY_BUFFER and that the buffer uses integer data instead of floating-point values. You can now create the index buffer for the four vertices as follows:

```
var ibo = webgl.createIndexBuffer(gl, [
    0, 1, 2,
    0, 2, 3
]);
```

Using models, views, and projections

Simply defining the model data isn't enough to render it in any meaningful way. You also need to transform the vertices so that the object is rendered at the desired position in the world with the desired rotation. The coordinates in the vertex data are all relative to the object's own center, so if you want to position the object 5 units above the (x, z) plane, you add 5 to the y component of all vertices. If the viewer is located in any other position than (0,0,0), that location must also be subtracted from the vertex position. Any rotation of both the viewer and the object itself must also be taken into account.

What if those values change, though? You could retransform the vertex data and send it to the GPU again, but transferring vertex data from JavaScript to the GPU is relatively expensive in terms of resources and can potentially slow down your application. Instead of updating the vertex buffer in each render cycle, the transformation task is usually delegated to the vertex shader. To transform the vertices into screen coordinates, you need to construct two matrices: the model-view matrix and projection matrix. The model-view matrix describes the transformations needed to bring a vertex into the correct position relative to the viewer. The projection matrix describes how to project the transformed points onto the 2D screen. The matrices can be declared as uniform variables in the shaders, so you just need to update those in each cycle.

Working with vectors and matrices in JavaScript isn't trivial because there is no built-in support for either. However, available libraries provide the most common operations, which means you don't have to deal with all the details of matrix manipulation and linear algebra. One such library is glMatrix, which was developed specifically with WebGL in mind and is, to quote the developer, "stupidly fast." You can read more about glMatrix at http://glmatrix.net.

The model-view matrix

To set up the model-view matrix, first you need some helper functions to work with matrices. Most of the matrices you use with WebGL will be 4x4 matrices. Such a matrix can be represented as an array of 16 values, 4 values for each row. Start by adding the createIdentityMat4() function that creates a new identity matrix. Listing 11-11 shows the function.

Listing 11-11 Creating new matrices

```
jewel.webgl = (function() {
    ...
    function createIdentityMat4() {
        return [
            1, 0, 0, 0,
            0, 1, 0, 0,
            0, 0, 1, 0,
            0, 0, 0, 1
```

continued

Listing 11-11   continued

```
        ];
    }
    . . .
})();
```

The identity matrix is all zeroes with a main diagonal of ones and will be the starting point of the model-view matrix.

```
var mvMatrix = createIdentityMat4();
```

Again, if you're not comfortable with matrices and vectors, I recommend paying a visit to linear algebra section at the Khan Academy (https://www.khanacademy.org/math/linear-algebra).

You also need a few functions for applying transformations to this matrix. The first transformation is translation, as shown in Listing 11-12.

Listing 11-12   Matrix translation

```
jewel.webgl = (function() {
    . . .
    function translateMat4(M, V) {
        var x = V[0], y = V[1], z = V[2];
        M[12] = M[0] * x + M[4] * y + M[8]  * z + M[12];
        M[13] = M[1] * x + M[5] * y + M[9]  * z + M[13];
        M[14] = M[2] * x + M[6] * y + M[10] * z + M[14];
        M[15] = M[3] * x + M[7] * y + M[11] * z + M[15];
    }
    . . .
})();
```

This function takes a matrix, M, and adds a translation by the three-dimensional vector V. Therefore, when you multiply a point with the resulting matrix, the vector V is added to the position.

```
translateMat4(mvMatrix, [1.5, 0, 7.3]);
```

You use this to add the position of the object you want to render, as well as the position of the virtual camera. Notice that vectors are also just regular JavaScript arrays.

Next up is rotation, which is a bit more complex. Listing 11-13 shows the `rotateMat4()` function that adds a rotation transformation to the matrix.

Listing 11-13 **Matrix rotation**

```
jewel.webgl = (function() {
    ...
    function rotateMat4(M, A, axis) {
        var x = axis[0], y = axis[1], z = axis[2],
            axisLength = Math.sqrt(x*x + y*y + z*z),
            sA = Math.sin(A),
            cA = Math.cos(A),
            t = 1 - cA;

        // normalize axis to unit vector
        x /= axisLength;
        y /= axisLength;
        z /= axisLength;

        // copy values
        var M00 = M[0], M01 = M[1], M02 = M[2],  M03 = M[3],
            M10 = M[4], M11 = M[5], M12 = M[6],  M13 = M[7],
            M20 = M[8], M21 = M[9], M22 = M[10], M23 = M[11];

        // rotation matrix
        var R00 = x*x*t+cA, R01 = y*x*t+z*sA, R02 = z*x*t-y*sA,
            R10 = x*y*t-z*sA, R11 = y*y*t+cA, R12 = z*y*t+x*sA,
            R20 = x*z*t+y*sA, R21 = y*z*t-x*sA, R22 = z*z*t+cA;

        // multiply matrices
        M[0]  = M00 * R00 + M10 * R01 + M20 * R02;
        M[1]  = M01 * R00 + M11 * R01 + M21 * R02;
        M[2]  = M02 * R00 + M12 * R01 + M22 * R02;
        M[3]  = M03 * R00 + M13 * R01 + M23 * R02;
        M[4]  = M00 * R10 + M10 * R11 + M20 * R12;
        M[5]  = M01 * R10 + M11 * R11 + M21 * R12;
        M[6]  = M02 * R10 + M12 * R11 + M22 * R12;
        M[7]  = M03 * R10 + M13 * R11 + M23 * R12;
        M[8]  = M00 * R20 + M10 * R21 + M20 * R22;
        M[9]  = M01 * R20 + M11 * R21 + M21 * R22;
        M[10] = M02 * R20 + M12 * R21 + M22 * R22;
        M[11] = M03 * R20 + M13 * R21 + M23 * R22;
    }
    ...
})();
```

The rotateMat4() function adds a rotation transformation by setting up a rotation matrix using the specified angle, A, and axis, and then multiplying that matrix with the matrix M. The angle must be given in radians, not degrees.

```
rotateMat4(mvMatrix, Math.PI / 4, [0, 1, 0]);
```

You can combine the operations to a setModelView() function for the webgl.js helper module, as Listing 11-14 shows.

Listing 11-14   Setting the model-view matrix
```
jewel.webgl = (function() {
    ...
    function setModelView(gl, program, pos, rot, axis) {
        var mvMatrix = createIdentityMat4();
        translateMat4(mvMatrix, pos);
        rotateMat4(mvMatrix, rot, axis);

        gl.uniformMatrix4fv(
            gl.getUniformLocation(program, "uModelView"),
            false,
            mvMatrix
        );
        return mvMatrix;
    }
    return {
        setModelView : setModelView,
        ...
    };
})();
```

After you apply the translation and rotation to the model-view matrix, the matrix is updated in the shaders with the gl.uniformMatrix4fv() function. The model-view function assumes that the uniform in the shader is called uModelView.

The projection matrix
There's more than one way to project a 3D point to a 2D surface. One often-used method is *perspective projection* where objects that are far away appear smaller than objects that are closer, simulating what the human eye sees. This method requires a projection matrix that must be multiplied with the model-view matrix. Listing 11-15 shows how to create this matrix.

Listing 11-15   Projection matrix helper function

```
jewel.webgl = (function() {
    ...
    function createPerspectiveMat4(fov, aspect, near, far) {
        var f = 1.0 / Math.tan(fov * Math.PI / 360),
            nf = 1 / (near - far);
        return [
            f/aspect,  0,    0,                 0,
            0,         f,    0,                 0,
            0,         0,    (far+near)*nf,     -1,
            0,         0,    (2*far*near)*nf,   0
        ];
    }

    function setProjection(gl, pgm, fov, aspect, near, far) {
        var projMatrix = createPerspectiveMat4(
                            fov, aspect, near, far);
        gl.uniformMatrix4fv(
            gl.getUniformLocation(pgm, "uProjection"),
            false,
            projMatrix
        );
        return projMatrix;
    }

    return {
        setProjection : setProjection,
        ...
    };
})();
```

The `fov` parameter is the field-of-view (FOV) value, an angular measurement of how much the viewer can see. This value is given in degrees and specifies the vertical range of the FOV. Humans normally have a vertical FOV of around 100 degrees, but games often use a lower number. Values between 45 and 90 degrees are commonly used, but the perfect value is subjective and depends on the needs of the game.

The `aspect` parameter is the aspect ratio of the output surface. In most cases, you want to use the width-to-height ratio of the output canvas. The `near` and `far` parameters specify the boundaries of the view area. Anything closer to the viewer than `near` or farther away than `far` isn't rendered.

Matrices in the vertex shader

To use the two matrices in the vertex shader, you can add the uniform declarations for uModelView and uProjection:

```
uniform mat4 uModelView;
uniform mat4 uProjection;
```

To transform the vertex position, multiply it by both matrices. Because they are 4x4 matrices, you need to turn the vertex into vec4 before multiplying. Listing 11-16 shows the complete vertex shader.

Listing 11-16 **Transforming the vertex position**

```
attribute vec3 aVertex;

uniform mat4 uModelView;
uniform mat4 uProjection;
varying vec4 vColor;

void main(void) {
    gl_Position = uProjection * uModelView * vec4(aVertex, 1.0);
    vColor = vec4((aVertex.xyz + 1.0) / 2.0, 1.0);
}
```

Rendering

Often, it's not enough to just set the model-view and projection matrices once at the beginning of the application. If the object is animated—for example, if it's moving or rotating—the model-view must be continuously updated. In Chapter 9, I show you how to make simple animation cycles with the requestAnimationFrame() timing function. You can use the same technique to create a rendering cycle for WebGL. An example of a cycle function is shown in Listing 11-17.

Listing 11-17 **The rendering cycle**

```
function cycle() {
    var rotation = Date.now() / 1000,
        axis = [0, 1, 0.5],
        position = [0, 0, -5];
    webgl.setModelView(gl, program, position, rotation, axis);
    draw();
    requestAnimationFrame(cycle);
}
```

In this example, the model-view matrix is updated each frame to adjust the rotation. The rotation applied to the matrix is based on the current time, so the object will rotate at an even rate, regardless of how often the cycle runs. After you update the model-view, a `draw()` function, or something similar, can take care of rendering the object. An initial `cycle()` call sets things in motion.

Clearing the canvas

The `cycle()` function in Listing 11-17 calls a `draw()` function to do the actual rendering. Before rendering anything, this function needs to clear the canvas. You do so with the `gl.clear()` function:

```
gl.clear(mask);
```

This function takes a single parameter that specifies what it clears. Possible values that you can use are the constants `gl.COLOR_BUFFER_BIT`, `gl.DEPTH_BUFFER_BIT`, and `gl.STENCIL_BUFFER_BIT`. These values refer to the three buffers (color, depth, and stencil) that have become standard in modern graphics programming. The color buffer contains the actual pixels rendered to the canvas. The depth buffer keeps track of the depth of each pixel when drawing overlapping elements at different distances from the viewpoint. The third buffer, the stencil buffer, is essentially a mask applied to the rendered content—for shadow effects, for example.

The `mask` parameter is a *bit-mask*. Bit-masks provide a resource-efficient way to specify multiple on/off values in a single numeric value. Each `gl.*_BUFFER_BIT` value corresponds to a different bit in the number. This way, you can pass more than one value to the function by using the bitwise OR (pipe) operator to combine values:

```
gl.clear(gl.COLOR_BUFFER_BIT | gl.DEPTH_BUFFER_BIT);
```

This function clears both the color buffer and depth buffer. The color of the canvas is reset to the color set with the `gl.clearColor()` function, as shown at the beginning of this chapter.

Next, you need to declare the viewport, which is the rectangular area of the canvas where the rendered content is placed:

```
gl.viewport(0, 0, canvas.width, canvas.height);
```

You don't actually need to set the viewport in each render cycle, but if the dimensions of the `canvas` element change after you set the viewport, it's not automatically updated. Setting the viewport in each cycle ensures that the viewport is set to the full canvas area before anything is rendered.

Drawing the vertex data

Now you're ready to draw some shapes. Before the vertex data is available to the vertex shader through the aVertex attribute, you must activate the vertex buffer. First, make sure the vertex buffer is bound to the gl.ARRAY_BUFFER target:

```
gl.bindBuffer(gl.ARRAY_BUFFER, vbo);
```

You can now assign the buffer data to the attribute value with the gl.vertexAttrib-Pointer() function:

```
gl.vertexAttribPointer(aVertex, 3, gl.FLOAT, false, 0, 0);
```

This function assigns the currently bound buffer to the attribute variable identified by aVertex, which is an attribute location retrieved with gl.getAttribLocation(). The five remaining parameters are as follows: attribute size, data type, normalized, stride, and offset. The attribute size is the number of components of each vector; in this case, each vertex has three components. The data type refers to the data type of the vertex components. Note, however, that the values are converted to float regardless of the data type. The normalized parameter is used only for integer data. If it's set to true, the components are normalized to the range [-1,1] for signed values or [0,1] for unsigned values. The stride is the number of bytes from the start of one vertex to the start of the next. If you specify a stride value of 0, WebGL assumes that vertices are tightly packed and there are no gaps in the data. The last parameter specifies the position of the first vertex.

That's it for the vertices—on to the index buffer, which just needs to be bound to the gl.ELEMENT_ARRAY_BUFFER target:

```
gl.bindBuffer(gl.ELEMENT_ARRAY_BUFFER, ibo);
```

This tells WebGL to use the buffer as indices instead of vertex data. You can now draw the triangles with the gl.drawElements() function:

```
gl.drawElements(gl.TRIANGLES, num, gl.UNSIGNED_SHORT, 0);
```

The gl.drawElements() function takes four arguments: the rendering mode, number of elements, data type of the values, and offset at which to start. The gl.TRIANGLES mode tells WebGL that a new triangle starts after every three index values. The data type corresponds to the type of the values used to create the buffer data. The index buffer was created from a Uint16Array() typed array, which corresponds to the gl.UNSIGNED_SHORT value in WebGL. Unless you're rendering only a subset of the triangles, you set the offset parameter to zero.

Combine these calls, and you get a `draw()` function like the one shown in Listing 11-18.

Listing 11-18 Drawing the object

```
function draw() {
    gl.clear(gl.COLOR_BUFFER_BIT | gl.DEPTH_BUFFER_BIT);
    gl.viewport(0, 0, canvas.width, canvas.height);

    gl.bindBuffer(gl.ARRAY_BUFFER, geometry.vbo);
    gl.vertexAttribPointer(aVertex, 3, gl.FLOAT, false, 0, 0);
    gl.bindBuffer(gl.ELEMENT_ARRAY_BUFFER, geometry.ibo);
    gl.drawElements(
        gl.TRIANGLES, geometry.num, gl.UNSIGNED_SHORT, 0
    );
}
```

In the file `01-cube.html`, you can find an example of how to use the techniques shown here to render a colored, rotating cube, as seen in Figure 11-1.

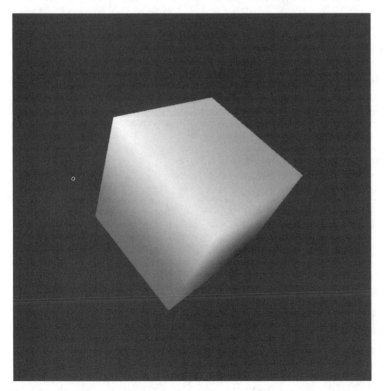

FIGURE 11-1: The procedures here, can be used to render this colored cube.

Other rendering modes

Rendering modes other than gl.TRIANGLES are available. WebGL can also render points and lines, and it has modes that interpret the vertex data in different ways. The available rendering modes are

- TRIANGLES

- TRIANGLE_STRIP

- TRIANGLE_FAN

- POINTS

- LINES

- LINE_LOOP

- LINE_STRIP

I don't go into detail on all these modes here, but I encourage you to play around with them. A mode like gl.TRIANGLE_STRIP is especially useful because it allows you to decrease the number of indices needed if you order the triangles so that the next triangle starts where the previous triangle ended. Other interesting modes are gl.POINTS, which is great for things such as particle effects, and gl.LINES mode, which you can use to render lines and wireframe-like objects.

In the previous example, WebGL needed a list of indices to be able to construct the triangles from the vertices. If the vertex data is packed so the vertices can be read from start to finish, you don't need the index data; instead, use the gl.drawArrays() function to render the geometry:

```
var vbo = createFloatBuffer([
    -0.5, -0.5, 0.0, // tri 1 ver 1
     0.5, -0.5, 0.0, // tri 1 ver 2
     0.5,  0.5, 0.0, // tri 1 ver 3 / tri 2 ver 1
    -0.5,  0.5, 0.0, // tri 2 ver 2
    -0.5, -0.5, 0.0  // tri 2 ver 3
]);
gl.drawArrays(gl.TRIANGLE_STRIP, 0, 5);
```

This example sets up the vertices needed to render a square as a triangle strip. Notice that the third vertex is used both as the third vertex in the first triangle and as the first vertex in the second triangle.

Loading Collada models

Specifying all the vertex and index values manually is feasible only for simple shapes, such as cubes, planes, or other basic shapes. It's better to import complex objects that require many triangles from external files. Be aware that 3D model formats are a dime a dozen, but only a few are easily parsed by JavaScript. The ideal solution would be JSON-based format, but I have yet to come across such a format supported in the major graphics applications.

XML, however, is also easy to use in JavaScript because you can parse it using the built-in DOM API. Collada is an XML-based model format maintained by the Khronos Group, the group that's responsible for WebGL. The format has gained popularity in recent years, and many 3D modeling applications can export their models as Collada files.

If you're new to 3D modeling and don't feel like shelling out hundreds or even thousands of dollars for a 3D graphics application, try Blender (`www.blender.org`), a free and open source 3D graphics package. It's available on several platforms, including Windows, Mac OSX, and Linux, and it has a feature set comparable to those found in many commercial applications. It also supports exporting and importing a variety of file formats, including Collada.

Fetching the model file

First, you need to load the model data, but you can easily take care of that with a bit of Ajax. The `webgl.loadModel()` function in Listing 11-19 shows the standard Ajax code needed to load a model file.

Listing 11-19 Loading the XML file

```
jewel.webgl = (function() {
    ...
    function loadModel(gl, file, callback) {
        var xhr = new XMLHttpRequest();
        xhr.open("GET", file, true);
        // override mime type to make sure it's loaded as XML
        xhr.overrideMimeType("text/xml");
        xhr.onreadystatechange = function() {
            if (xhr.readyState == 4) {
                if (xhr.status == 200 && xhr.responseXML) {
                    callback(parseCollada(gl, xhr.responseXML));
                }
            }
        };
        xhr.send(null);
    }
```

continued

Listing 11-19   continued

```
    return {
        loadModel : loadModel,
        ...
    };
})();
```

When the file finishes loading, the XML document is available in the `responseXML` property of `xhr`. This document is passed on to a `webgl.parseCollada()` function, which must parse the XML document and create the necessary buffer objects.

Parsing the XML data

The `parseCollada()` function can use Sizzle to extract the relevant nodes, and from there, it's a matter of constructing arrays with the values. I don't go into details of the Collada XML format and the `parseCollada()` function. However, you can find more on the Collada specification at `www.khronos.org/collada`. You can find the full parsing function in the `webgl.js` module in the code archive for this chapter, but please note that it implements a very small subset of the format to get the test model loaded. Listing 11-20 shows the return value from the parsing function.

Listing 11-20   Parsing Collada XML data

```
jewel.webgl = (function() {
    ...
    function parseCollada(gl, xml) {

        ... // XML parsing

        return {
            vbo : createFloatBuffer(gl, vertices),
            nbo : createFloatBuffer(gl, normals),
            ibo : createIndexBuffer(gl, indices),
            num : indices.length
        };
    }
    ...
})();
```

The return value of `webgl.parseCollada()` is a small object with the three buffer objects `vbo`, `nbo`, and `ibo`, as well as a number indicating the number of indices. The `vbo` and `ibo` buffers contain the vertex and index data; the third buffer, `nbo`, contains the *normal vectors*. You see how these normal vectors are used in the next section when I show you how to enhance the rendering with textures and lighting effects. The example in the file 02-collada.html uses the Collada loading code to load and render a model of a sphere. The resulting image is shown in Figure 11-2.

FIGURE 11-2: This sphere model was loaded from a Collada file.

You cannot access local files with Ajax requests. This example needs to run from a web server in order to work.   `REMEMBER`

Using Textures and Lighting

The two examples you've seen so far have been a bit bland and flat. To really bring out the third dimension in the image, the scene needs lighting. The color scheme of the surface isn't very interesting either. In many cases, the surface should be covered by a texture image to simulate a certain material. First, however, look at the lighting issue.

Adding light

You can use many different methods to apply lighting to a 3D scene, ranging from relatively simple approximations to realistic but complex mathematical models. I stick to a simple solution called *Phong lighting*, which is a common approximation of light reflecting off a surface.

The Phong model applies light to a point on a surface by using three different components: ambient, diffuse, and specular light. Ambient light simulates the scattering of light from the surrounding environment—that is, light that doesn't hit the point directly from the source but bounces off other objects in the vicinity. Diffuse light is the large, soft highlight on the surface that appears when light coming directly from the light source hits the surface. This light component simulates the diffuse reflection that happens when the surface reflects incoming light in many different directions. Specular light depends on the position of the viewer and simulates the small intense highlights that appear when light reflects off the surface directly toward the eye. The color of a surface point is then determined as the surface color multiplied by the sum of the three lighting components:

```
gl_FragColor = color * (ambient + diffuse + specular);
```

The ambient component is the easiest to implement because it's simply a constant. The diffuse and specular components require a bit of trigonometry, however.

Angles and normals

The diffuse light component uses the angle between the light ray hitting the object's surface and the surface normal. The normal to a point on the surface is a vector that's perpendicular to the surface at that point. For example, a surface that's parallel to the ground has a normal vector that points straight up. Normal vectors are normalized, so the norm, or length, of the vector is exactly 1:

```
length = sqrt(v.x * v.x + v.y * v.y + v.z * v.z) = 1.0
```

This is also called the *unit length,* and a vector with unit length—for example, a normal vector—is called a *unit vector*.

Because the 3D geometry is made of triangles and vertices and not smoothly curved surfaces, the normals are actually vertex normals in the sense that each vertex has a normal perpendicular to a plane tangent at that vertex position. The Collada loading function shown earlier already creates a normal buffer object with the normal data found in the model file.

In the vertex shader, you access the vertex normals through an attribute variable, just as you access the vertices themselves:

```
attribute vec3 aNormal;
```

You also activate and enable the normal buffer in the same way you do the vertex buffer:

```
var aNormal = gl.getAttribLocation(program, "aNormal");
gl.enableVertexAttribArray(aNormal);
```

The code that binds the buffer data and assigns it to the aNormal attribute shouldn't come as a surprise either:

```
gl.bindBuffer(gl.ARRAY_BUFFER, nbo);
gl.vertexAttribPointer(aNormal, 3, gl.FLOAT, false, 0, 0);
```

When the vertex data is transformed by the model-view matrix, you also need to transform the normals. If you haven't applied any scaling on the model-view matrix, which the examples shown here don't do, you can just use the upper-left 3x3 part of the model-view matrix. If the model-view has been scaled, you need to use the *inverse transpose* of the model-view matrix. Listing 11-21 shows the setNormalMatrix() function for the helper module.

Listing 11-21 **Setting the normal matrix**

```
jewel.webgl = (function() {
    ...
    function toMat3(M) {
        return [
            M[0], M[1], M[2],
            M[4], M[5], M[6],
            M[8], M[9], M[10],
        ];
    }

    function setNormalMatrix(gl, program, mv) {
        var normalMatrix = toMat3(mv);
        gl.uniformMatrix3fv(
            gl.getUniformLocation(program, "uNormalMatrix"),
            false,
```

continued

Listing 11-21　**continued**

```
            normalMatrix
        );
        return normalMatrix;
    }

    return {
        setNormalMatrix : setNormalMatrix,
        ...
    };
})();
```

Per-vertex lighting

With the normal vector accessible in the vertex shader, you're able to use it to calculate the amount of light that hits a given vertex. First, I show how you can implement the diffuse part of Phong lighting in the vertex shader. The examples I show you next use a single static light source. The light position is specified as a uniform variable, uLightPosition. The final diffuse light value is passed to the fragment shader via a varying variable, vDiffuse.

Start by transforming the normal by multiplying it with the normal matrix. Make sure you renormalize it after the multiplication:

```
vec3 normal = normalize(uNormalMatrix * aNormal);
```

The direction of the light ray is easily determined by subtracting the transformed vertex position from the position of the light:

```
vec3 lightDir = normalize(uLightPosition - position.xyz);
```

Now use the dot product of these two vectors to calculate the amount of diffuse light at this vertex:

```
vDiffuse = max(dot(normal, lightDir), 0.0);
```

If the light direction is parallel to the surface, the normal and light direction vectors are orthogonal, causing the dot product to be zero. The closer the two vectors are to being parallel, the closer the diffuse value gets to 1. The result is that the lighting is more intense where the light hits the surface straight on. Listing 11-22 shows the complete vertex shader.

Listing 11-22 **Calculating per-vertex diffuse light**

```
attribute vec3 aVertex;
attribute vec3 aNormal;

uniform mat4 uModelView;
uniform mat4 uProjection;
uniform mat3 uNormalMatrix;
uniform vec3 uLightPosition;

varying float vDiffuse;
varying vec3 vColor;

void main(void) {
    vec4 position = uModelView * vec4(aVertex, 1.0);
    vec3 normal = normalize(uNormalMatrix * aNormal);
    vec3 lightDir = normalize(uLightPosition - position.xyz);
    vDiffuse = max(dot(normal, lightDir), 0.0);
    vColor = aVertex.xyz * 0.5 + 0.5;
    gl_Position = uProjection * position;
}
```

In the fragment shader, shown in Listing 11-23, applying the light is just a matter of multiplying the pixel color with the sum of the ambient and the diffuse components.

Listing 11-23 **Lighting in the fragment shader**

```
#ifdef GL_ES
precision mediump float;
#endif

uniform float uAmbient;
varying float vDiffuse;
varying vec3 vColor;

void main(void) {
    gl_FragColor = vec4(vColor * (uAmbient + vDiffuse), 1.0);
}
```

You can find this example in the file `03-lighting-vertex.html`. It produces the result shown in Figure 11-3.

FIGURE 11-3: This sphere has per-vertex lighting.

Adding per-pixel lighting

As you can see in Figure 11-3, it's easy to make out the triangles in the band where the transition from light to shadow occurs. One solution to this problem is to move the calculations to the fragment shader. This is called *per-fragment* or *per-pixel* lighting because the light is calculating per pixel rather than per vertex. Doing calculations in the fragment shader can often produce better results, but doing so comes at the cost of using extra resources. Although the vertex shader needs only three calculations to cover a triangle, the fragment shader must calculate for every pixel drawn on the screen.

Diffuse light

The fragment must be able to access the vertex normal. Listing 11-24 shows the revised vertex shader with the calculations removed and the normal exported to a varying variable.

Listing 11-24 **Vertex shader for per-pixel lighting**

```
attribute vec3 aVertex;
attribute vec3 aNormal;

uniform mat4 uModelView;
uniform mat4 uProjection;
uniform mat3 uNormalMatrix;

varying vec4 vPosition;
varying vec3 vNormal;
varying vec3 vColor;

void main(void) {
    vPosition = uModelView * vec4(aVertex, 1.0);
    vColor = aVertex.xyz * 0.5 + 0.5;
    vNormal = uNormalMatrix * aNormal;
    gl_Position = uProjection * vPosition;
}
```

The calculations in the fragment shader, shown in Listing 11-25, are almost identical to those from the vertex shader in Listing 11-22.

Listing 11-25 **Diffuse light in the fragment shader**

```
#ifdef GL_ES
precision mediump float;
#endif

uniform vec3 uLightPosition;
uniform float uAmbient;

varying vec4 vPosition;
varying vec3 vNormal;
varying vec3 vColor;

void main(void) {
    vec3 normal = normalize(vNormal);
    vec3 lightDir = normalize(uLightPosition - vPosition.xyz);
    float diffuse = max(dot(normal, lightDir), 0.0);
    vec3 color = vColor * (uAmbient + diffuse);
    gl_FragColor = vec4(color, 1.0);
}
```

Now that you've moved to the fragment shader, you can also add the specular component to get a shiny highlight.

Specular light

To calculate the intense specular light component, you need two new vectors: the *view direction* and *reflection direction*. The view direction is a vector pointing from the view position to a point on the surface. If vPosition is the position relative to the eye, the direction is just -vPosition, normalized to unit length:

```
vec3 viewDir = normalize(-vPosition.xyz);
```

The reflection direction is the direction the light reflects off the surface. If you know the surface normal and direction of the incoming light, GLSL provides a reflect() function that calculates the reflected vector:

```
vec3 reflectDir = reflect(-lightDir, normal);
```

The amount of specular light that needs to be added to the surface point depends on the angle between these two vectors. As with the diffuse light, you can use the dot product of the vectors as a specular light value:

```
float specular = max(dot(reflectDir, viewDir), 0.0);
```

You can control the shininess of the surface by raising the specular value to some power:

```
specular = pow(specular, 20.0);
```

Finally, add the specular component to the lighting sum. Listing 11-26 shows the additions to the fragment shader.

Listing 11-26   Specular light in the fragment shader

```
...
void main(void) {
    ...
    vec3 viewDir = normalize(-vPosition.xyz);
    vec3 reflectDir = reflect(-lightDir, normal);
    float specular = max(dot(reflectDir, viewDir), 0.0);
    specular = pow(specular, 20.0);
```

```
    vec3 color = vColor * (uAmbient + diffuse + specular);
    gl_FragColor = vec4(color, 1.0);
}
```

The result is shown in Figure 11-4. Moving the light calculations to the fragment shader gives a much smoother transition between the different shades, and the addition of a specular component adds a nice, shiny look to the surface. The code for this example is located in the file 04-lighting-fragment.html.

FIGURE 11-4: The transitions are smoother in this sphere with per-pixel lighting.

Creating textures

It's time to get rid of that boring color gradient on the sphere and slap on something a bit more interesting. To use a texture image, start by creating a texture object:

```
var texture = gl.createTexture();
```

The texture object needs to be bound to a target to let WebGL know how you want to use it. The target you want is `gl.TEXTURE_2D`:

```
gl.bindTexture(gl.TEXTURE_2D, texture);
```

The functions `gl.texParameteri()` and `gl.texParameterf()` enable you to set parameters that control how the texture is used. For example, you can specify how WebGL should scale the texture image when it's viewed at different distances. The parameters `gl.TEXTURE_MIN_FILTER` and `gl.TEXTURE_MAG_FILTER` specify the scaling method used for minification and magnification, respectively:

```
gl.texParameteri(
    gl.TEXTURE_2D, gl.TEXTURE_MIN_FILTER, gl.LINEAR
);
gl.texParameteri(
    gl.TEXTURE_2D, gl.TEXTURE_MAG_FILTER, gl.LINEAR
);
```

The value `gl.NEAREST` toggles the fast nearest-neighbor method, whereas `gl.LINEAR` chooses the smoother linear filter.

A term you'll probably encounter now and then is *mipmaps*. Mipmaps are previously calculated, downscaled versions of the texture image you can use to increase performance. You can make WebGL generate the mipmaps automatically by calling the `gl.generateMipmaps()` function:

```
gl.generateMipmaps(gl.TEXTURE_2D);
```

You can then set the minification parameter to one of the values:

- `gl.NEAREST_MIPMAP_NEAREST`
- `gl.LINEAR_MIPMAP_NEAREST`
- `gl.NEAREST_MIPMAP_LINEAR`
- `gl.LINEAR_MIPMAP_LINEAR`

NOTE If you do use mipmapping, the dimensions of your textures must be powers of two, such as 512x512, 256x256, or 2048x1024. The mipmap images are entered into mipmap levels where each level contains a version that scales to $1/2^n$, where *n* is the level number.

Loading image data

You're now ready to load some pixels into the texture object. You do this with the texImage2D() function:

```
gl.texImage2D(
    gl.TEXTURE_2D, 0, gl.RGBA, gl.RGBA, gl.UNSIGNED_BYTE, image
);
```

The second parameter specifies the mipmap level into which this data should be loaded. Because you're not using mipmaps here, the data should be loaded into level 0. The third parameter is the pixel format used internally by the texture, and the fourth parameter is the pixel format used in the image data. It's not actually possible to convert between formats when loading data, so the two arguments must match. Valid formats are gl.RGBA, gl.RGB, gl.ALPHA, gl.LUMINANCE, and gl.LUMINANCE_ALPHA. The fifth parameter specifies the data type of the pixel values, usually gl.UNSIGNED_BYTE. Consult Appendix B or the WebGL specification for detailed information on pixel formats and types. The last parameter, image, is the source of the image data and can be an img element, a canvas element, or a video element.

You can also use gl.texImage2D() to load pixel values from an array. In that case, the function uses a few additional parameters that specify the dimensions of the texture data:

```
// create array that can hold a 200x100 px RGBA image
var image = new Uint8Array(200 * 100 * 4);
// fill array with values
...
// and load the data into the texture
gl.texImage2D(
    gl.TEXTURE_2D, 0, gl.RGBA,
    200, 100, 0, // width, height, border
    gl.RGBA, gl.UNSIGNED_BYTE, image
);
```

The type of the array passed to gl.texImage2D() must match the data type specified in the call. For example, gl.UNSIGNED_BYTE requires a Uint8Array. Listing 11-27 shows the texture creation combined in a function for the helper module.

Listing 11-27   Creating texture objects

```
jewel.webgl = (function() {
    ...
    function createTextureObject(gl, image) {
        var texture = gl.createTexture();
        gl.bindTexture(gl.TEXTURE_2D, texture);
        gl.texParameteri(
            gl.TEXTURE_2D, gl.TEXTURE_MIN_FILTER, gl.LINEAR);
        gl.texParameteri(
            gl.TEXTURE_2D, gl.TEXTURE_MAG_FILTER, gl.LINEAR);
        gl.texImage2D(gl.TEXTURE_2D, 0,
            gl.RGBA, gl.RGBA, gl.UNSIGNED_BYTE, image);
        gl.bindTexture(gl.TEXTURE_2D, null);
        return texture;
    }

    return {
        createTextureObject : createTextureObject,
        ...
    }
})();
```

When you're loading data from an `img` element, the image must be fully loaded before calling `gl.texImage2D()`. Just wait until the `load` event fires on the `img` element before you create the texture:

```
var image = new Image();
image.addEventListener("load", function() {
    // create and load texture data...
}, false);
image.src = "earthmap.jpg";
```

You can also add a listener to the `error` event on the `img` element if you want to catch loading errors.

In the code archive for this chapter, you'll find the texture of the Earth's surface, which I downloaded from NASA's Visible Earth website (`http://visibleearth.nasa.gov`). The images you find there are generally not copyrighted and you are free to use them in your own projects. Figure 11-5 shows the texture map. In the following example, I show you how to apply this texture map to the sphere to make a rotating planet.

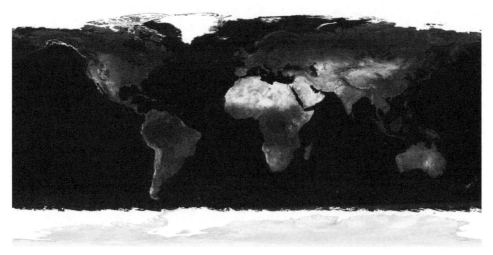

FIGURE 11-5: You can apply this Earth texture map to a sphere.

Using textures in shaders

Textures are referenced in the fragment shader using a uniform variable with a special data type. The `sampler2D` type is a handle that points to the texture data and can be used with a function called `texture2D()` to sample color values from the texture image.

```
uniform sampler2D uTexture;
gl_FragColor = texture2D(uTexture, vTexCoord);
```

The second parameter to `texture2D()` is a `vec2` with `x` and `y` values between 0 and 1, specifying the point on the texture image that should be sampled. The upper-left corner is given as (0.0, 0.0) and the lower-right corner as (1.0, 1.0). Texture coordinates are often created as buffers and accessed in the vertex shader alongside the vertices. You can use a varying variable to transfer and interpolate the coordinates to the fragment shader to create continuous texture mapping across the surface of the triangle. For example, to map an image to a flat rectangle, you specify the texture coordinates (0.0, 0.0) at the upper-left vertex, (1.0, 0.0) at the upper-right vertex, and so on.

Calculating texture coordinates

For intricate 3D objects, the modeler or texture artist often assigns texture coordinates in the modeling application and then exports them with the rest of the model data. Almost all model formats, including Collada, are able to attach texture coordinates to the vertices. However, because I'm dealing with a simple sphere in this example, I instead show how you can calculate these coordinates manually in the shader.

You do the calculations in the fragment shader, but first you need a bit of information from the vertex shader. The texture coordinates on the sphere depend on the position of the given point. For calculating spherical coordinates, the surface normal is just as good, so the vertex shader should export the normal to a varying vector. The normal must be the original, unmodified normal. Listing 11-28 shows the new varying variable in the vertex shader.

Listing 11-28   Passing the normal to the fragment shader

```
...
varying vec3 vOrgNormal;

void main(void) {
    ...
    vOrgNormal = aNormal;
}
```

The fragment shader calculates the spherical coordinates from the normal and uses those as texture coordinates. In a spherical coordinate system, a point is described by a radial distance and two angles, usually denoted by the Greek letters θ and π. The relation between Cartesian (x,y,z) and spherical coordinates is as follows:

```
radius = sqrt(x*x + y*y + z*z)
theta = acos(y / radius)
phi = atan(z / x)
```

All points on the surface of a sphere are at the same distance from the center, so only the two angles are important. Because you used the normal rather than the vertex position, you know the radius is equal to 1, so the conversion simplifies to

```
theta = acos(y)
phi = atan(z / x)
```

If you apply these equations to the normal vector in the fragment shader, you can use `theta` and `phi` as texture coordinates, as shown in Listing 11-29.

Listing 11-29   Fragment shader with spherical texture

```
...
varying vec3 vOrgNormal;
uniform sampler2D uTexture;
```

```
void main(void) {
    ...
    float theta = acos(vOrgNormal.y);
    float phi = atan(vOrgNormal.z, vOrgNormal.x);
    vec2 texCoord = vec2(-phi / 2.0, theta) / 3.14159;

    vec4 texColor = texture2D(uTexture, texCoord);

    vec3 color = texColor.rgb * (uAmbient + diffuse + specular);
    gl_FragColor = vec4(color, 1.0);
}
```

Texture coordinates range from 0 to 1, but the theta and phi angles are given in radians. The theta angle goes from zero to pi, and phi goes from zero to 2 pi. To account for this, both coordinates are divided by pi, and phi is further divided by 2. The pixel value is then fetched from the texture image using the texture2D() function and the newly calculated texture coordinates. The file 05-texture.html contains the full sample code for rendering the textured sphere shown in Figure 11-6.

FIGURE 11-6: Sphere with planet texture.

This concludes the walkthrough of the WebGL API, and you now have a basic understanding of how you can use WebGL to create 3D graphics for your games and applications. The next section shows you how to use WebGL to add a new display module to Jewel Warrior.

Creating the WebGL display

You now know the basics of WebGL, so it's time to get to work. The new display module, shown in Listing 11-30, goes in the file display.webgl.js. It uses the same functions as the canvas display module, so the two can be used interchangeably.

Listing 11-30   The WebGL display module

```
jewel.display = (function() {
    var animations = [],
        previousCycle,
        firstRun = true,
        jewels, cursor,
        paused;

    function initialize(callback) {
        paused = false;
        if (firstRun) {
            setup();
            firstRun = false;
        }
        jewels = [];
        requestAnimationFrame(cycle);
        callback();
    }

    function cycle() { }
    function setup() { }

    function setCursor() { }
    function levelUp() { }
    function gameOver() { }
    function redraw() { }
    function moveJewels() { }
    function removeJewels() { }

    return {
```

```
        initialize : initialize,
        redraw : redraw,
        setCursor : setCursor,
        moveJewels : moveJewels,
        removeJewels : removeJewels,
        refill : redraw,
        levelUp : levelUp,
        gameOver : gameOver
    };
})();
```

The WebGL display module can borrow the addAnimation() and renderAnimations() functions from the canvas module, so they can be copied from display.canvas.js without any changes. If you find yourself copying behavior like this, consider whether it would be better to move it to a separate module. In this case, I just copied the animation functions.

Loading the WebGL files

Now that you have two different display modules, you need to alter the loading sequence in index.html to load the correct module, which depends on whether the browser supports WebGL. First, add a feature detection method in jewel.js, as shown in Listing 11-31.

Listing 11-31 **Detecting WebGL support**

```
var jewel = (function() {
    ...
    function hasWebGL() {
        var canvas = document.createElement("canvas"),
            gl = canvas.getContext("webgl") ||
                canvas.getContext("experimental-webgl");
        return !!gl;
    }

    return {
        hasWebGL: hasWebGL,
        ...
    };
})();
```

You can use this test to determine which display module to load in index.html. Listing 11-32 shows the changes.

Listing 11-32   **Loading the WebGL display module**

```
window.addEventListener("load", function() {
    jewel.load("scripts/dom.js");
    if (jewel.isStandalone()) {
        ...
        if (jewel.hasWebGL()) {
            jewel.load("scripts/webgl.js");
            jewel.load("scripts/display.webgl.js");
        } else {
            jewel.load("scripts/display.canvas.js");
        }
        ...
    } else {
        ...
    }
});
```

The game now automatically loads the WebGL display module if the browser supports it and falls back to the 2D canvas module if WebGL isn't available.

Creating the jewel objects

The jewels list in the WebGL display differs from that in the canvas display. Instead of the two-dimensional array structure, jewels is now just an array of jewel objects. The create-Jewel() function in Listing 11-33 adds new jewels to the list.

Listing 11-33   **Creating new jewels**

```
jewel.display = (function() {
    ...
    function createJewel(x, y, type) {
        var jewel = {
            x : x,
            y : y,
            type : type,
            rnd : Math.random() * 2 - 1,
            scale : 1
        };
        jewels.push(jewel);
        return jewel;
    }

    function getJewel(x, y) {
        return jewels.filter(function(j){
```

```
            return j.x == x && j.y == y;
        }) [0];
    }
    ...
}) ();
```

You can use the `rnd` property on the jewel object to add variation to the jewels so they don't all look exactly alike—for example, by making the rotation of each jewel slightly different. The `getJewel()` function is a helper function that searches the list for jewels matching a given set of coordinates. Both of these functions are used in the `redraw()` function, as shown in Listing 11-34.

Listing 11-34 **Redrawing the board**

```
jewel.display = (function() {
    ...
    function redraw(newJewels, callback) {
        var x, y,
            jewel, type;
        for (x = 0; x < cols; x++) {
            for (y = 0; y < rows; y++) {
                type = newJewels[x][y];
                jewel = getJewel(x, y);
                if (jewel) {
                    jewel.type = type;
                } else {
                    createJewel(x, y, type);
                }
            }
        }
        callback();
    }

    function setCursor(x, y, selected) {
        cursor = null;
        if (arguments.length > 0) {
            cursor = {
                x : x,
                y : y,
                selected : selected
            };
        }
    }
    ...
}) ();
```

The redraw() function iterates over all positions on the board. If a jewel object exists in the given position, its type is changed; otherwise, a new jewel object is created. Listing 11-34 also shows the setCursor() function, which is almost identical to the one from the 2D canvas display.

Setting up WebGL

Now that the basic functionality for creating the jewel data is in place, you can move on to setting up the WebGL environment. The first step to setting up the WebGL display is adding a new canvas element and getting a WebGL context object for the canvas. You do so by using the setup() function, as shown in Listing 11-35.

Listing 11-35 Setting up the WebGL display

```
jewel.display = (function() {
    var canvas, gl, cols, rows,
        . . .

    function setup() {
        var $ = jewel.dom.$,
            boardElement = $("#game-screen .game-board")[0];

        cols = jewel.settings.cols;
        rows = jewel.settings.rows;

        canvas = document.createElement("canvas");
        gl = jewel.webgl.createContext(canvas);

        jewel.dom.addClass(canvas, "board");
        boardElement.appendChild(canvas);

        var rect = canvas.getBoundingClientRect();
        canvas.width = rect.width;
        canvas.height = rect.height;

        setupGL();
    }

    . . .
})();
```

The setup() function ends by calling a setupGL() function. This function, shown in Listing 11-36, is responsible for setting up the WebGL context so that it's ready to render the game display.

Listing 11-36 **Initializing the WebGL context**

```
jewel.display = (function() {
    var program,
        geometry,
        aVertex, aNormal,
        uScale, uColor,
        ...

    function setupGL() {
        var webgl = jewel.webgl;
        gl.enable(gl.DEPTH_TEST);
        gl.enable(gl.CULL_FACE);
        gl.enable(gl.BLEND);
        gl.blendFunc(gl.SRC_ALPHA, gl.ONE);

        program = setupShaders();
        setupTexture();
        gl.useProgram(program);

        aVertex = gl.getAttribLocation(program, "aVertex");
        aNormal = gl.getAttribLocation(program, "aNormal");
        uScale = gl.getUniformLocation(program, "uScale");
        uColor = gl.getUniformLocation(program, "uColor");

        gl.enableVertexAttribArray(aVertex);
        gl.enableVertexAttribArray(aNormal);

        gl.uniform1f(
            gl.getUniformLocation(program, "uAmbient"),
            0.12
        );
        gl.uniform3f(
            gl.getUniformLocation(program, "uLightPosition"),
            20, 15, -10
        );

        webgl.loadModel(gl, "models/jewel.dae", function(geom) {
            geometry = geom;
        });
        webgl.setProjection(
            gl, program, 60, cols/rows, 0.1, 100
        );
```

continued

Listing 11-36 **continued**
```
    }

    function setupTexture() {}

    function setupShaders() {}
    ...
})();
```

Note that a few of the uniform locations as well as the attribute locations are stored for later use. You store them so you don't have to look them up in each render cycle. The locations don't change, so you don't need to query them more than once.

Rendering jewels

Figure 11-7 shows the jewel model that the WebGL display uses. You can find this isolated jewel renderer in the file 06-jewel.html.

FIGURE 11-7: The WebGL display uses this jewel model.

Blending and transparency

In the `setupGL()` function, notice that two new settings are enabled: `gl.BLEND` and `gl.CULL_FACE`. Both are used to give the jewels a semitransparent appearance.

Enabling `gl.BLEND` lets you set rules for how the color output from the fragment shader is blended with the color value underneath the fragment. You set the blending rule with the `gl.blendFunc()` function. This function takes two parameters, a source factor and a destination factor, that describe how the two colors are computed. The destination is the existing color, and the source is the incoming color drawn on top. Setting the source factor to `gl.SRC_ALPHA` means that the RGB values in the fragment color are multiplied by the alpha value; setting the destination factor to `gl.ONE` means that the existing color is just multiplied by 1. You can find the full list of blends in Appendix C, which is part of the online bonus content on the book's companion website.

The `gl.CULL_FACE` setting enables face culling, which essentially removes the triangles facing away from the viewpoint. The direction in which a triangle faces depends on whether it's drawn clockwise or counterclockwise on the screen. The default mode is that triangles that are drawn counterclockwise facing the viewer, whereas clockwise triangles face away. When culling is enabled, you can switch between culling front-facing and back-facing triangles with the `gl.cullFace()` function. This function takes a single argument, which is either `gl.FRONT` or `gl.BACK`. If you cull the front-facing triangles, only the internal surface of the object is visible. If you then do another render on top of that with blending enabled and back-facing triangles culled, the effect is a translucent object where the backside is visible through the model.

Drawing jewels

The render cycle is similar to the cycle from the canvas display, but it calls only the `draw()` function after the model file finishes loading and the `geometry` object is ready. Listing 11-37 shows the `cycle()` function.

Listing 11-37 The render cycle

```
jewel.display = (function() {
    var paused = false,
        ...

    function cycle() {
        var now = Date.now();
        if (!paused) {
            renderAnimations(now, previousCycle);
            if (geometry) {
                draw();
```

continued

Listing 11-37 **continued**

```
                }
            }

            previousCycle = now;
            requestAnimationFrame(cycle);
        }

        function pause() {
            paused = true;
        }
        function resume(pauseTime) {
            paused = false;
            for (var i=0;i<animations.length;i++) {
                animations[i].startTime += pauseTime;
            }
        }

        return {
            pause : pause,
            resume : resume,
            ...
        };
    })();
```

Despite its name, the `draw()` function doesn't actually do any drawing. Its task is to clear the canvas and bind the buffers. Listing 11-38 shows the function.

Listing 11-38 **Preparing for the next frame**

```
jewel.display = (function() {
    ...
    function draw() {
        gl.clear(gl.COLOR_BUFFER_BIT | gl.DEPTH_BUFFER_BIT);
        gl.viewport(0, 0, canvas.width, canvas.height);

        gl.bindBuffer(gl.ARRAY_BUFFER, geometry.vbo);
        gl.vertexAttribPointer(
            aVertex, 3, gl.FLOAT, false, 0, 0);

        gl.bindBuffer(gl.ARRAY_BUFFER, geometry.nbo);
        gl.vertexAttribPointer(
            aNormal, 3, gl.FLOAT, false, 0, 0);
```

```
        gl.bindBuffer(gl.ELEMENT_ARRAY_BUFFER, geometry.ibo);

        jewels.forEach(drawJewel);
    }
    ...
})();
```

All the jewels use the same geometry, so you need to bind the buffers only once. You can then draw the model as many times as you want. The draw() function finishes by calling drawJewel() on all jewels. This function is shown in Listing 11-39.

Listing 11-39   Drawing a single jewel

```
jewel.display = (function() {
    ...
    var colors = [
        [0.1, 0.8, 0.1],
        [0.9, 0.1, 0.1],
        [0.9, 0.3, 0.8],
        [0.8, 1.0, 1.0],
        [0.2, 0.4, 1.0],
        [1.0, 0.4, 0.1],
        [1.0, 0.9, 0.1]
    ];

    function drawJewel(jwl) {
        var webgl = jewel.webgl,
            x = jwl.x - cols / 2 + 0.5,   // make position
            y = -jwl.y + rows / 2 - 0.5, // relative to center
            scale = jwl.scale,
            n = geometry.num;

        var mv = webgl.setModelView(gl, program,
            [x * 4.4, y * 4.4, -32], // scale and move back
            Date.now() / 1500 + jwl.rnd * 100, // rotate
            [0, 1, 0.1] // rotation axis
        );
        webgl.setNormalMatrix(gl, program, mv);

        // add effect for selected jewel
        if (cursor && jwl.x==cursor.x && jwl.y==cursor.y) {
            scale *= 1.0 + Math.sin(Date.now() / 100) * 0.1;
        }
```

continued

Listing 11-39   continued

```
        gl.uniform1f(uScale, scale);
        gl.uniform3fv(uColor, colors[jwl.type]);

        gl.cullFace(gl.FRONT);
        gl.drawElements(gl.TRIANGLES, n, gl.UNSIGNED_SHORT, 0);

        gl.cullFace(gl.BACK);
        gl.drawElements(gl.TRIANGLES, n, gl.UNSIGNED_SHORT, 0);
    }
    ...
})();
```

First, the model-view and normal matrices are updated to match the position of the current jewel. The jewel position is also scaled and moved back to get the full 8x8 grid of jewels to fit within the confines of the canvas. The rotation of the jewel is a function of the current time. Adding the jewel's own rnd number to the rotation avoids having all the jewels rotating in sync.

If the jewel happens to be selected—that is, if its position matches that of the cursor—the jewel scale is multiplied by a sine function to create a throbbing effect. The uniform scale factor is applied in the vertex shader. By multiplying the vertex position from the aVertex attribute with the uScale variable, you can control the size of the rendered jewel:

```
vPosition = uModelView * vec4(aVertex * uScale, 1.0);
```

When the matrices and uniforms are updated, the drawing can commence. The rendering is split in two passes. The first pass renders the backside of the jewel, and the second pass renders the front of the jewel.

Creating the jewel surface

The shaders are created in the setupShaders() function and build off the ones you saw already in the lighting and texturing examples. The flat faces of the jewel don't require the high-resolution per-pixel lighting, however, so the lighting is done per-vertex. This type of lighting also gives a better specular light in this particular scenario. The shader code is too big to include here, but you can find the complete code for setupShaders() in the display. webgl.js file included in the code archive for this chapter. The fragment shader uses a mix of a solid color and texture, as shown in Figure 11-8, to color the jewel. The texture provides noise to the jewel, simulating a bit of structure in the jewel.

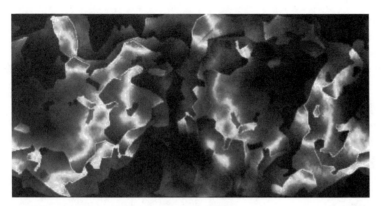

FIGURE 11-8: Noise texture for the jewels adds structure.

The texture is created in the `setupTexture()` function shown in Listing 11-40.

Listing 11-40   **Setting up the jewel texture**

```
jewel.display = (function() {
    ...
    function setupShaders() {
        var vsource = "... vertex shader source ...";
        var fsource = "... fragment shader source ...";

        var webgl = jewel.webgl,
            vshader = webgl.createShaderObject(
                        gl, gl.VERTEX_SHADER, vsource),
            fshader = webgl.createShaderObject(
                        gl, gl.FRAGMENT_SHADER, fsource);

        return webgl.createProgramObject(gl, vshader, fshader);
    }

    function setupTexture() {
        var webgl = jewel.webgl,
            image = new Image();
        image.addEventListener("load", function() {
            var texture = webgl.createTextureObject(gl, image);
            gl.uniform1i(
                gl.getUniformLocation(program, "uTexture"),
                "uTexture", 0
            );
            gl.activeTexture(gl.TEXTURE0);
```

continued

Listing 11-40   **continued**

```
            gl.bindTexture(gl.TEXTURE_2D, texture);
        }, false);
        image.src = "images/jewelpattern.jpg";
    }
    ...
})();
```

The solid color that is mixed with the jewel texture comes from the uniform variable set by the drawJewel() function:

```
uniform vec3 uColor;
```

The shader fetches a sample from the texture image using the spherical coordinates you saw earlier. It's the brightness of the texture that's important, and because the texture is gray-scale, you need only one of the RGB channels:

```
float texColor = texture2D(uTexture, texCoord).r;
```

The texture color acts as an extra light component and just adds to the sum of lights:

```
float light = uAmbient + vDiffuse + vSpecular + texColor;
```

Finally, the lighting is applied to the jewel color, and the result is assigned to the fragment:

```
gl_FragColor = vec4(uColor * light, 0.7);
```

The 0.7 alpha value in the fragment color makes the color semitransparent so the backside of the jewel shines through. Figure 11-9 shows the game board as rendered with the WebGL display.

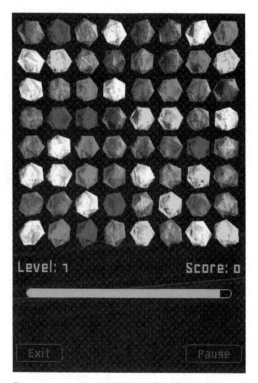

FIGURE 11-9: The WebGL renders the jewel board.

Animating the jewels

The last step is to implement the animations for the various game actions.

Moving and swapping jewels

The moveJewels() function, shown in Listing 11-41, is similar to its canvas counterpart. It adds a new animation for each moving jewel, moving the jewel toward its destination in the render() function.

Listing 11-41 Moving jewels

```
jewel.display = (function() {
    ...
    function moveJewels(movedJewels, callback) {
        var n = movedJewels.length;
        movedJewels.forEach(function(mover) {
            var jwl = getJewel(mover.fromX, mover.fromY),
```

continued

Listing 11-41   continued

```
                dx = mover.toX - mover.fromX,
                dy = mover.toY - mover.fromY,
                dist = Math.abs(dx) + Math.abs(dy);

            if (!jwl) { // new jewel entering from the top
                jwl = createJewel(mover.fromX, mover.fromY,
                        mover.type);
            }
            addAnimation(200 * dist, {
                render : function(pos) {
                    pos = Math.sin(pos * Math.PI / 2);
                    jwl.x = mover.fromX + dx * pos;
                    jwl.y = mover.fromY + dy * pos;
                },
                done : function() {
                    jwl.x = mover.toX;
                    jwl.y = mover.toY;
                    if (-n === 0) { // last one calls callback
                        callback();
                    }
                }
            });
        });
    }
    ...
})();
```

When you're iterating over the list of moving jewels, the relevant jewel object is fetched from the jewels list using the getJewel() function. The getJewel() function returns undefined if the search fails; in that case, a new jewel is created. This handles the case where new jewels move in from the top of the screen.

Removing matched jewels

In the canvas display module, removing jewels causes a spinning and shrinking effect on the jewels. The removeJewels() function in Listing 11-42 adds a variation of that to the WebGL display.

Listing 11-42   **Removing jewels**

```
jewel.display = (function() {
    ...
    function removeJewels(removedJewels, callback) {
```

```
        var n = removedJewels.length;
        removedJewels.forEach(function(removed) {
            var jwl = getJewel(removed.x, removed.y),
                y = jwl.y, // original coordinates
                x = jwl.x;
            addAnimation(400, {
                render : function(pos) {
                    jwl.x = x + jwl.rnd * pos * 2;
                    jwl.y = y + pos * pos * 2;
                    jwl.scale = 1 - pos;
                },
                done : function() {
                    jewels.splice(jewels.indexOf(jwl), 1);
                    if (-n === 0) { // last one calls callback
                        callback();
                    }
                }
            });
        });
    }
    ...
})();
```

The animation added by the removeJewels() function makes the jewel fall toward the bottom while shrinking. The pos value goes from 0 to 1 over the course of the animation, so subtracting it from the jewel scale causes the jewel to shrink until it disappears. The vertical movement uses the pos factor squared to simulate downward acceleration because of gravity:

```
jewel.y = y + pos * pos * 2;
```

In addition to the vertical movement, you can use the random rnd value to add a bit of horizontal movement so the jewel doesn't fall straight down:

```
jewel.x = x + jewel.rnd * pos * 2;
```

You can increase or decrease the two factors, currently set to 2, to speed up the movement in either direction.

When the animation ends and the done() function is called, the jewel is removed from the jewels list using the splice() array method.

Leveling up and ending the game

Three functions remain: `refill()`, `gameOver()`, and `levelUp()`. There are endless possibilities for what the refill animation could look like. I leave that one up to you as an exercise. The current implementation simply redirects the call to the `redraw()` function:

```
function refill(newJewels, callback) {
    redraw(newJewels, callback);
}
```

This function works fine but is, of course, not very exciting.

You can use the animation from the `removeJewels()` function to implement the `gameOver()` function, as shown in Listing 11-43. Just call `removeJewels()` on the entire list of jewels to make the whole board fall apart.

Listing 11-43　**Removing all jewels**

```
jewel.display = (function() {
    . . .
    function gameOver(callback) {
        removeJewels(jewels, callback);
    }
    . . .
})();
```

That leaves the `levelUp()` function. Now add a highlight effect to all the jewels by increasing the ambient light component. This causes all jewels to briefly light up. Listing 11-44 shows the animation.

Listing 11-44　**The level up animation**

```
jewel.display = (function() {
    . . .
    function levelUp(callback) {
        addAnimation(500, {
            render : function(pos) {
                gl.uniform1f(
                    gl.getUniformLocation(program, "uAmbient"),
                    0.12 + Math.sin(pos * Math.PI) * 0.5
                );
            },
            done : callback
        });
```

```
    }
    ...
}) () ;
```

That's the last of the WebGL display module. You now have two different options for display-ing the game graphics.

Using Third-Party WebGL Engines

With WebGL getting more and more attention, middleware for this particular technology is also popping up. Considering that WebGL is relatively new, the number of 3D engines and libraries based on it is surprising. One example is Three.js (http://threejs.org/) by Ricardo Cabello, aka Mr. Doob (http://www.mrdoob.com/). Three.js removes a lot of the complexity of working with WebGL, and the road from blank page to a basic 3D scene can be very short. Listing 11-45 shows the code necessary to render a rotating sphere. You can find this example in the file 07-threejs.html.

Listing 11-45 A basic Three.js example

```
var canvas = document.getElementById("scene"),
    ratio = canvas.width / canvas.height,
    camera = new THREE.PerspectiveCamera(60, ratio, 1, 10000),
    scene = new THREE.Scene(),
    renderer = new THREE.WebGLRenderer({ canvas : canvas }),
    geometry = new THREE.SphereGeometry(300, 40, 20),
    material = new THREE.MeshPhongMaterial({
                    color: 0x00dddd,
                    shading : THREE.FlatShading
                }),
    mesh = new THREE.Mesh(geometry, material),
    light = new THREE.DirectionalLight(0xffffff, 1.2);

camera.position.set(0, 0, 1000);
light.position.set(500, 500, 1000);
scene.add(mesh);
scene.add(light);

function render() {
    requestAnimationFrame(render);
    mesh.rotation.set(0.3, Date.now() / 800, 0);
    renderer.render( scene, camera );
}

render();
```

This code is quite different from the elaborate code you've seen throughout this chapter. Three.js takes care of setting up buffer objects and shaders, leaving a much simpler interface for you to work with. Despite the simplified rendering flow, Three.js has been used in some very intricate projects—for example, interactive music experiences for artists such as Danger Mouse (`www.ro.me`), Arcade Fire (`http://thewildernessdowntown.com`), and Ellie Goulding (`http://lights.elliegoulding.com`). Three.js is free, and the code is licensed under the MIT license.

Three.js includes a number of built-in primitives that you can generate, such as cubes, spheres, and cylinders. It doesn't have functionality for loading external model files other than its own custom JSON format, but exporters are available for some 3D graphics applications such as Blender and 3ds Max. Alternatively, there is a converter that will convert OBJ files to JSON that can then be loaded directly into Three.js.

Three.js doesn't just stick to pure graphics, though. In the examples, you'll also find things like sound emitters that can be placed in the 3D environment. Three.js then automatically adjusts the volume and balance based on the player's position, using the Web Audio API you find in Chapter 10.

One area that leaves a bit to be desired is the documentation. The Three.js documentation site (`http://threejs.org/docs`) has only a very brief example and a terse API reference. However, the project archive available from the GitHub project page contains more than one hundred examples that range from very simple to quite advanced. On the project page, you can find even more user-contributed examples that demonstrate advanced features such as reflective materials, normal mapping, and particle effects. Learning Three.js (`http://learningthreejs.com`) is another interesting site that regularly posts short videos demonstrating how to create different things with Three.js.

Summary

You're now equipped to start using WebGL in your applications and games. This chapter introduced you to the basics of the WebGL API, the GLSL language used in shaders, and a few techniques you can use to add textures, lighting, and blending effects to your rendered objects. It also showed how to use WebGL to create a more advanced display module for the Jewel Warrior game.

With Internet Explorer 11 adding WebGL to its feature set, all major desktop browsers finally have WebGL. Mobile platforms are also slowly getting up to speed, although it will be some time before you can safely take WebGL support on smartphones and tablets for granted.

Part IV
Local Storage and Multiplayer Games

Chapter 12

Local Storage and Caching

In This Chapter

- Introducing Web Storage
- Storing data in cookies versus in local storage
- Adding persistent data to the game
- Making a high score list
- Enabling offline play with application caching

HTTP COOKIES HAVE traditionally solved the problem of storing data in the browser. In this chapter, you learn how to use Web Storage, another technology born out of the HTML5 movement, to achieve some of the same functionality. You also find out how to use Web Storage to make the game remember where the player left off and how to add a high score list.

The final section discusses the application cache introduced by HTML5 and how you can use it to make your games accessible, even without a network connection.

Storing Data with Web Storage

Web Storage is often lumped in with other technologies under the HTML5 umbrella, although it has now been moved to its own specification (www.w3.org/TR/webstorage) and is being developed independently from HTML5.

Unlike cookies, data stored in Web Storage remains on the client and is never transferred to the server. Cookies, in contrast, are sent back and forth between the browser and the server with each HTTP request. This limits the amount of data you can store as cookies, and if the server has no use for the data, the bandwidth used to transmit the cookies is wasted. Browsers impose hard limits on the number and size of cookies. To stay on the safe side, store no more than 50 cookies and 4K per domain.

Using Web Storage solves both of these problems. First, the data never leaves the browser. Second, it allows you to store a larger amount of data. The W3C currently recommends a limit of 5MB, but browsers are allowed to prompt the user for permission if more space is needed. Current browsers allow at least 2MB of Web Storage data.

There are other storage-related developments as well. The File API (www.w3.org/TR/FileAPI) is another proposed specification that aims to become a W3C Recommendation. The File API provides a set of objects that make it easy to work with files and binary data. Add the IndexedDB API (www.w3.org/TR/IndexedDB) to the mix, and you can even create a virtual file system for easy storing of files on the client. The IndexedDB API provides the functionality needed for storing large amounts of data as well as the ability to perform fast searches on this data. All major desktop browsers support the File API, and all but Safari support the IndexedDB API.

If you're storing only small amounts of data, however, Web Storage is usually enough and is available in all current versions of desktop browsers as well as Android and iOS.

Using the storage interface

The Web Storage specification describes two storage objects—the local storage and the session storage—accessible through the global objects `localStorage` and `sessionStorage`. The storage objects use the same interface, which means that anything you can do with `localStorage`, you can also do with `sessionStorage`, and vice versa.

Using the storage API

The storage objects are essentially doors to different data containers maintained by the browser. The `localStorage` object is tied to the domain, and the stored data is kept alive until you remove it.

The storage API consists of just a few functions. To change a value or to add a new value, use the `localStorage.setItem()` method:

```
localStorage.setItem("myData", "This is my data")
```

The first argument is a unique key that identifies the data, and the second argument is the data you want to store. You can now retrieve the data with the `localStorage.getItem()` method:

```
var data = localStorage.getItem("myData");
```

Even if you close the browser, reload the page, or call `localStorage.getItem()` from another page (on the same domain), the data is still there.

Alternatively, you can access the data using square brackets notation. All the stored values are available as properties on the storage object:

```
var data = localStorage["myData"];
localStorage["myData"] = "This is my data";
```

You can, of course, also use dot notation:

```
var data = localStorage.myData;
localStorage.myData = "This is my data";
```

If you need to remove a stored value from the storage object, you can do so with the `localStorage.removeItem()` method:

```
localStorage.removeItem("myData");
```

Use the `localStorage.clear()` method if you need to clear everything from a storage object:

```
localStorage.clear(); // remove all stored data
```

Encoding complex data types

Web Storage is limited to string values, so you can't store other data types without converting them to a string representation. You can easily get around this limit if you encode your data as JSON:

```
var data = {
    key1 : "string",
    key2 : true,
    key3 : [1,2.3]
};
localStorage.setItem("myData", JSON.stringify(data));
```

When you read the data back, just remember to decode the JSON string:

```
var data = JSON.parse(localStorage.getItem("myData"));
```

Iterating over stored values

The `length` property of the storage object is equal to the number of key/value pairs that you have saved:

```
var numValues = localStorage.length;
```

The `localStorage.key()` method takes a single argument, an index between 0 and `length-1`, and returns the name of the key in that position:

```
var data = localStorage.key(0); // name of key at index 0
```

There's no guarantee that keys are in the order you added them, but the method can still be useful if, for example, you need to iterate over all the stored values:

```
for (var i=0,key,value;i<localStorage.length;i++) {
    key = localStorage.key(i);
    value = localStorage.getItem(key);
    console.log(key, value);
}
```

NOTE The browser determines the order of the key/value pairs and can change when you add or remove an item. As long as you just read or write to existing keys, the order is untouched.

Creating a simple text editor

Time for a quick example. Listing 12-1 shows the code for a crude text editor that remembers the text entered into a `textarea`. This example is in the file `01-localStorage.html`.

Listing 12-1   **Saving data in the local storage**

```
<textarea id="input"></textarea>

<script>

var input = document.getElementById("input");

input.value = localStorage.getItem("mytext") || "";

input.addEventListener("keyup", function() {
    localStorage.setItem("mytext", input.value);
}, false);

</script>
```

When you load the page, the text is loaded into the `textarea` element from the `local Storage` object. The `keyup` event handler updates the stored value whenever you type in the field. Because the data is continuously saved in `localStorage`, you can close the window at any time and resume writing when you open the page again.

You can even read the same data from a different page. Listing 12-2 shows a read-only version that loads the text every 50 milliseconds. Find the code for this example in the file `02-localStorageReader.html`.

Listing 12-2 **Reading data from another page**

```
<textarea id="input" disabled></textarea>

<script>

var input = document.getElementById("input");

setInterval(function() {
    input.value = localStorage.getItem("mytext") || "";
}, 50);

</script>
```

If you load the two pages in separate windows and place them side by side, you see that the second window automatically updates as you type in the first.

Using session storage

The session storage is available through the `sessionStorage` object and uses the same interface as `localStorage`. The difference between session storage and local storage lies in the lifetime and scope of the data. Data in the local storage is available to all browser windows and tabs that are viewing pages on the given domain, even after the user closes and opens the browser window. Session storage, in contrast, is tied to the browser session and is cleared when the browser session ends, which typically occurs when the window closes.

Session storage is useful for data that you need to store temporarily but you want to be able to access as the user clicks through different pages. A common use case could be a shopping basket that persists across page views but is emptied when the user closes the browser window.

You access the session storage the same way you access the local storage. Listing 12-3 shows the example from Listing 12-1 modified to use session storage. You can find this example in the file `03-sessionStorage.html`.

Listing 12-3   Using the session storage

```
<textarea id="input"></textarea>

<script>

var input = document.getElementById("input");

input.value = sessionStorage.getItem("mytext") || "";

input.addEventListener("keyup", function() {
   sessionStorage.setItem("mytext", input.value);
}, false);

</script>
```

When you enter text, it's still there after you reload the page. If you close the browser or the tab, however, the text is cleared.

Building a storage module

To implement the high score list, you need a storage module. This module is very simple and is essentially a wrapper for the localStorage object. You get around the string value limitation by encoding the values as JSON strings before saving them. This approach lets you store complex types such as objects and arrays. Just beware of host objects such as DOM elements; these objects have no meaningful JSON representation. Listing 12-4 shows the storage module storage.js.

Listing 12-4   The storage module

```
jewel.storage = (function() {
    var db = window.localStorage;

    function set(key, value) {
        value = JSON.stringify(value);
        db.setItem(key, value);
    }

    function get(key) {
        var value = db.getItem(key);
        try {
            return JSON.parse(value);
        } catch (e) {
```

```
            return;
        }
    }

    return {
        set : set,
        get : get
    };

})();
```

Load the storage module with the other scripts in `index.html` as shown in Listing 12-5.

Listing 12-5 Loading the storage module
```
window.addEventListener("load", function() {
    jewel.load("scripts/dom.js");
    if (jewel.isStandalone()) {
        ...
        jewel.load("scripts/storage.js");
    } else {
        ...
    }
});
```

Making the Game State Persistent

In its current state, the game forgets everything when the player leaves or reloads the page. It would be nice if the game remembered the state of the active game so the player can stop playing, exit the game, and come back later to resume playing. In this section, you implement a feature that stores the game state and asks the user if he wants to continue the previous game.

Saving the game data

The `saveGameData()` function in `screen.game.js`, shown in Listing 12-6, stores the values necessary to restore the game state the next time the player loads the game. The function is called in the `exitGame()` function just before returning to the menu. You should also clear the data in the `gameOver()` function.

Listing 12-6 Saving the game

```
jewel.screens["game-screen"] = (function() {
    ...
    function saveGameData() {
        jewel.storage.set("activeGameData", {
            level : gameState.level,
            score : gameState.score,
            time : Date.now() - gameState.startTime,
            endTime : gameState.endTime,
            jewels : jewel.board.getBoard()
        });
    }

    function exitGame() {
        ...
        if (confirmed) {
            saveGameData();
            jewel.showScreen("main-menu");
        }
    }

    function gameOver() {
        ...
        jewel.storage.set("activeGameData", null);
    }
    ...
})();
```

These four values are all you need to restore the game state, and they should all be self-explanatory. When a new game starts, the startGame() function must check whether there's a previous game that the player can resume. You can't be sure that the player actually wants to do so, so it's best to ask. If the player chooses to resume the game, use the stored values to set up the game. Listing 12-7 shows the changes to the startGame() function. The new code goes just before the updateGameInfo() call.

Listing 12-7 Loading the state from the previous game

```
jewel.screens["game-screen"] = (function() {
    ...
    function startGame() {
        ...

        var activeGame = storage.get("activeGameData"),
```

```
            useActiveGame,
            startJewels;

        if (activeGame) {
            useActiveGame = window.confirm(
                "Do you want to continue your previous game?"
            );
            if (useActiveGame) {
                var now = Date.now();
                gameState.level = activeGame.level;
                gameState.score = activeGame.score;
                gameState.startTime = now - activeGame.time;
                gameState.endTime = activeGame.endTime;
                startJewels = activeGame.jewels;
            }
        }

        updateGameInfo();
        jewel.audio.initialize();
        board.initialize(startJewels, function() {
            display.initialize(function() {
                cursor = { x : 0, y : 0, selected : false };
                display.redraw(board.getBoard(), function() {
                    if (useActiveGame) {
                        setLevelTimer();
                    } else {
                        advanceLevel();
                    }
                });
            });
        });
    }
    ...
})();
```

If the player confirms that she wants to resume the previous game, the level, score, and timer values are restored. The initial `advanceLevel()` call should happen only if the player starts a new game. If it's a previous game, just call `setLevelTimer()` to start the timer. You should also restore the jewels on the board, but that's a bit trickier because currently there's no way to initialize the board module with a given set of jewels. The board module can start only with its own randomly generated board. Modifying the board module in `board.js` to allow an initial jewel set is easy, however, as shown in Listing 12-8.

Listing 12-8 Passing the initial jewels to the board module

```
jewel.board = (function() {
    ...
    function initialize(startJewels, callback) {
        settings = jewel.settings
        numJewelTypes = settings.numJewelTypes,
        baseScore = settings.baseScore,
        cols = settings.cols;
        rows = settings.rows;
        if (startJewels) {
            jewels = startJewels;
        } else {
            fillBoard();
        }
        callback();
    }
    ...
})();
```

The `initialize()` function now takes an additional parameter, and if you pass a set of jewels, it uses them in place of the randomly filled board.

The board module can also run as a web worker, so the `board.worker-interface.js` script that interacts with the worker also needs a slight modification, as shown in Listing 12-9.

Listing 12-9 Sending the initial jewels to the worker

```
jewel.board = (function() {
    ...
    function initialize(startJewels, callback) {
        ...
        var data = {
            settings : jewel.settings,
            startJewels : startJewels
        };
        post("initialize", data, callback);
    }
    ...
})();
```

Whereas the `initialize()` function in the worker received only a `settings` parameter, it now receives an object holding both the `settings` and the `startJewels` values. The worker script, `board.worker.js`, is modified as shown in Listing 12-10.

Listing 12-10   **Using the initial jewels in the worker**

```
...
addEventListener("message", function(event) {
    var board = jewel.board,
        message = event.data;

    switch (message.command) {
        case "initialize" :
            jewel.settings = message.data.settings;
            board.initialize(
                message.data.startJewels, callback
            );
            break;
        ...
    }
    ...
}, false);
```

The game now saves the state when the player exits to the main menu, allowing her to resume the game when she returns.

You may also want to consider the case where the player simply closes the window or browser. In that case, any progress is lost. If you want to save the game continually, you can add `saveGameData()` calls in relevant places, such as `setLevelTimer()` and `playBoardEvents()`.

TIP

Creating a High Score List

When the game ends because the timer expires, the game must switch automatically to the high score screen, passing along the final score. The high score module checks the score against the stored list of scores, and if the score is high enough to make it onto the list, the player is asked to enter her name. The high score module enters the score into the list along with the player name and displays the top 10 scores.

Building the high score screen

The high score screen consists of a title, an ordered list, and a footer with a button that leads back to the main menu. Listing 12-11 shows the new screen in `index.html`.

Listing 12-11   **Adding the high score markup**

```
<div id="game">

    ...

    <div class="screen" id="high-scores">
        <h2 class="logo">High score</h2>
        <ol class="score-list">
        </ol>
        <footer>
            <button name="back">Back</button>
        </footer>
    </div>

</div>
```

Now you can populate the ol element with list items in the high score module. Add the CSS rules shown in Listing 12-12 to main.css to style the list.

Listing 12-12   **Styling the high score list**

```
/* High score */
#high-scores h2 {
    margin-top : 0.25em;
    font-size : 1.25em;
}
#high-scores ol.score-list {
    font-size : 0.65em;
    width : 75%;
    margin : 0 10%;
}
#high-scores ol.score-list li {
    width : 100%;
}
#high-scores ol.score-list li span:nth-child(1) {
    display : inline-block;
    width : 70%;
}
#high-scores ol.score-list li span:nth-child(2) {
    display : inline-block;
    width : 30%;
    text-align : center;
}
```

```
#high-scores footer button.back {
    float: left;
}
```

When the list items are added later, they all contain two child span elements: one for the player name and one for the score. Once again, you can make the necessary adjustments for landscape orientation on your own.

Transitioning to the high score screen

First, you need to actually switch to the high score screen from the game screen. Return to the screen.game.js script and change the gameOver() function as shown in Listing 12-13.

Listing 12-13   **Transitioning to the high score screen**

```
jewel.screens["game-screen"] = (function() {
    ...
    function gameOver() {
        jewel.audio.play("gameover");
        jewel.storage.set("activeGameData", null);
        jewel.storage.set("lastScore", gameState.score);
        jewel.display.gameOver(function() {
            announce("Game over");
            setTimeout(function() {
                jewel.showScreen("high-scores");
            }, 2500);
        });
    }
    ...
})();
```

After the announce() function displays the "Game over" text, the game screen automatically switches to the high score list. The final score is also stored in the storage module so it can be accessed from the high score screen.

Adding the new module

Listing 12-14 shows the high score screen module, screen.high-scores.js. The basic structure should be familiar.

Listing 12-14   **The high score screen module**

```
jewel.screens["high-scores"] = (function() {
    var firstRun = true;

    function setup() {
        var $ = jewel.dom.$,
            backButton = $("#high-scores button[name=back]")[0];
        jewel.dom.bind(backButton, "click", function() {
            jewel.showScreen("main-menu");
        });
    }

    function run() {
        if (firstRun) {
            setup();
            firstRun = false;
        }
        populateList();
        var score = jewel.storage.get("lastScore");
        if (score) {
            checkScores(score);
            jewel.storage.set("lastScore", null);
        }
    }

    return {
        run : run
    };
})();
```

The high score screen needs to be viewable in two modes, one where the player enters his name and one where he just views the scores from the main menu. The `run()` function checks the storage module, and if a score value is present, this function calls the `checkScores()`, which will be responsible for adding the new score to the high score list.

Remember to load the new screen module in `index.html`.

Storing the high score data

You can now implement the `enterScore()` function. Listing 12-15 shows the function.

Listing 12-15   Entering a new high score entry

```javascript
jewel.screens["high-scores"] = (function() {
    var numScores = 10,
        ...

    function getScores() {
        return jewel.storage.get("scores") || [];
    }

    function addScore(score, position) {
        var scores = getScores(),
            name, entry;

        name = prompt("Please enter your name:");
        entry = {
            name : name,
            score : score
        };
        scores.splice(position, 0, entry);
        jewel.storage.set(
            "scores", scores.slice(0, numScores)
        );
        populateList();
    }

    function checkScores(score) {
        var scores = getScores();
        for (var i=0;i<scores.length;i++) {
            if (score > scores[i].score) {
                addScore(score, i);
                return;
            }
        }
        if (scores.length < numScores) {
            addScore(score, scores.length);
        }
    }
    ...
})();
```

You use the getScores() function to fetch the high score list from the storage module. If no scores are stored yet, getScores() simply returns an empty array.

The checkScores() function goes through the list of saved scores until it encounters a score that's smaller than the player's score and then adds the score by calling addScore(). If a smaller score isn't found, it checks for room at the bottom of the list.

In addScore(), the player is prompted for a name. The name and score are then inserted at the specified position using the splice() method. The function then uses slice() to get the first 10 elements and stores them in the storage module. Finally, it calls the populateList() function to update the list on the screen.

Displaying the high score data

Now you just need to render the list of scores. That happens in populateList(), as shown in Listing 12-16.

Listing 12-16   Populating the list of high scores

```
jewel.screens["high-scores"] = (function() {
    ...
    function populateList() {
        var scores = getScores(),
            list = jewel.dom.$("#high-scores ol.score-list")[0],
            item, nameEl, scoreEl, i;

        // make sure the list is full
        for (i=scores.length;i<numScores;i++) {
            scores.push({
                name : "&#x2014;",
                score : 0
            });
        }

        list.innerHTML = "";
        for (i=0;i<scores.length;i++) {
            item = document.createElement("li");

            nameEl = document.createElement("span");
            nameEl.innerHTML = scores[i].name;

            scoreEl = document.createElement("span");
            scoreEl.innerHTML = scores[i].score;
```

```
            item.appendChild(nameEl);
            item.appendChild(scoreEl);
            list.appendChild(item);
        }
    }
    ...
})();
```

After `populateList()` retrieves the scores from the storage module, it makes sure that `numScores` entries appear in the list. That way, the high score list appears to be prefilled with scores with 0 points. The `list` element itself is simply filled with list items, each with two `span` elements. Figure 12-1 shows the resulting high score screen.

FIGURE 12-1: The high score list updates when the game is over.

Application Cache

The final section of this chapter discusses another form of local data, the *application cache*. The application cache is a way for you to specify which resources the browser can cache locally and which ones it must always fetch from the server. Being able to cache files locally has the obvious advantage of decreasing network traffic on subsequent visits, but it also allows the application to function if no network connection exists at all.

The relevant part of the HTML5 specification is available from the W3C at www. w3.org/TR/2011/WD-html5-20110525/offline.html.

The cache manifest

The application cache and offline web applications use a cache manifest to control which resources are cached and which ones aren't. The manifest is a basic text file with a simple syntax. Listing 12-17 shows the basics of the manifest format.

Listing 12-17   The cache manifest for jewel warrior

```
CACHE MANIFEST
# Jewel Warrior cache manifest

CACHE:
images/jewels32.png
images/jewels40.png
images/jewels64.png
...


NETWORK:
...


FALLBACK:
...
```

You can find the complete manifest for Jewel Warrior in the file manifest.appcache. The first line of the manifest is required and must be CACHE MANIFEST. Any line that starts with a # is treated as a comment and is ignored. The rest of the manifest is divided into three sections—CACHE, NETWORK, and FALLBACK, each starting with the section name followed by a colon. The CACHE section lists the resources the browser must download and store in the cache. The NETWORK section lists the resources that should be accessed online, and the FALLBACK section specifies a page to load if the application needs online access but no network connection is available.

Adding the manifest to the HTML page

When you have a valid manifest, you must add a reference to it in the html element on the main page. Just add an attribute called manifest and let the value be the path to the manifest file:

```
<html manifest="manifest.appcache">
```

Currently, no official extension is required when naming your manifest file. Some sites use `.manifest`, whereas others use `.appcache`. However, I recommend that you use the latter because an unrelated Microsoft technology also uses the `.manifest` extension.

More important, the web server sends the manifest file with the MIME type `text/cache-manifest`. Otherwise, you risk causing errors that stop your application from loading. If your web server sends an incorrect MIME type, consult the documentation or contact your server administrator. For web servers such as Apache and Nginx, you can add the following line to the `mime.types` configuration file:

```
text/cache-manifest appcache
```

The page that points to the cache manifest—for example, `index.html`—is automatically cached, so you don't need to add that file to the `CACHE` section.

Handling online resources

Using a cache manifest fundamentally changes the way a browser loads resources.

It's not necessary to cache all files in the application cache. For instance, if you always need the latest data, you may not want to cache pages generated dynamically. You need to add these resources to a whitelist so the browser knows that it must retrieve the resource from the network. These resources go in the `NETWORK` section of the manifest. The following snippet shows a counter script added to the online whitelist so the browser can access it when online:

```
NETWORK:
# allow online access only to this file
counter.php
```

You can also use a wildcard to indicate that you want to allow access to all online URLs if they're not found in the cache:

```
NETWORK:
# allow online access to all URLs
*
```

However, what if the browser needs to access a resource that hasn't been cached and no network connection is available? Well, you can't just create the resource out of thin air, but you do have a bit of control over how the browser reacts. The optional `FALLBACK` section of the manifest specifies a page shown when online resources are unreachable. Consider the following example from the HTML5 specification:

```
CACHE MANIFEST
FALLBACK:
/ /offline.html
NETWORK:
*
```

This manifest makes the browser add pages and files to the application cache as the user visits them. Every time the user visits a new page, it's added to the cache. When the user goes offline, only those pages remain accessible. If the user tries to visit any other page on the site, he sees the offline.html page instead, where a helpful message could be displayed.

On one hand, this functionality frees you from specifying every single file in the manifest and forcing the browser to download everything. On the other hand, the user has offline access only to the content he's already seen. The limited offline availability can be useful for websites with many pages where the user doesn't necessarily need offline access to everything. If you want to be certain that the needed resources are available offline, it's better to declare them explicitly in the CACHE section of the manifest.

TIP No rules dictate how you order the sections in the manifest. You can mix them up any way you want and even create multiple CACHE sections. Additionally, you can leave out the CACHE: header and simply list the cache resources under the CACHE MANIFEST line.

Forcing cache updates

Just because you change the contents of a file listed in the manifest doesn't mean that the browser automatically picks up the change. The cache manifest must change also. That might seem counterintuitive when you haven't changed the name of the file in question. Nevertheless, the manifest needs to change for the browser to recheck the cached files. Changing as little as one character in a comment is enough to trigger the check, so one solution is to keep a revision number near the top of the file and just increment it whenever you modify a file listed in the manifest. See Listing 12-18 for an example.

Listing 12-18   Cache manifest with revision number

```
CACHE MANIFEST
# Jewel Warrior cache manifest, rev 47

CACHE:
images/jewels32.png
images/jewels40.png
...
```

Triggering a cache update makes the browser check all the files listed in the manifest. The files that have changed since they were last cached are downloaded, but the rest are skipped. These checks are done using the regular cache-related HTTP headers such as `If-Modified-Since`.

Because cached files aren't automatically updated in the cache unless you modify the manifest, developing with the application cache turned on can be a challenging experience. If it gives you trouble, simply disable it while working on the game—for example, by removing the `manifest` attribute from the `html` element.

Summary

In this chapter, you saw how the Web Storage specification lets you store client-side data that persists across browser sessions. You discovered how to use local storage to save data that remains until actively removed and how the related session storage keeps the data alive only until the current browser session ends.

In addition, you saw how to use these features to add a persistent, local high score screen and how to save the game state so the game remembers where the player left off. Finally, this chapter covered the application cache and how you can use it to make your games playable, even when the user goes offline.

Chapter 13

Going Online with WebSockets

In This Chapter

- Using WebSockets for online communication
- Introduction to Node.js and server-side JavaScript
- Creating a simple chat application

IN THIS CHAPTER, I introduce you to WebSockets and Node, two relatively new technologies that make creating network applications and server-side scripting a much better experience than it has been in the past.

In the first half of the chapter, I take you through the WebSocket API and show you how to establish and manage a connection to a server as well as how to communicate with the server by sending and receiving data.

I then show you how to use Node to create server-side JavaScript applications. By the end of the chapter, you will know how to create a chat server and client using Node and WebSockets.

Using WebSockets

Traditionally, whenever network communication outside regular Ajax requests was needed, the solution was either plug-in-based or a workaround using existing `XmlHttpRequest` technology, possibly involving long-lived connections that wait for responses from the server. HTTP wasn't really designed with polling in mind, and HTTP requests and responses carry a lot of overhead. When all the HTTP headers, cookies, and other request data are combined, an HTTP request can easily have 1K of overhead data. That's a lot if you want to send only a short status update.

WebSockets were created to provide an alternative geared specifically toward persistent connections and low-latency communication. WebSockets keep the connection alive and use only two bytes of overhead for each message, a drastic reduction. Another cool thing about WebSockets is that they allow for bidirectional communication. Both the client and server can send messages to each other at the same time via the same connection. The HTTP protocol limits you to sending a request and getting a response.

> **TIP** WebSockets enable low-latency connections between server and client but do not let you communicate directly between clients. For this, you can turn to WebRTC, a new specification that is currently being drafted at the W3C. WebRTC is an API that provides real-time communication between browsers, allowing things such as video chat, peer-to-peer file sharing, and more. You can read more about WebRTC at `www.webrtc.org/`.

The protocol used to communicate via WebSocket connections is being standardized by the Internet Engineering Task Force (IETF). You can find the full specification for this protocol at `http://tools.ietf.org/html/rfc6455`. This is the data protocol that is used behind the scenes. You will usually not have to deal with this directly but will instead work with the JavaScript WebSocket API.

WebSockets are available in all major desktop browsers as well as Safari on iOS. Android did not support WebSockets out of the box in versions prior to Android 4.4, although both Chrome for Android or Firefox for Android can be installed to gain WebSockets support on those devices. In Android 4.4+, the default browser is based on Chrome and therefore also supports WebSockets. As always, refer to CanIUse (`http://caniuse.com/#feat=websockets`) for the latest information.

Connecting to servers

In the browser, WebSockets are available via a standardized API. The W3C developed and maintains the WebSocket API. You can access the most recent version at `www.w3.org/TR/websockets`. There isn't an API for server applications. Server developers are free to implement WebSockets any way they choose, as long as they follow the IETF protocol.

Establishing the connection

Setting up a WebSocket connection is easy. Just create a new `WebSocket` object and pass the URL of the server as the first argument:

```
var ws = new WebSocket("ws://www.myserver.com:9999/");
```

This creates a new `WebSocket` object and attempts to establish a connection to www. myserver.com on port 9999. The WebSocket constructor takes an optional second argument that specifies a list of sub protocols.

WebSockets can operate in both a secure and non-secure manner. The `ws://` prefix in the URL indicates a non-secure connection. Use the `wss://` to establish secure connections. This is similar to the `http://` and `https://` protocols used for HTTP connections. Note that secure connections require that server support.

If you've worked with Ajax and the `XmlHttpRequest` object, you're probably familiar with the concept of the ready state. The ready state, which can be read from the `ws.readyState` property, is a numeric value that indicates the current state of the connection. Table 13-1 lists the four ready states defined by the WebSocket API.

Table 13-1 **WebSocket ready states**

Status code	Numeric	Description
CONNECTING	0	The client is establishing the connection.
OPEN	1	The connection is open, and you can use the `send()` method and the `message` event to communicate with the server.
CLOSING	2	The connection is in the process of being closed.
CLOSED	3	The connection is closed, and you can no longer communicate with the server.

When you first create a new `WebSocket` object, its ready state is set to CONNECTING. When the connection to the server is established, the ready state switches to OPEN, and you can start communicating with the server. You can use the following snippet to check whether the connection is open or closed:

```
if (ws.readyState === 1) {
    // connection is open
}
```

Alternatively, you can use the status code properties available on the `WebSocket` object:

```
if (ws.readyState === ws.OPEN) {
    // connection is open
}
```

Closing the connection

When you want to close the connection, simply call the ws.close() method:

```
ws.close();
```

Calling the ws.close() method switches the ready state to CLOSING until the connection is completely shut down, after which the ready state is CLOSED. Call the ws.close() method only after the connection is opened; otherwise, you get an error.

When the connection is closed by calling the ws.close() method or by some other event—for example, if the server closes the connection or the connections fails—the WebSocket object emits a close event:

```
ws.addEventListener("close", function() {
    console.log("Connection closed");
}, false);
```

A connection may suddenly close for many different reasons, so it can be useful to know whether the connection closed because it was supposed to or whether an error forced it to close. For that purpose, the WebSocket protocol defines a number of status codes used to indicate the reason the connection was closed. Table 13-2 shows the currently defined status codes.

Table 13-2　Status codes for close events

Status code	Description
1000	The connection was closed normally—that is, not because of a problem.
1001	The endpoint is moving away. For the server, this could be a server shutdown; for the client, it could be because the user is navigating to a new page.
1002	The connection was closed because of a protocol error.
1003	The endpoint received unsupported data—for example, binary data when it accepts only text.
1004	Reserved for future use.
1005	This status code is reserved for use when no status code was received but one was expected.
1006	This status code is reserved for use where the connection was closed without sending the close frame.
1007	The connection was closed because the endpoint received invalid UTF-8 text data.

Status code	Description
1008	This status code can be used when no other status code fits or if there is a need to hide the real reason.
1009	The connection was closed because the endpoint received a message that is too big to process.
1010	The connection was closed because the server did not negotiate one or more expected extensions.
1011	The connection was closed because something unexpected happened that stopped the server from processing the request.
1015	The connection was closed due to a failure to perform a TLS handshake, for example if the server certificate cannot be verified.

You can use these codes and the `e.wasClean` property to determine whether the connection closed cleanly and why the connection was closed. If necessary, you can take appropriate action:

```
ws.addEventListener("close", function(e) {
    if (!e.wasClean) {
        console.log(e.code + " " + e.reason);
    }
}, false);
```

You also can define and use your own status codes. The 4000–4999 range is reserved for private use, so if you want to implement a custom status code for your application, feel free to use a code in that range. The `ws.close()` method takes two optional parameters: the status code and a reason. Note that the reason string can be no more than 123 characters.

```
ws.close(4100, "Player disconnected");
```

Of course, you're responsible for intercepting the close event on the server and checking for these codes. Because no standard API is defined for WebSocket servers, exactly how this works on the server depends on the frameworks and libraries you use.

Communicating with WebSockets

Because WebSockets are full-duplex, bidirectional connections, you need to create only one connection to be able to send and receive data. This is contrasted by, for example, long-polling with HTTP connections, where you need one connection that waits for messages *from* the server while another connection is used to send messages *to* the server.

Sending messages

When the connection is open, you can send data to the server with the `ws.send()` method. This function takes a single argument that can be a UTF-8 string, an `ArrayBuffer`, or a binary `Blob` object:

```
ws.send("Hello Server!"); // send a string to the server
```

If strings aren't enough and you want to send more complex data types, you can, of course, always encode your JavaScript objects as JSON and decode it on the server-side. The following function takes whatever you pass in the data parameter and sends it as JSON:

```
function sendData(ws, data) {
    var jsonData = JSON.stringify(data);
    ws.send(jsonData)
}
```

The following snippet sends an update data structure for a hypothetical game. The update data contains the current direction of movement and information about whether the player character is firing a weapon:

```
sendData(ws, {
    move : {x : 0.79, y : -0.79},
    firing : true,
    weapon : 7
});
```

In addition to string data, you can send binary data using either `ArrayBuffer` objects or `Blob` objects. Both of these data types are often used with the File API but can be used to send any kind of data. In this chapter, you work only with strings.

Whenever you send a message with the `ws.send()` method, the data is placed in a buffer. The `WebSocket` object feeds data from this buffer to the network connection as fast as it can, but there's a chance the buffer won't be empty when you send the next piece of data. If you try to send data and the buffer is completely full, not only is the data not sent, but also the connection is closed. The `ws.bufferedAmount` property tells you how much data is currently stored in the buffer. One possible use of this value is to limit the rate at which messages are sent. If, for example, your game sends an update to the server at a certain interval, checking that the buffer is empty before sending the data can help you avoid flooding the connection with more data than it can handle:

```
setInterval(function() {
    if (ws.bufferedAmount == 0) {
        var data = getUpdate();
        ws.send(data);
    }
}, 100);
```

Even though the interval is set to 100 ms, the preceding example sends the update data only if the buffer is empty, thereby avoiding potential congestion.

Receiving messages

When the server sends a message, a `message` event is fired on the `WebSocket` object. The event object passed to any handlers has a `data` property that contains the message from the server. Attach an event handler to the `message` event and process the data any way you want:

```
ws.addEventListener("message", function(e) {
    console.log("Received data: " + e.data);
}, false);
```

Using Node on the Server

WebSockets aren't very useful without a server to which they can connect. Many server libraries and frameworks are available already for a variety of platforms and programming languages. Node (`http://nodejs.org`), or Node.js as it's also called, is a JavaScript-based framework for the server and is perfect for this purpose, not least because it lets you code in the same language on both the client and server.

Node emphasizes asynchronous patterns, which should be familiar to any JavaScript programmer who is used to developing for the browser. In the browser, Ajax and DOM events, for example, all function asynchronously. The process of attaching event handlers and passing callback functions is second nature to many, if not most, web developers. In the server-side setting of Node, this means that whenever you request access to some I/O resource (such as a file on the disk, a database, or a network connection), you pass a callback function to the given function. The function immediately returns and calls the callback function when the task is done. Listing 13-1 illustrates how you can use Node to read data from a file.

Listing 13-1 **Reading data from a file with node**

```
var fs = require("fs");

fs.readFile("./myfiles/mystuff.txt", function(err, data) {
    if (err) {
        // something bad happened
    } else {
        // process file data
    }
});
```

Most of the asynchronous built-in functions follow this pattern of adding a callback function at the end of the parameter list. Similarly, callback functions usually have an error value as the first parameter followed by any other parameters that make sense in that particular context.

The `require()` function imports a module. In Listing 13-1, the file system module is made available through the variable `fs`. Node comes with many built-in modules; you can see a complete list and read more about the functionality they provide in the API documentation: `http://nodejs.org/docs/latest/api/index.html`.

Installing Node

You need a server to be able to use Node, preferably one to which you have enough access that you can install new programs. The exact way to install Node depends on the server platform. Node is available for Windows, OS X, and Linux. You can find installers for all platforms on the Node web site (`http://nodejs.org/download/`). I used Node 0.10.20 when creating the examples in this chapter.

After you install Node on your server, you can try it out immediately by entering `node` at a command prompt. This command gives you a Node console where you can type any line of JavaScript you want to execute.

Using third-party modules

As mentioned previously, Node has a lot of built-in functionality, and you can get pretty far with what's available out of the box. However, the built-in functions are all relatively low level; for example, no database functionality is built in. Instead, Node includes all the building blocks you need to make add-on modules that provide features such as database integration, web servers, and so on. Node also comes with the Node Package Manager (npm), which is a useful tool that makes managing your modules a breeze. You can read more about npm at the project's website (`http://npmjs.org`), where you can also search its extensive module registry.

Open a console/terminal window and use the `npm install` command to install modules. For example, to install the WebSocket module that you use later in this chapter, enter the following command:

```
npm install websocket
```

Similarly, you can use the `npm remove` command to remove any module you want to uninstall:

```
npm remove websocket
```

The `npm list` command gives you a full list of all installed modules. You can browse all the modules available through npm at `http://search.npmjs.org`.

Node hosting

Don't despair if you don't have the required access to your server and don't have a Linux machine to experiment with. A few options are available if you just want to play around with Node.

Nodejitsu (`www.nodejitsu.com`) is a Node platform-as-a-service (PaaS) provider that can host your Node application for a reasonable price. The lowest tier costs $9 per month, but you get a free 30-day trial version, which should be enough for you to see whether it's the right choice. If your game or application is open source software, Nodejitsu will even host it for free. This service is similar to the Node SmartMachines service that Joyent, the company behind Node, had until they recently shut the service down.

If you'd rather experiment with a Linux server, you can use Amazon's Elastic Compute Cloud (EC2) service. With EC2, you can launch a virtual server called an *instance* whenever you need it and shut it down when you're done so you don't waste server resources. Amazon provides a free tier that lets you use an EC2 Micro Instance free for a year. Read more about this at `http://aws.amazon.com/free`.

Follow the instructions on the Amazon Web Services site to set up an EC2 instance. You get to choose from a variety of different Amazon Machine Images (AMI), some created by Amazon and others created by the community. Ubuntu provides images for Amazon EC2 at `http://cloud-images.ubuntu.com/locator/ec2`. Clicking the AMI ID links takes you straight to the AWS console and initiates the AMI launch process.

If you choose an Ubuntu image, you can install Node and the `websocket` module with two simple commands:

```
sudo apt-get install nodejs
npm install websocket
```

Don't be alarmed if npm complains that the native code compile failed, the module will work fine. Now you can get started with the first example. For something simple yet potentially useful, I show you how to create a basic HTTP server that always responds with the same message before moving on to creating a WebSocket application.

 TIP There are many options for hosting your Node applications. Joyent has put together a Github page that lists and compares many of these hosting options: `https://github.com/ joyent/node/wiki/node-hosting`.

Creating an HTTP server with Node

Node provides a networking module called `net`. This module provides low-level socket functionality that lets you create network clients as well as server applications. Node also includes an HTTP module implemented on top of the `net` module. You can use this module to create servers that implement the HTTP protocol. However, the server functionality provided by this module goes only as far as managing the connection. How to interpret the requests is up to you.

Import the HTTP module with the `require()` method and use its `createServer()` method to create a new HTTP server object:

```
var server = require("http").createServer();
```

Use the `server.listen()` method to start accepting connections. This method takes three parameters: a port number, an optional hostname, and an optional callback function. If the hostname is left out, the server listens on all available IP addresses:

```
server.listen(9999); // listen on port 9999 on all interfaces
```

The server object fires a `connection` event whenever a client connects to the server. Node lets you attach event handlers by using the `on()` method on the target object. For example, to attach a handler to the `connection` event on the server object, use the following:

```
server.on("connection", function(socket) {
    console.log("Connection from: ", socket.address().address);
});
```

When the server receives a valid HTTP request, it fires a `request` event, passing a `request` object and a `response` object to the event handlers. The `request` object enables you to access information about the HTTP request, such as the request path, HTTP headers, and so on. The `response` object is used to write the HTTP response to the client socket. The response object has three important methods: `response.writeHead()`, `response.write()`, and `response.end()`.

The `response.writeHead()` method writes the HTTP header to the socket. The function takes two parameters: an HTTP status code (such as 200 for a successful request or 404 for "file not found" errors) and a JavaScript object containing the response headers.

```
response.writeHead(200, {
    "Content-Type" : "text/plain"
});
```

The `response.write()` method writes the actual response data:

```
response.write("It Works!");
```

Finally, the `response.end()` method closes the connection. Listing 13-2 shows the full code for the HTTP server. You can find this example in the file `01-httpserver.js`.

Listing 13-2   A basic HTTP server

```
var server = require("http").createServer();

server.on("connection", function(socket) {
    console.log("Connection from: ", socket.address().address);
});

server.on("request", function(request, response) {
    console.log("Request:", request.method, request.url);

    response.writeHead(
        200,
        {
            "Content-Type" : "text/plain"
        }
    );

    response.write("It Works!");

    response.end();
});

server.listen (9999); // listen on port 9999
```

Run the server by executing the command:

```
node 01-httpserver.js
```

If you are running the server on your local machine, you can now connect to the server by pointing your browser to http://127.0.0.1:9999/. When you connect to the server, you should see the text "It Works!" displayed, no matter what file or path you request.

Creating a WebSocket chat room

In the second example, I show you how to use Node and WebSockets to create a simple chat application. If you haven't done so already, make sure the websocket module is installed by executing the following command at a command prompt in the same folder as your application:

```
npm install websocket
```

You can also use the -g option to install the module globally so you won't have to install it for every new project:

```
npm -g install websocket
```

You can now import the websocket module into your Node applications:

```
var WebSocketServer = require("websocket").server,
    WebSocketClient = require("websocket").client,
    WebSocketFrame = require("websocket").frame,
    WebSocketRouter = require("websocket").router;
```

You use only the WebSocketServer constructor in this example, but the others are useful in other scenarios—for example, if you need to use the Node as a client to connect to a third-party server.

Creating the server

First, use the WebSocketServer constructor to create a new WebSocket server object. You also need an HTTP server:

```
var ws = new WebSocketServer(),
    server = require("http").createServer();
```

Next, you need to make a link between the WebSocket server and HTTP server. The WebSocket server essentially attaches to the HTTP server and processes all requests it receives. To create a link between the servers, you *mount* a server configuration object:

```
ws.mount(serverConfig);
```

`serverConfig` is a simple JavaScript object that specifies a number of options and parameters for the WebSocket server, the most important being the reference to the HTTP server:

```
var serverConfig = {
    httpServer : server,
    autoAcceptConnections : true
};
```

Setting `autoAcceptConnections` to `true` means that the server will accept all connections, regardless of what sub protocol versions they use. In a real production setting, you should consider a stricter approach to avoid problems. For this example, being forgiving is acceptable.

If you need to stop accepting new WebSocket connections, you can unmount the server by using the `ws.unmount()` method. This function breaks the link to the server configuration so no new connections can be established. Any existing connections are left untouched. You can use the `ws.closeAllConnections()` method if you also want to close existing connections. Finally, the `ws.shutDown()` performs both these tasks in one call.

As an alternative to using the `ws.mount()` method, you can pass the server configuration object directly to the WebSocketServer constructor. Listing 13-3 shows the code needed to set up the chat server so it accepts connections on port 9999. If you have a firewall running, make sure that you use an open port. You can find the complete code for this example in the file `02-websocketserver.js`.

Listing 13-3   Setting up the server

```
var WebSocketServer = require("websocket").server;

// create a HTTP server
var server = require("http").createServer();

// and a WebSocket server
var ws = new WebSocketServer({
    httpServer : server,
    autoAcceptConnections : true
});
```

continued

Listing 13-3   continued
```
console.log("Chat server listening on port 9999!");

server.listen(9999);
```

When a new client connects to the server, a connect event is fired on the `WebSocketServer` object. This event carries a connection object that you must use to communicate with that client. Listing 13-4 shows the connection handler for this event.

Listing 13-4   Handling new connections
```
// create the initially empty client list
var clients = [];

ws.on("connect", connectHandler);

function connectHandler(conn) {
    // set the initial nickname to the client IP
    conn.nickname = conn.remoteAddress;

    conn.on("message", messageHandler);
    conn.on("close", closeHandler);

    // add connection the client list
    clients.push(conn);

    // send message to all clients
    broadcast(conn.nickname + " entered the chat");
}
```

The `connectHandler()` function starts by assigning a nickname to the client. This is the name that you use when sending messages to the other clients. Initially, this is set to the client's IP address, which is available in the `conn.remoteAddress` property. I get back to the handlers for the message and close events shortly. The `connectHandler()` function finishes by adding the connection object to the `clients` array and broadcasting a message to all clients that a new person has entered the chat room. Listing 13-5 shows the `broadcast()` function.

Listing 13-5   **Broadcasting the messages to all clients**

```
function broadcast(data) {
    clients.forEach(function(client) {
        client.sendUTF(data);
    });
}
```

This function simply iterates over all the connected clients and sends the message. Note that the method used to send the data is called `client.sendUTF()`; if you're sending binary data, you must use the `client.sendBinary()` method, which accepts a Node `Buffer` object.

All clients are added to the `clients` array when they connect, so they must also be removed when the connection closes. Listing 13-6 shows the event handler for the `close` event attached in Listing 13-4.

Listing 13-6   **Removing disconnected clients**

```
function closeHandler() {
    var index = clients.indexOf(this);
    if (index > -1) {
        clients.splice(index, 1);
    }
    broadcast(this.nickname + " left the chat");
}
```

After removing the client connection from the `clients` array, `closeHandler()` sends a message to the remaining clients that the person has left the chat room.

When a client sends data to the WebSocket server, it fires a `message` event on the client connection object. Listing 13-7 shows the `messageHandler()` function attached as the handler for this event.

Listing 13-7   **Handling client messages**

```
function messageHandler(message) {
    var data = message.utf8Data;
    broadcast(this.nickname + " says: " + data);
}
```

The event handler receives a single argument, an object containing the message. String messages keep the data in the `message.utf8Data` property, whereas messages with binary content keep the data as a Node `Buffer` object available in the `message.binaryData` property.

The `messageHandler()` function in Listing 13-7 simply broadcasts the message to all clients, prefixed with the nickname of the sender. To make things a bit more interesting, introduce a couple of commands that clients can issue. In particular, add the following two commands:

```
/nick newnickname
/shutdown
```

The `/nick` command changes the client's nickname to *newnickname*. The `/shutdown` command simply shuts down the chat server. If this were a real application, you would probably restrict access to such a command. The modified `messageHandler()` function is shown in Listing 13-8.

Listing 13-8   Intercepting commands

```
function messageHandler(message) {
    var data = message.utf8Data.toString(),
        firstWord = data.toLowerCase().split(" ")[0];
    // is this a command?
    if (data[0] == "/") {
        // if so, which command is it?
        switch (firstWord) {
            case "/nick" :
                // new nickname is the second word
                var newname = data.split(" ")[1];
                if (newname != "") {
                    broadcast(this.nickname
                        + " changed name to " + newname);
                    this.nickname = newname; // set new nick
                }
                break;
            case "/shutdown" :
                broadcast("Server shutting down. Bye!");
                ws.shutDown(); // shut down the WebSocket server
                server.close(); // and the HTTP server
                break;
```

```
        default :
            this.sendUTF("Unknown command: " + firstWord);
    }
} else {
    broadcast(this.nickname + " says: " + data);
}
}
```

You can find the complete Node server script in the file `02-websocketserver.js`.

Creating the WebSocket client

It's time to create the chat client, starting with the HTML shown in Listing 13-9. The HTML is available in the file `03-websocketclient.html`.

Listing 13-9   **Chat client markup**

```
<!DOCTYPE HTML>
<html lang="en-US">
<head>
    <meta charset="UTF-8">
    <meta name="viewport"
        content="width=device-width,user-scalable=0">
    <title>Chapter 13: WebSocket Chat</title>
    <link rel="stylesheet" href="03-websocketclient.css">
    <script src="03-websocketclient.js"></script>
</head>
<body>
    <h1>Very Simple Chat</h1>
    <input id="input" placeholder="Enter message..."/>

    <textarea id="response" disabled></textarea>
</body>
</html>
```

The HTML is just a basic `input` field that the user enters messages into and a `textarea` element used to display the output. Listing 13-10 shows the content of the CSS file `03-web-socketclient.css`.

Listing 13-10   Styling the chat client

```
#input, #response {
    border : 1px solid black;
    padding : 2px;
    display : block;
    width : 600px;
}

#response {
    height : 300px;
}
```

The JavaScript file `03-websocketclient.js` contains all the code needed to set up the chat client. When the page finishes loading, the `setupChat()` function shown in Listing 13-11 creates the WebSocket connection and attaches the relevant event handlers. Remember to change the URL passed to the `WebSocket()` constructor, if necessary.

Listing 13-11   Setting up the client code

```
function setupChat() {
    var ws = new WebSocket("ws://127.0.0.1:9999/");

    setupInput(ws);

    write("Welcome to Very Simple Chat!");

    ws.addEventListener("open", function () {
        write("Opened connection");
    }, false);

    ws.addEventListener("message", function(e) {
        write(e.data);
    }, false);

    ws.addEventListener("close", function() {
        write("Connection closed");
    }, false);
}

window.addEventListener("load", setupChat, false);
```

The `setupInput()` function attaches a function to the `keydown` event on the `input` field. Whenever the user presses Enter, which has the key code 13, the text in the field is sent to the server and the field is cleared. Listing 13-12 shows the function.

Listing 13-12 **Setting up the input field**

```
function setupInput(ws) {
    var input = document.getElementById("input");

    input.addEventListener("keydown", function(e) {
        if (e.keyCode == 13) {
            ws.send(this.value);
            this.value = "";
        }
    });
}
```

Listing 13-13 shows the last function, `write()`, which simply writes a line of text to the output `textarea`, prefixing the string with a time stamp.

Listing 13-13 **Writing output messages**

```
function write(str) {
    var response = document.getElementById("response"),
        time = (new Date()).toLocaleTimeString();
    response.value += time + " - " + str + "\r\n";
}
```

Now you can try opening `03-websocketclient.html` in a browser while the server is running. Start the server with this command:

```
node 02-websocketserver.js
```

If all goes well, you should see the welcome message followed by a message informing you that the connection is established. In the input field, you can type messages that are then sent to the server. If you open a second browser (perhaps on a different computer) with the chat client, you see that the messages are, in fact, sent to all connected clients and that the basic chat system works.

Summary

In this chapter, you learned about the server-side JavaScript environment Node and the WebSocket API that enables you to create better network-enabled web applications than do traditional HTTP-based solutions.

This chapter showed you how to use WebSockets to create connections to a server and how to send and receive data. You also found out how WebSockets provides a better experience than the methods used in the past when persistent connections were needed.

In introducing Node, this chapter showed you how to create a simple HTTP server in just a few lines of code. Finally, you discovered, through creating a basic chat application, how Node and WebSockets can work together to create powerful web applications with efficient, low-latency network communication.

Index